NEGOTIATING FOR INDIA

Negotiating for India

Resolving problems through diplomacy (seven case studies 1958–1978)

JAGAT S. MEHTA

MANOHAR
2007

First published 2006
Reprinted 2007

ISBN 81-7304-672-7

Published by
Ajay Kumar Jain for
Manohar Publishers & Distributors
4753/23 Ansari Road, Daryaganj
New Delhi 110002

Typeset by
A J Software Publishing Co. Pvt. Ltd.
New Delhi 110005

Printed at
Lordson Publishers Pvt. Ltd.
Delhi 110007

Distributed by
FOUNDATION BOOKS
4381/4 Ansari Road,
Daryaganj, New Delhi 110002
and its branches at Mumbai, Hyderabad,
Bangalore, Chennai, Kolkata

To my father who, for me and my children
left an example of unflinching integrity,
commitment to responsible citizenship and
public-spirited values.

Contents

Acknowledgements 9

Introduction 13

1. Catalyzing Graduated Modernization through Diplomacy: Nehru's Trek to Bhutan – 1958 35
2. Diplomatic Advocacy in a Crisis of Mutual Misperceptions: Negotiating the India-China Boundary Question – 1960 54
3. Diplomacy for Compensation for Indians: Negotiating with Idi Amin's Government – 1975 123
4. Diplomacy to Restore Severed Links and Mutual Confidence: The Normalization of India-Pakistan Relations – 1976 147
5. Fresh Water Diplomacy for Resource Optimization: The Salal Hydel Project – 1976 197
6. Diplomacy for Equitable Allocation on International Riparian Flows: The Sharing of the Ganga Waters at Farakka – 1976-1977 219
7. Diplomacy between Landlocked and Unequal Countries: Separating Transit and Trade with Nepal – 1978 249
8. Some Unforgettable Diplomatic Contemporaries 274

Index 287

Acknowledgements

The negotiations described in this book took place between 1958 and 1978. I have relied on memory but whenever possible I have consulted colleagues who were with me or are knowledgeable on the background in order to refresh, or refine the recall. While I take full responsibility for the presentations but I want to acknowledge my gratitude to those who at my request reviewed the specific studies.

Dileep Mehta, who was Ambassador to Bhutan in the 1990s and his wife Nandini very kindly, went through the paper about Prime Minister Nehru's trek to Bhutan in 1958. Both have a scholarly understanding of the country and told me that the visit remains embedded in the national memory of Bhutan. Old and young, born after Nehru's visit, look upon it as a milestone in Bhutan's history. The late King and Jigme Dorji, then Prime Minister, passed away decades ago. Her Majesty, the Queen mother, is happily still with us, and was in the prime of her elegance at the time of the visit of Panditji's and Mrs Gandhi but she took no part in the discussions. My photograph of the present king was taken when he was three years old, he was sitting in the lap of Major Malhotra, the doctor in our team, both watching the archery competition.

None of the five-member team involved in the six month long discussions with China in 1960, including Dr S. Gopal my deputy are still around. Our interpreter, V.V. Pranjpe, remains in good health, full of memories of all high-level conversations with China between 1953 and 1993. In our protracted and complex discussions, Vasant Pranjpe was never once stumped for the appropriate Chinese word or corrected by Chieh his Chinese opposite number. In the archives of the ministry, the 3,000-page verbatim record is available in print, but I did not ask permission to consult it or my reporting telegrams. However, without the then Foreign Secretary's authorization, I took C.V. Rangnathan, who had just over one year service, to sit through the Delhi session and get a feel of the evidence marshalling exercise. He had chosen Chinese as his language but this was before he went to Hong Kong to start the learning process. Subsequently he not only developed fluency in Chinese but deep insights on the country and India-China problems. He eventually became our ambassador to China. I requested him to go through my recollection with a critical eye. He would not necessarily endorse every contention in the paper but he has been a great friend and mentor on China. I am truly grateful for his labour of love.

I tried to contact H.K. Singh, who was the High Commissioner in Kampala in 1975 (and in whose architecturally special residence I stayed for a month after deliberate harassment compelled me and my colleague Rangachari to move out of the Kampala Hilton Hotel). Singh was a great support in the talks on the compensation for the expelled Indians, but I was shocked to learn from Mrs Singh that her husband had passed away not so long ago. Rangachari who, in 1975 was the Assistant Custodian of Enemy Property in the Ministry of Commerce stationed in Mumbai, was my sole adviser. He was extremely knowledgeable on valuation principles but, alas, he too is no more. There is no one else who could help me recall those tortuous sessions, often lasting into the small hours everyday for five weeks, appraising the thousand odd claims. Oboth-Offembi, the Finance Minister, who sat behind the curtain and was my real opposite number, was killed in a deliberate ambush along with the Archbishop of Uganda soon after our negotiations. There was a team of 15 officials including seven or eight permanent secretaries sitting opposite the three or four of us. Even if any of the Ugandans still survive, I cannot trace them. The then Indian Foreign Minister Y.B. Chavan and my immediate superior Keval Singh who summoned me back at the last minute because of legal anxieties are also no more.

On the momentous comprehensive negotiation in May 1976 for the India-Pakistan normalization, the key coordinator was I.P. Singh, Joint Secretary dealing with Pakistan. It was fortunate that, unlike many others, he was throughout on the same wavelength as myself. Alas, he passed away four years ago who after retirement was appointed as ambassador to Nepal. I gratefully record my gratitude and tribute to him.

I.P. Singh was also with me for the Salal talks in October

1976. R. Rangachari, then a Senior Civil Engineer with the Central Water and Power Commission and later its Chairman, though now retired, is still intellectually engaged in India's Water and River Development problems. He kindly scrutinized the draft of the paper on Salal. Leela Poonappa, then Under Secretary (Pakistan) along with Rangachari, did the meticulous calculations, sitting all through the night to provide me with the arguments which I marshalled to Z.A. Bhutto, the Pakistan Prime Minister, which reversed the deadlock. Leela has now moved from Bangkok to take over as Ambassador in The Hague. I have sent the draft of the paper to her to refine my recollection, but she has not volunteered any correction.

Muchkund Dubey was Joint Secretary (Bangladesh) and a great intellectual support in the many shuttles between Dhaka and New Delhi on Farakka in 1976-7. At the time, he had some honest reservations on the allocation criteria and the guarantee clause if the Ganga flow went below the past statistical average. Muchkund Dubey also accompanied me to New York in November 1976 for the discussions of the Farakka item in the General Assembly agenda. In the body of the paper on Farakka, I acknowledge my gratitude to him. I greatly appreciated that many years later he was gracious enough to concede that on balance, my overruling him to reach a compromise was not really repugnant to our wider national interests.

I also owe a debt of gratitude to C.V. Ranganathan, this time for his counsel as Joint Secretary dealing with Nepal in 1978. He helped in the negotiations to separate the Trade and Transit treaties. He scrutinized my essay on the subject and supplemented my memory. I also requested K.V. Rajan who until a few years ago was Ambassador to Nepal to look through the paper for its political backdrop. I absolve both of them of the frank criticism of our bilateral diplomacy on relations with Nepal.

This acknowledgement omits mention of the Herculean labour of the junior colleagues during the final sessions of the talks with the Chinese as they figure in the body of the case study itself. It culminated in Prime Minister Nehru specially coming to office on Christmas day in 1960 to be photographed with the entire delegation before some of them dispersed out of Delhi.

I would not be surprised if my publishers Ramesh and Ajay Jain and the editors B.N. Varma and later Siddharth Chowdhury were exasperated during the torturous process of editing the manuscript. They have been very patient and encouraging throughout. My sincere thanks for their tact and forbearance.

Finally, I would like to place on record my deep appreciation to S.S. Bolia in Udaipur who has cheerfully typed these essays between 2002 and 2004. He re-typed them umpteen times. As Galbraith once said with deliberate exaggeration, it is only in the seventeenth draft that there is real spontaneity!

29 August 2005 JAGAT S. MEHTA

Introduction
India's Role in Contemporary Diplomacy

EVOLUTION OF DIPLOMACY IN THE TWENTIETH CENTURY: INDIA'S NATURAL ADVANTAGE SLIPPED AWAY

This book is pegged around seven cases of privileged responsibilities entrusted to me during my career in the Foreign Service of India and so the account must necessarily be a subjective one. But even this limited experience illustrated how India was slow to comprehend and adjust to the sea-change world politics underwent during the twentieth century. The old notion of a prestigious calling, accustomed to residing abroad in luxury, enjoying plenipotentiary latitudes as guardians of national egos, has been undermined by technology and the enlarging of the international community. Envoys now must work with democratic governments and sometimes non-elected rulers. At the time of the Congress of Vienna (1815), the effort of five European great powers and their ambassadors more or less ensured peace for a century; but since WW-II, sovereign entities have quadrupled and there is a cacophony of upward of 20,000 excellencies resident in over 190 odd capitals, many pursuing only narrow parochial interests. The old notions of power providing the sanction for diplomacy have been faced with defiance of the militarily strong. Instant communications and jet age travel by heads of government and ministers have narrowed ambassadorial discretion. The differential between a few developed and a vast number of developing countries has sharpened and the old sense of binding common identity of the diplomatic corps is left for ritual farewell gatherings of departing colleagues. Sovereign equality and presuming non-interference was implicit in the Treaty of Westphalia (1648), but the few affluent and many poor nations are both willy-nilly affected by economic and technical globalization with baffled responses to the politics of immigration, competition and unemployment. Independence and interdependence thrive side by side.

National sovereignty, however, remains resilient. The Communist ideology claimed solidarity across national frontiers but the Sino-Soviet alliance splintered within 10 years and even after 40 years of Soviet military domination and presence, the Berlin Wall was demolished by pick-axes, mocking the might of a nuclear power. The Warsaw Pact itself collapsed but NATO survived and even so, its members do not invariably march to the trumpet of their protector, the United States. The US defence budget roughly equals that of the rest of the world put together, but there is independence in Foreign Policy even amongst economically dependent nations. Under the Charter, the UN affirms equality between its member states and, though often stumped by the veto of the five permanent members of the Security Council, it does not mean they are always dutifully compliant. USA could decide whether to consult the Security Council or to act unilaterally, but this does not hamstring the groundswell of anti-Americanism. Technology has, of course, greatly improved war-making and Intelligence capabilities of a country like the USA, but this has not ensured the return to the old centralized decision-making as in 'Empires'. In Vietnam and Chechnya, we have seen powerful nations being stalled and defeated by nationalism and in Iraq even by the defiance of motivated individuals. In 1945, after Hiroshima and Nagasaki, nuclear weapons were hailed as the ultimate arbiter of international politics but the monopoly did not last long. Even after expending trillions of dollars in their further sophistication (and continuing with programme for Star Wars), the unprecedented destructive capability looks paralysed and condemned to remain in silos or basements. The nuclear weapon countries themselves are really alarmed at accidental ignition or deliberate abuse by rogue states or non-state actors controlling nuclear proliferation and it is now the most baffling diplomatic challenge for the future peace of the world. The world is, no doubt, less prone to major organized conflicts but after being so enmeshed, peace-keeping is often impotent against sporadic violence and bush conflicts. The democratization of weak nations has in fact enfeebled the strong. The paradox is transparent: when conventional wisdom expected that diplomacy would marginalize the independent discretion of nations, in fact, the scope, the responsibility and the imperative for negotiations for international problem-solving through 'persuasion' is now greater than ever.

The essence of diplomacy was always plurality of sovereignties and compromise in conflict resolution. India's civilizational personality with its old salad bowl of faiths and tradition of toleration, and its more recent pioneering role in decolonization should have given the country a natural advantage in diplomacy in the contemporary world. Gandhiji's aversion to violence and placing premium on peaceful dialogue approximated to the method of negotiated persuasion. Though indefatigably opposed to imperialism, Gandhiji's non-hate for the instruments and 'messengers' is not far removed from the immunities of envoys critical to the practice of diplomacy. But, if we are honest, we would recognize that in six decades of independence, India has not optimized its international standing. We showed poor comprehension and inconsistent adherence to the diplomatic method. There are of course good many reasons but scapegoatism in acknowledging our own share of misperceptions is often not conceded. The hurried Partition of a 'naturally' united and culturally enmeshed subcontinent meant that democratic India got preoccupied with countering the appeal of the breakaway Islamic Pakistan; we also slipped into the imitation of the old European practice of insensitivity towards the small surrounding neighbours, overlooking our own proclaimed approach of universalized right of national self-fulfilment. In fact after the experience with China and Pakistan we too came close to rely on condign power. Under the hypnosis of the big Cold War, while proclaiming detachment from military blocs, we came to assume that bipolarity was permanent and so our non-alignment resorted to tactical improvisations. We presumed on the West and tilted towards the East and this at least in the eyes of the beholders almost resembled blackmail. Except in conference declarations, we abandoned the crusade for general and at least nuclear disarmament. (It would have been consistent with our earlier position if India had anticipated the Reagan-Gorbachev formulation 'that nuclear wars should never be started as they can never be won'.) The international community came to see India as having renounced its natural leadership of the Third World and adherence to enlightened internationalism. Instead of urging all countries to follow India, we got handicapped by defending 'exceptionalism'. No country was better placed to prophetically anticipate the twenty-first century reality of political equality in the face of economic and military inequality. The future of the global village depends on working peacefully and purposefully through diplomacy in order to promote greater fulfilment of people's expectations and social progress in an interdependent world. This cannot be done by nuclear weapons or military compulsion.

The American President Woodrow Wilson brought from across the Atlantic the notion, that diplomacy must adopt the practice of 'Open covenants openly arrived at' but the American President soon realized that relations between independent nations demanded confidentiality and compromise. The Treaty of Versailles adopted revanchist provisions and laid the seeds of WW-II, but even the half-enlightened vision of the League of Nations was killed by the non-ratification by the US Senate. More relevant, the Information Revolution got underway and this started the spread of people's political awareness. The practice of 'official' lies was started by Dr Goebbels, the Nazi minister, and public relations became part of the official preoccupation of all governments. It has meant a tightrope walk between 'raison d'état' confidentiality and 'openness' to people and democracy. The media ferrets out information and then has the compulsion to print or broadcast it instantly, sometimes even without verification. Diplomacy on the other hand must resist the desire of wanting to play to the domestic gallery and forgo the splash of an accompanying photograph. Sound bytes and tabloids which play into populism can and do complicate prophylactic diplomacy and negotiated problem solving. 'My country right or wrong', which for centuries became strident only in times of war, inhibits constructive resolution of international problems.

European diplomacy was based on a shared cultural heritage and common faith in Christianity. The United Nations Charter is now the nearest approximate in the enlarged international system. The UN document entitled 'Threats, Challenges and Change' and in the 'Millennium Project of the Secretary General', there is recognition of interconnectivity between Security, Development and Human Rights, but finally state sovereignty alone can help in peace enforcement and establishing a Peace-Keeping Commission. A nation state has also the latitude to perpetuate genocide and tribal or religion-based violence. The UN and its manifold other institutional rotaries reflect the patient quest to better manage the inequities of globalized interdependence, but parochial nationalism frequently obstructs international enlightenment. After 9/11, the most dangerous development, is the discovery of non-state international linkages supporting terror. This international Frankenstein monster dwarfs the earlier nationally restricted disaffection. Two strong international irrationalities—anti-Americanism and Islamaphobia—are new but we may be inviting greater frustration if the anti-terror campaign is divorced from enlightened internationalism. The paradox is further deepened that so much of the world hates the country, which remains the greatest magnet for migrants and the indispensable trading partner for all nations. The world must turn to patient diplomacy for the resolution of terror.

No grand reflections on modern diplomacy were ever part of the brief in the assignments, which came my way. The directions on the particular issue on the agenda if given at all were narrowly specific. My own personal approach, however permeated with the conviction that it was in our national interest to overcome inherited deadlocks through diplomacy. The purpose throughout was not to surcharge the issue with self-righteous populism, or treat diplomacy as only public relations and—as happens not infrequently—make it a dialogue of the deaf, but make serious effort to identify the perception and misperception of the adversaries. The lessons distilled from the negotiated exercises are summarised in this introduction.

II

JSM IN THE ROULETTE OF HAPPENSTANCE

Before embarking on an analytical overview of the specific case studies, may I digress to recall my own entry in the Foreign Service, which happened to coincide with the transition period before our independence.

In 1945, when in the Navy, I applied for the war-reserved vacancies in the ICS. I also gave a preference for the Indian Political Service (IPS). It was my vague hope that, if selected and placed reasonably high in the merit list, after independence, which was then on the horizon, the successor of this most exclusive British dominated service might open avenues for a career in diplomacy. While at Cambridge where I went after getting demobilized from the Navy in 1946, I learnt that my name was on the list of 62 successful candidates of the ICS announced in October 1946. It was my further good fortune to be amongst the thirteen who were approved for the Political Service and, so appointed to its natural successor, the Indian Foreign Service. Most of those on the approved list were called to Metcalfe House for the foundation course training in March 1947. This was, of course, before the Partition; three out of the group accepted for the political service went to Pakistan and like the ten in India, became the nucleus of the two Foreign Services. Thus began my journey in diplomacy.

In the sitting room of Professor John Kenneth Galbraith, there is a plaque embroidered by a lady admirer and prominently displayed on top of the bookshelves, which reads: 'Galbraith's first law: Modesty is an overrated virtue.' This, of course, does no justice to one whose *Life in Our Times* has made him an icon of liberalism and worldwide social concerns but the plaque makes visitors sit up as it highlights Galbraith's style of self-deprecatory humour. It was this tongue-in-the-cheek boast which inspired me to conceive of Jagat Mehta's 'Law on Bureaucracy', which runs somewhat as follows: 'In any erupting crisis, there is every likelihood that, regardless of merit or relevance of experience, government will assign the nearest conveniently available idiot for the job.'

Some officers are, of course, identified early for their exceptional ability and get assigned to a succession of responsible posts. In my experience, Sir G.S. Bajpai, my first chief, H.V. Iengar, H.M. Patel, L.P. Singh, L.K. Jha come to mind, but also R. Venkateswaran, who topped the list in the first IFS/IAS examination in 1948 and opted for the Foreign Service. (Alas all of them are no more.) Any one familiar with the working of an administration—ours and I imagine most others—will have come across plenty of instances of how square pegs are placed in round holes. Ability and experience go un-recognized and un-rewarded; some turn cynical; others wallow in frustration and public interest often suffers.

Looking back, I honestly believe I was undeservedly lucky in being entrusted with more hard negotiating responsibilities than any other service colleague, some of which came when I was at a comparatively junior level. Most of these assignments are only explicable by the roulette of happenstance. The particular circumstances of the seven negotiating exercises, the tactical steps, and the subsequent fall-outs are described in the respective essays but, by no stretch of my egotistical imagination, was I the most qualified for these difficult responsibilities. In fact four cases fully illustrate my 'law' where the burden fell on my shoulders simply because I happened to be conveniently around.

My involvement in China is a case in point. As it is not lacking in connected public interest let me recall the virtually forgotten background. When in September 1946 Nehru became Vice-President and member-in-charge of the External Affairs Department (EAD) in the Governor-General's Council, he immediately decided on the constitution of a separate Foreign Service (IFS). The EAD was then largely manned by British officers of the Political Service. Nehru asked Humphrey Travelyan (who later had an exceptional career in the British Foreign Service ending in the House of Lords and being made a knight of the Garter) to draw up plans and the rules for the IFS. The Indian missions in London, Washington and Chungking already existed but Moscow, with Mrs Vijayalakshmi Pandit as Ambassador was opened in April 1947 even before independence. The subordinate infrastructure of superintendents, assistants, private secretaries, stenographers, etc., were deputed from the Central Secretariat Service (CSS), the first preference going to those serving in the EAD. Many readily volunteered as the new missions were in 'attractive' capitals like New York, Moscow, Paris, Bern, etc. I was the first IFS officer to be sent to the Administration division in 1949, which until then was officered by the Audit and Accounts Service or promotees from the CSS. I was to succeed M. O'Meally, an Anglo-Indian, who finally retired after 43 years of service including nine extensions having started as a clerk in 1906 in the old Foreign and Political Department. O'Meally chose the supporting staff for the new missions at his own sweet discretion. Soon after I took over, when extending our diplomatic network, I found there was hesitation and even refusals to go to the not so glamorous posts. I realized we must have an IFS (B) so that the option of working in MEA as with the IFS (A) would carry the automatic obligation to go wherever posted or they should move horizontally to another ministry. In consultation with the Home Department, I did the complex spadework to prepare a scheme to separate IFS (B) from the CSS.

Let me further complicate this historical digression. In 1947, the frontier areas of India like the North-West Frontier Province (NWFP) and the North-East Frontier Agency (NEFA) and Nagaland were part of EAD because of their linkages with neighbouring countries or Tibet. The NWFP, of course, went to Pakistan. Though not for the same reason as for the British Indian administration, Nehru did not want the tribal areas to be bureaucratized and 'commercialized' by the elaborate paraphernalia as in the districts in the states. He, wanted NEFA and Nagaland, though constitutionally within India, to remain with External Affairs. He appointed Verrier Elwin, the famous anthropologist (who had worked in the tribal area of Central India) as Adviser for NEFA with instructions to study and preserve the customs and existing institutions of the different tribes. He also ordered the continuation of the post by which a senior bureaucrat based in Shillong, reporting directly to the Governor of Assam, should superintendent over the NEFA Secretariat. A single-line administration was to be evolved for harnessing calibrated development in the NEFA, and the Nagaland and, to do so, a separate Indian Frontier Administrative Service (IFAS) liable for postings only in the frontier region was to be constituted. These officers, mostly volunteers from the army, were chosen for their unusual 'adventurous' aptitudes. They were to have long tenures in the frontier divisions and during which they were to learn the dialect and so win the confidence of the inhabitants of the hills and forests. In the ministry under the Joint Secretary (East), a Deputy Secretary had responsibilities for NEFA and the recruiting and administering of the IFAS. It was probably my experience of planning IFS (B) that at the end of 1956, I was nominated as Deputy Secretary (East). I remember the then Joint Secretary (East) (T.N. Kaul, who was a distinguished and dynamic member of the ICS and had opted for the Foreign Service in 1947 and later became the Foreign Secretary) telling me, 'Forget Europe; move East.' (Until then my service experience and languages were West European). In my Deputy Secretarial charge, there was an Under Secretary for (NEFA and Nagaland) and three others; one Under Secretary each for Nepal (N), Bhutan, Sikkim and Tibet (with acronym BST), and East Asia (EA) dealing with China, Japan, Mongolia, and the Koreas. The last was the lightest of the four branches. As explained in the second case study, it just happened that when the China crisis broke in March 1959, B.K. Acharya, who since 1957 was the successor of T.N. Kaul as head of the division, had gone on leave prior to proceeding as ambassador to Prague. K.L. Mehta, who was the Adviser to the Governor of Assam for NEFA was to become Acharya's successor but for some reason was held up in Shillong, and could not join for four months. Though the Foreign Secretary suggested it, apparently the Prime Minister did not want Acharya to be recalled to the ministry as he was well into the preparations for his posting abroad. I therefore found myself operationally in-charge of the Division when the Dalai Lama surreptitiously left Lhasa and arrived in Bumla on our frontier on 31 March 1959. This precipitated the crisis in our relations with China, I got pitchforked into concentrating on China and in due course had to drop the other branches. I simply had to grow up with the magnitude of the job. For the next two years, I lived with China—sometimes working 18 hours a day including half-the-night. China remained in my horoscope until I retired two decades later. Anyway it was simply this happenstance that after Chou En-lai's visit I was asked to lead the Indian team in 1960.

My association with the Pakistan negotiations also began by an accident of timing. Following the destruction of an highjacked IAC plane we had suspended over-flights across Indian airspace. Had Bhutto withdrawn the complaint filed in 1971 with the International Civil Aviation Organization, in January or February instead of on 27 March 1976—four days before I took over as Foreign Secretary—it is more than likely that Kewal Singh, my predecessor (a Punjab Cadre ICS, and ex-High Commissioner to Pakistan) would have handled the restoration of diplomatic relations and other broken ties with Pakistan. His approach might have been different but the point I want to substantiate is that my 'law' is not a false modesty!

III

FASHIONING NEGOTIATING STRATEGIES: MAXIMIZING OPPORTUNITIES

Even when the timing was accidental the negotiating approaches required careful preparations. What were to be the overall goals? What subjects to concentrate on and what to slur over? What should be the acceptable bottom line and when rupture merited some forethought? India has to be grateful to China for Panditji's visit to Bhutan. The Chinese refusal gratuitously gave seven days for formal and informal talks at the heads of government level, which would otherwise have been inconceivable. Even though Bhutan has voted differently to India on some occasions in the General Assembly, the result of Panditji's visit has ensured Bhutan is the only neighbour with whom India's relations have had no serious setback. Our crisis with China erupted six months later, and so I speculate that if Panditji had not trekked across the mountains in September 1958, an Indian Prime Ministerial visit might never have taken place. In 1958, we had not resiled from the hypnosis of 'Hindi-Chini bhai bhai'. So China could not object to the overnight transit halts in Yatung in the Chumbi Valley (till then this was the normal route to Bhutan). Without Panditji's visit to Paro, the direct road from Phuntsholing through the malarial hills and jungles, would not even have started; the Chuka hydel project might never have been possible without construction equipment being taken overland from India. Incidentally

Panditji told me afterwards that of all his official travels, he had never enjoyed a trip so much as the three-week trek to Bhutan but I still have shivers if, as the Foreign Secretary Subimal Dutt feared what if like R.K. Nehru, his own predecessor, Panditji suffered an heart attack on one of the 12,000 feet passes. After all his kidney failure was less than six years away. With hindsight, the Chinese must regret that, notwithstanding the hazard of Nehru coming to hear about the insurgency in Kham, if they had let him come to Lhasa they might have pre-empted the consolidation of India's relations with Bhutan. The chances are that Bhutan might by now have been Tibetanised.

Idi Amin's letter had asked Indira Gandhi to send her Foreign or Finance Minister to 'settle' the question of compensation for the expelled Indians. I was singularly unsuited for the assignment because until the previous year, I was accredited to Tanzania, and President Julius Nyerere was Amin's *bete noire*. Even so, I was 'ordered' to go and that too when it was known that Uganda was nearing bankruptcy. It is another instance of the role of happenstance in my assignments which gave me the opportunity and the latitude for negotiated improvisations. I felt it was prudent to be expeditious and not risk delay in bargaining or dwelling on the more controversial items in the claims under our joint scrutiny. I readily agreed to the palpably unreasonable demand that amortization of built-up properties be limited to only 10 years after construction; the dropping of all claims on immovable assets (which included many Mercedes Benz cars,) not insisting on scrutiny of bank lockers, etc. I concentrated on easily verifiable items like bank accounts. Above all, it was humouring Amin's lure for an improved international image, which substantially increased the limits for compensation for the expelled Indians. Had we however, not completed our negotiations in five weeks, I dare say, the cheque we received eventually might have bounced.

In two cases,—Salal and the separation of Trade and Transit with Nepal, I took the initiative to recommend to the respective Prime Ministers the reversal of inherited decisions. Whereas in 1976 Mrs Gandhi readily agreed to do so on Salal, but in 1978, it led to a Cabinet 'battle' and required Morarji Desai over-ruling H.M. Patel, the Finance Minister. The end result negotiations was substantial power availability for India in Salal but the two treaties on Transit and Trade and the separate agreement on smuggling were only cosmetic and procedural, but the political dividends were immense. We must have suffered hundreds of thousands of crores in opportunity costs for the eight years deadlock on Salal and incalculably in distrust in Nepal.

With Pakistan, in 1976 instead of stringing them out over months which was in line with advice given and conventional adversarial caution, I myself thought there was great potential advantage in dramatically enlarging the scope of the talks. After overcoming the inconvenience of denial of formal contacts and flights across India I imagined Pakistan would have been quite content to postpone the people-to-people contact by land communications and, periodically, repeating the old refrain on Kashmir. By making the normalization comprehensive in a time-bound MOU, in other words taking the tide at the flood, we cleared, at least a little, of the stale fog of rigidity and prejudice and put Pakistan in a more responsive mood to recommence the dialogue on Salal.

Adjusting to Small Country Nationalism

Most of these case studies are with neighbours. We had inwardly imbibed the notions from European history of the advantage of size and comparative strength and did not fully appreciate that the twentieth century reality was that economics of dependence had been over-trumped by the political pride of newly-found independence. The British could enforce detachment but with our crusade of decolonization we should have anticipated the rise of new political sensitivity at being India-locked, which had placed visible limitation on Nepal's sovereign discretion. Having taken the initiative to sponsor Nepal for membership of the UN, we had become wooden to its unavoidable consequences of providing Nepal with the opportunity to learn of the rights of other landlocked countries. The subsequent estrangement of Nepal has many reasons but it is an example of the penalty of not making diplomacy contemporaneous. In Bangladesh, notwithstanding the gratitude for the help in its liberation, we unthinkingly squandered the good will and allowed the rise of fear of Indian hegemonism. What baffled us in both cases was that our positive roles were forgotten and predictably psychological resistance had developed because of the differential in size. It requiring sensitive diplomacy of equality to overcome the reality of inequality.

Another lesson learnt was that, if problem solving is the goal it was prudent not to rejoice in causing embarrassment or humiliation to the other side. We were right to resist the temptation not to humiliate Z.A. Bhutto, which would have been the interpretation if we had insisted on his coming to Delhi to sign the MOU in 1976. Our press was bound to have reminded him that he had gone back on the informal understanding reached with Mrs Gandhi in Simla in 1972 to confirm the LOC. (It was incidentally unfortunate for India to have resurrected the reminder of Simla in 2004.) In 1976 on Salal I volunteered that the prevalence of Emergency in India might come in handy in not publicly crowing about the Pakistan Prime Minister having come down on the eight-year refusal on Salal. Good diplomacy must aim at a win-win situation for both parties.

At times it may be necessary to risk rupture and try brinkmanship in negotiations but it has to be carefully calibrated and never overplayed. I hinted at stopping the talks in Peking when China showed reluctance to provide her own certified maps of what the Chinese delegation considered to be the frontiers of China. (Of course, I wanted to undercut the untenable Chinese contention that boundaries are not valid unless formally delimited.) In Kampala I actually booked passage home when Oboth-Offembi arbitrarily stopped the scrutiny of the bank ledgers and so I asked for a farewell interview with President Amin. Attempted brinkmanship must however be couched in regret and rationality so that when there is a climb-down, it is not trumpeted as humiliation for the adversary. On my plea Amin asked all ledgers to be produced but we consciously resisted the temptation to gloat over our triumph. Rubbing the nose of a sovereign country or its representative in mud is not good diplomacy.

Importance of Harmony within a Delegation

In six out of seven cases described in these studies, I was the team leader, but there were colleagues, from other ministries and juniors of my own. To use a rugger expression, I was simply the 'hooker'—the leader in the centre of the scrum—others were also 'pushing' for India. Team leadership demands sensitive intra-delegation diplomacy, specially with large delegations as in the negotiations with Pakistan, Nepal and Bangladesh. The technical inputs and limitations are important and therefore the cooperation of the others necessary but the MEA must exercise overall direction to bring in non-parochial considerations. Had the junior members of the delegation from the MEA and the Central Water and Power Commission not cooperated, at times in defiance of some senior officers, we would never have been able to marshall the telling statistics on Salal and Farakka; nor overcome the exaggerations on smuggling from the open border with Nepal. In the Bhutan visit, Panditji himself was the 'hooker' and, Apa Pant, the Political Officer in Gangtok and I were the only side collaborators. On return to Delhi, to continue the rugger metaphor became the 'scrum half', I was responsible for passing the 'ball' to the appropriate wings (agencies) of the Government of India and then pushing them with reminders of Prime Ministerial interest and urgency to obtain optimisation of results.

It is also great satisfaction to me that in two, probably three, cases (Salal, Farakka, Trade and Transit with Nepal), there was actual or imminent possibility of the internationalization of stalemated bilateral problems (new 'Kashmirs') which the timely agreement averted. The end-result in all cases described here was better than the government or I had dared to expect but, I hope, it will reinforce the conviction that sensitive diplomacy is the natural means to advance India's interest in the twenty-first century.

I have dealt at length in the discussion of the boundary question on the background to the Sino-India relations, which after ups and downs culminated in the War of 1962. I have always believed that it was the professional duty in the MEA in loyalty to a non-replicable national hero like Nehru to volunteer dissent. Earlier we should have followed and probed the deflecting statement of Chou En-lai in 1956-7 that erroneous maps to which Nehru had referred were based on Kuomintang surveys. There were inherent constitutional problems on the Indian side before 1959. On the basis of 'mutual' accommodation an agreement might have been reached. The hurriedly drafted communiqué gave a near impossible task to the official team; it was no more than a holding diplomacy. During the six months of talks, the climate in the frontier areas never degenerated into tensions; there were no more border incidents all through 1960.

The India-China boundary question remains unresolved but relations have improved after 43 years. I have personally differed from the view that the border question was at the heart of the 1962 conflict or that its persistence was responsible for seriously obstructing the improvement. Even conceding there were some provocations by India in Dhola in 1962, the India-China relations between 1954-62—and up to 1976—remain the grossest example of mis-anticipation and wishfulness in our diplomacy. The guilt is however both in India and China. The massive attack all along the boundary was politically punitive. China's professing faith in Peaceful Co-existence has been scarcely justified. This, however, should not come in the way of genuine two-way cooperation between neighbours in the future but as I speculate in the conclusion of the essay on Sino-Indian Boundary question this complementarily may still conceal divergent diplomatic and national ambitions and long-term rivalry.

Plenipotentiary Latitude in Negotiations

All negotiations discussed in the following studies except the one session of the China talks, were held in the other or third country capitals. I received no written brief but I had some idea of our national interests. Keeping in mind the absence of clear directions, the negotiating postures, sometimes with policy implications had to be improvised. After one instance of no timely reply being received to a query sent to Delhi from Peking, rather than seeking postponement in the schedule of talks, I decided to run the risk of taking a decision on the spot. On return to headquarters the decision makers in Delhi crossed-examined me and, in the case of China, along with Gopal, but never repudiated the line taken when abroad. The one serious exception was in the negotiations in Kampala and that too when a few hours later, Amin was scheduled to handover the cheque of the agreed amount to me. After a month long silence and non-interest in our tedious protracted scrutiny of the claims, this last-minute repudiation posed the most serious political anxiety in all the negotiations entrusted to me. For insulting President Amin face-to-face, I thought I might well be destined for the dinner of the Nile crocodiles! On the Farakka allocation also, in September 1977, I faced the possibility of a last-minute breakdown. At the eleventh hour, Shri Charan Singh, the Finance Minister in Morarji Desai's Cabinet urged a change in the duration of the agreed release schedules. It was truly embarrassing because, with the prior Cabinet approval, the text of the draft agreement had been transmitted to Bangladesh. Knowing that there were higher-ups in both countries who did not want the suggested compromise settlement, it gave me a very anxious day. I was relieved when Abbas, the leader of the Bangladesh delegation, was able to get the approval from President Zia-ur-Rahman on the telephone to our requested modification. In general, for all negotiations when specific directions do not exist, plenipotentiary latitude should be exercised fearlessly by the leader. It is not possible to negotiate with hands tied at the back.

Importance of Transparency and Personal Trust between Negotiators

From the case studies, it must also emerge that success in diplomacy requires, as a pre-condition, the creation of a climate conducive to harmonious personal trust between the principal negotiators. Mental rigidity in one of them becomes the enemy of feasible compromises. Not revealing all the relevant factors may be tactically justified, but it is entirely counter-productive to rely on falsehood or deliberate deception. Truthfulness and calm are essential qualities which foster confidence in the diplomatic method. We, in India, are sometimes apt to take advantage of our greater drafting skills in English but, I found in Germany, that in the end it gets discovered and actually frustrated more generous aid terms. It is worth recalling Jules Cambon, the legendary head of the Quai d' Orsay who said, long ago 'Moral integrity of a man of strict honour wins the confidence essential for diplomacy.'

IV

OVERRIDING IMPORTANCE OF A LONG-DISTANT VISION IN ALL NEGOTIATIONS

There is an important but unexpressed second part to the jocularly formulated Jagat Mehta's Law of Happenstance. 'Success in negotiations ultimately hinge on the overriding inspiration of the long distant goal of national destiny.' Tactical improvisation may be made but scoring brownie points to satisfy populist public opinion must not, even unthinkingly, compromise the distant vision. When in 1989, we contrived so that both Trade and Transit Treaties expired together and we followed it up by closing all but two entry points into Nepal, we struck what was understably interpreted by the people of the country a high-handed posture and slighted the claim of permanent interdependence with Nepal. Following the terrorist attack on our Parliament, it was apparently considered necessary to reflect a harsh and angry attitude and so we advanced all our forces to Forward posts on the Pakistan frontier. (I myself thought it was an unthinking over-reaction). This deployment, though extravagant, caused short-term alarm in Pakistan, but as no operations were launched, and we could withdraw at our discretion. But when some advisers suggested that we should abrogate the Indus Treaty, it might have foreclosed the post-2004 improvement with Pakistan. (Fortunately, at the last minute, we rescinded the proposed impetuous move.) It was good that despite the 1962 War we didn't break diplomatic relations with China: nor in the face of the wholly irrational Red Guard court condemnation of Raghunath and Vijay in 1967. It would have been tortuous to find propitious reasoning and circumstances to restore relations, once they had been broken.

In hawkish opinions it is often overlooked, that there is a fundamental difference between internal governance and diplomacy. Diplomacy is not like military operations demanding victory and unconditional surrender. We (and others like Pakistan) have made fatal mistakes in veering round the old notion that real power only flows from the barrel of a gun. The Clauswitzian precept 'War is politics by other means' is now out-of-date. Diplomacy remains, more than ever the craft of managing international relations by bringing intelligence to problem solving. Navigating by the distant star should not get deflected by a temporary squalls or tempests. I am aware that this view is controversial but at least in all the cases here described, it will be seen that diplomatically stooping to conquer led to agreements and in the bargain improved India's international standing.

Nehru was in my view correct in his long distance vision of relations with China, perhaps he was even more prophetic than the Chinese themselves realized until, after the cultural Revolution and the advent of Deng-Hsio-Ping. Nehru's short term perspective on China was flawed and wishful but with Bhutan, in both the tactics and vision, he was correct. With Nepal, Bangladesh and even Sri Lanka while a vision for the longterm relationship has existed in India but diplomacy has had avoidable ups and downs, which vitiated the vision of constructive interdependence. With Pakistan a vision in India for the relations only emerged with the Vajpayee visit in 1978; it retreated with Pakistan's intrusions and Indian unprincipled responses in the subsequent 20 years, but it is now crystallizing into a rational vision of geographical and functional interdependance. With America our attitude was ambivalent but today India is a better guardian of America's values and natural potential than many of the American people themselves realize. For decades we had the wrong reason for admiration of USSR but now we may be in the process of finding the right basis for friendship with Russia. If India had only recognized before or even after partition that our long-term greatness could only be realized if South Asia, as a whole prospered together in mutual trust and that hinged on contemporaneously adjusted diplomacy.

I should like to have also included reference to Afghanistan where after the Saur revolution in 1978, by quick diplomatic initiatives, we managed to pre-empt the remilitarization of Pakistan. This is described more fully in a separate book, but the knee-jerk false reactions in 1980, which led to the chaos in Afghanistan and still bedevils the country and was teleologicatlly responsible for 9/11. Afghanistan remains one of the greatest unforced international errors—an avoidable blunder—of the twentieth century.[1] We are now piggy-backing on America but Pakistan can neither fully own nor publicly disown the American connection. The USA and NATO contigents are making very halting success in getting to *status quo* ante in Afghanistan. Afganisthan has been a terrible case of a succession of faulty diplomacy.

V

COMPARING AMERICAN AND INDIAN DIPLOMACY

At a conference organized in 2002 by the American Institute of Peace outside Washington DC on 'US Negotiating Behaviour' to which I was invited, all participants were provided months in advance five scholarly books on the historical experience of the national diplomacies of Britain, Germany, Czarist Russia (with its difference with that of Soviet Union), China and North Korea. The three-day discussions with a gathering of experienced diplomats from many countries along with scholars who had followed international affairs provided thoughtful analyses which I will refrain from summarizing here.

It occurred to me at the conference how many problems of India's diplomacy resemble those of United States, except that our difficulties were regional whereas America's were global. Both countries drew their original national strength from moral values, universal ideals, and non-ulterior principles; both shared the historical experience of protesting against British Imperialism and had an instinctive revulsion against the politics of brute militarism. However, in recent times, both have come to be suspected of being arrogant, hegemonistic and crudely relying on size and superior strength, and moving away from the diplomacy of equality, plurality and non-selfish values.

Kissinger in his seminal work on Diplomacy describes two

[1]J.S. Mehta, *The March of Folly in Afghanistan*, New Delhi: Manohar, 2001.

running strains in US diplomacy: the 'Crusader' motivation as exemplified by Theodore Roosevelt and the 'Beacon' inspiration symbolized by Woodrow Wilson.[2] The two strains have blended and alternated both with India and USA. India was a crusader for the end of imperialism and racial discrimination and started as a beacon for Third World internationalism. We intervened unthinkingly in Sri Lanka and earned the reputation of not desisting from playing the big brother. We are now baffled by Nepal, but we have at least been sagacious not to yield to intervention. There has been no greater nemesis than the US political frustration in Iraq. The world however does not understand why when so many countries like Canada and those in Scandinavia have subscribed to the treaty banning anti-personnel landmines, India remains detached; or why we refuse to accept the jurisdiction of the International Criminal Court; or why we showed no concern for genocide in Burundi nor for human right abuses or starvation in Dafur or non-selfish concern for global Environmental degradation. It is salutary for India to note that Nelson Mandela, the most respected contemporary statesman confesses that his inspiration is Mahatma Gandhi. India's standing has been highest when the world has recognized that we live by principled internationalism.

VI

RECALL NEHRU'S FAITH IN DIPLOMACY– RESIST EXCEPTIONALISM

There is a wide consensus in India to consign Nehru to history, but his faith in problem solving through diplomacy has, to my mind abiding validity. Nehru now looks far more prophetic today than Mao-tse-Tung, Stalin or John Foster Dulles. Atal Behari Vajpayee became a convert to Nehruism, when he publicly disowned his own old idea of seeing Pakistan undermined. Swallowing an instinctive revulsion at another military takeover in Pakistan he has repeatedly made conciliatory gestures and extended the hand of friendship to Pakistan. The

[2]Henry Kissinger, *Diplomacy*: New York: Simon & Schuster, 1994.

accord reached in January 2004 was historic. There is continuation of this policy and giving it bipartisan legitimacy as seen in the meetings between Manmohan Singh with Musharraf in September 2004 and in the visit of the Pakistan President in April 2005.

The world has been surprised at the India-Pakistan thaw, but it is proof of statesmanship on both sides. It is showing the restored resilience of the subcontinental civilization. President Musharraf, when he came to Delhi to witness the last one-day India-Pakistan cricket match, spoke that he came to Delhi with a new heart and that the present process was 'almost irreversible'. Rediscovering the logic of neighbourly interdependence is a shift towards greater faith in diplomacy. As has been argued in this book, India's interest and strength have always been in giving priority but limited to sufficiency in defence. It requires shrewd balancing: in order to meet internal disaffection we must stop preparing for the 'last' war and must become diplomatically contemporaneous on the ascendancy of economics and social justice.

China is commanding more and more respect by demonstrating priority to economic rationality. India is already being seen as a potential economic super power. In the Nehru vision, national strength ultimately depended on democratic participation and just governance. We do harm to Nehru by using his name to legitimize post-Nehru nuclear policy. Despite all our advertised warts, India will regain greater respect in the Third World by demonstrating openness and democracy, which genuinely exemplifies plurality. To go back to Kissinger's alternatives, India must remain true to the Woodrow Wilsonian beacon principles specially when the United States itself has gone back to the old approach associated with Theodore Roosevelt. The right of pre-emptive intervention has compromised the international moral appeal of the US. India may be singularly well-placed to show that globalization, urbanization, religious toleration, and international cooperation for humanitarianism is predicated on faith in the diplomacy of equality. Each case is pegged around a particular set of negotiations but success in resolving deadlocks or effecting improvements flowed from a coherent integrated vision of foreign policy. Each paper is sought to be self-contained.

Inevitably there is overlap and repetition but it is my hope that it brings out and reinforces the role more than ever in the past that diplomacy will be necessary as we move into the twenty-first century.

In the final chapter of this monograph, I go on to recall some eminent diplomats from other countries whom I encountered during my career. They include my negotiating opponents but also others who through vigorous representation of their respective countries struck me as men with conviction and genuinely enlightened international perspectives. I believe they shared my faith in the growing relevance of sensitive diplomacy.

This introductory survey on diplomacy as illustrated by specific case studies would be incomplete if once again I did not acknowledge the privilege of having been entrusted with these negotiating responsibilities. Whether it was being deputed to accompany Panditji on the tough trek to Bhutan or acting as an advocate with China or innovating international law with Idi Amin, or negotiating comprehensive normalization with Pakistan or for sharing the Ganges waters with Bangladesh, or accepting Nepal's sovereign rights even as a landlocked country, I was deeply gratified for the trust reposed in me by successive Prime Ministers. As I near the end of my days, I can only pray that India reverts to its old original Nehruvian approach to conflict resolution. We should not hesitate to recognize that we would have done better for our own people had we not tilted away from the logic of paying deference to other nationalisms. Our heritage of political plurality in the international system was a unique asset in a nervous polarized world. The great challenge of terror—internal and international—demands sagacious blend of defence, development and greater reliance on sophisticated diplomacy.

CHAPTER 1

Catalyzing Graduated Modernization through Diplomacy

Nehru's Trek to Bhutan – 1958

HISTORICAL AND POLITICAL BACKDROP

No Prime Minister has, in defiance of medical caution and governmental hesitation, embarked on the kind of hazardous and physically demanding diplomatic mission, as Nehru did when he visited Bhutan in September 1958. He was already 69. On the most frequented and convenient route, no mechanized transport could be used beyond the Sikkim border. The long traverse around altitudes of 10,000 ft involved riding mountain ponies, using yaks to go up steep gradients and down sharp descents, and strenuous walking and climbing along narrow stony pathways. The helicopters then available to the Indian Air Force could not cross even the outer ranges of the Himalayas. It was only Nehru, confident of his democratic popularity, and with his youthful spirit of adventure, who could insist on undertaking this diplomatic mission to a land that had rejoiced in a self-imposed detachment. The Prime Minister's exertions proved to be a turning point not just in India's relations with Bhutan and in the survival of Bhutan's distinct identity, but also, in the light of developments that followed, crucial to the security of India.

Bhutan was the last closed country in the world. In the eighth century, Guru Padmasambhava propagated the message of Buddha with a long stay in Bhutan and then travelled across the Himalaya into Tibet and established the domain of

* First published in *World Affairs*, New Delhi, 2000.

Mahayana Buddhism. It was only in the first decade of the twentieth century that the diarchy was superseded by a unified authority, when the able Tongsa Penlop of the Wangchuk family, supported by the British because of his help to the Younghusband expedition to Tibet in 1903-4, was consecrated the Druk Gyalpo (King) of Bhutan. Since no incarnation of the previous Deb Raja was known, the ecclesiastical hierarchy concurred in the establishment of the monarchy.

In the nineteenth century there were periodic intrusions from Bhutan into Cooch-Behar in north Bengal, which led to conflicts and ended in the Treaty of Sinchula in 1865. By this treaty Bhutan had to cede the Dooars to the British but was promised an annual subsidy of Rs. 50,000. This reflected the general policy of the British—alternating the punitive stick with an ameliorative carrot. While the British were vigilant and maintained a dominating influence in Tibet, as illustrated by the Younghusband expedition of Lhasa, the strategic interest of British India was served by keeping Bhutan as a quiescent buffer. This suited Bhutan's own inclination to introverted insulation.

The same detached approach was cherished after India became independent, but to show due courtesy, the Bhutanese King paid a visit to New Delhi in 1948. A new treaty was negotiated and signed in Darjeeling in 1949, in which India recognized Bhutan's independence, reverted the Dooars, and significantly increased the subsidy to Rs. 5 lakh. In turn Bhutan readily reaffirmed in Article II, 'it will be guided by India in its external relation'—using precisely the same words as in the 1910 treaty with British India.

Located as Bhutan was, south of the high Himalayan range that stretches in a 2,000-mile unbroken arc from the Karakoram to Arunachal, and which in many segments forms the watershed boundary of India, Bhutan's integrity, like that of Nepal, had become a national security concern for New Delhi. Nehru's visit in 1958 was a recognition of Bhutan's strategic importance but the irony is that the visit was triggered by happenstance and was only a last-minute improvisation.

THE SUBSTITUTION OF BHUTAN FOR THE PLANNED VISIT TO TIBET

In order to propitiate the two thousand and five hundredth anniversary of the birth of the Buddha, the Dalai Lama and the Panchen Lama had both come to India in November 1956. Following the Chinese military action and occupation of Tibet in 1950, grave anxieties had troubled the Dalai Lama and the Tibetan Cabinet (Kashag) about the future of Tibet's faith and institutions. These apprehensions had not been assuaged even after the 17-point agreement promising internal autonomy to Tibet which had been signed in Peking in 1951. During the Buddha Jayanti visit in 1956-7, the Dalai Lama persistently expressed the wish to stay on in India, if only until the Chinese intentions towards Tibet became clear. Deeply concerned at the possible setback to the developing India-China friendship by giving Dalai Lama even temporary asylum, Nehru persuaded him to go back to Lhasa. However, with his interest in Buddhism and the Tibetan civilization, Nehru readily accepted the invitation of the Dalai Lama to visit Tibet. In January 1958 Chou En-lai told the Indian Ambassador in Peking that he hoped himself to accompany the Indian Prime Minister on the visit. Three weeks in September 1958 had been blocked for the proposed visit. Months went by, but no official invitation came to us in Delhi. Finally in July 1958, the Chinese Embassy informed the ministry that the visit was not convenient and should be postponed.

I was then Deputy Secretary in the Eastern Division dealing with East Asia and the Himalayan states. I was called by the then Special Assistant to the Prime Minister, M.O. Matthai, to throw light on the possible reasons for the refusal and I confirmed that from reports which we had been receiving, the Kham and Amdo areas, east of Tibet proper, were posing a challenge to the process of integration with the mainland administrative structure. To our knowledge, however, the road to Lhasa was free of incident. The Chinese obviously did not want even a whiff of internal disturbance adjoining Tibet to reach the Indian Prime Minister's party. I spontaneously let slip that three weeks was exactly the period required for a visit to Bhutan, and added there were imperatives to build stronger contact with the King of Bhutan and his government. Nehru jumped at the suggestion.

The next morning, I was summoned by the Foreign Secretary, Subimal Dutt, and roundly admonished for my impetuous suggestion. Mr Dutt recalled that his own predecessor as Foreign Secretary, R.K. Nehru, had gone to Bhutan with his wife and had suffered an angina attack on one of the high passes. The implication clearly was that should the Prime Minister, much older than R.K. Nehru, suffer from the effects of high altitude, it would be very serious for the country and the blame would squarely be pinned on the ministry. But Nehru being the man he was would not hear of any suggestion to cancel the prospect of an adventurous trek in the lap of the Himalayas and a meaningful mission to Bhutan.

On official visits the Prime Minister has been invariably accompanied by the Secretary-General or the Foreign Secretary. A senior Joint Secretary was head of the division. I was therefore surprised and gratified when I was told that it had been decided that I should go with the Prime Minister to Bhutan. I was conscious of the rare privilege of being on the sidelines and perhaps occasionally providing some background detail when the Prime Minister would be making a journey which in purpose was historic, and, in hazards and beauty of surroundings, unmatched.

But the only viable route posed the problem of obtaining China's consent to transit, albeit just for one night, on the outward and return journeys, through the Chumbi Valley in the extreme south of Tibet. The Chinese authorities in their refusal had probably never contemplated the substitution of Bhutan for the visit to Lhasa, but it would have heaped insult on discourtesy if transit were denied to the Indian Prime Minister. The Chinese hesitated but eventually signified their consent to the transit through Tibet.

Paradoxically, the substitution of a visit to Bhutan had far greater political importance. A visit to Lhasa would have been exhilarating, sightseeing on the roof of the world and viewing the 1,000-room Potala Palace and it might have provided insights to the Prime Minister on Tibetan civilization and some feel for Dalai Lama's dilemmas in preserving his position in one of the last holds of a theocratic form of governance. At that time our crystal balls gave no inkling of the Sino-Indian crisis, which was precipitated barely six months later, following the escape of the Dalai Lama from Lhasa.

Much of the burden of the arrangements fell on the Royal Government of Bhutan. It required the hiring of a dozen yaks for high altitudes (crossing four passes around 14,000 ft), many riding ponies and 100 pack animals to carry the luggage, rations, tents, crockery, collapsible furniture, etc. Experienced advice came from Apa Pant, the Political Officer in Gangtok, who had travelled the route before. Incidentally no one was seriously concerned about security, but some precautions were taken for the safety of the Prime Minister.

The Prime Minister decided that the party must be kept small. Mrs Gandhi was to accompany the Prime Minister, both to play hostess and as health guardian for her father. Apart from Apa Pant, G.C. Dutt, a Deputy Director from the Intelligence Bureau, Major Malhotra from the Army Medical Corps and as already decided, myself from the ministry, were in the senior party. Nari Rustamji, the Diwan of Sikkim, independently joined the party in Gangtok at the special invitation of the Bhutanese Prime Minister. In addition, there were a number of junior staff members like photographers, secretarial staff but the Prime Minister did not want to take even a personal attendant. It was the Prime Minister himself who told me to caution all members of the party not to take steel or sharp-edged suitcases as they could wound the pack animals.

THE LONG HIMALAYAN TRAVERSE THROUGH TIBET INTO BHUTAN

We flew in the Prime Minister's special aircraft from Delhi to Bagdogra. On the drive to Gangtok we were held up because of a post-monsoon landslide and had to walk across and continue in substitute vehicles to the other side of the blocked passage. The first engagement of the Prime Minister in Gangtok was to open the Namgyal Institute of Tibetology, where in a beautiful Sikkimese/Tibetan style building, an extensive collection of Tibetan manuscripts and artefacts had been assembled under the guidance of the Maharajkumar of Sikkim and the dedicated scholarship of Dr Nirmal Sinha, an eminent Indian Tibetologist. It had symbolic significance that, at a time when Tibetan monasteries were being emasculated, the Government of India had provided funds and support to preserve elements of Tibetan heritage.

The next morning, in the presence of the Maharaja of Sikkim, Nehru cut the tape to inaugurate the motorable road to Nathula. The construction of this road had begun after the 1954 Agreement was signed. It was indicative of India's faith in the potential of suspicion-free relations with the Tibet region after the imperial advantages had been readily surrendered by India. The hope was that better land communications would optimise the traditional border exchanges and regional trade, as also two-way pilgrimages. But the work on the connecting link on the Chinese side, from Yatung up to Nathula in the Chumbi Valley never started. This was an early sign that India and China were not on the same political wavelength as regards future relations with Tibet. Even during the years 1954-9, when relations between the governments were full of friendship—as manifested during Nehru's visit in 1955 and the Vice-President Radhakrishnan's visit in 1957 to China, and Chou En-lai's visit to India in 1956-7—the authorities in Tibet had no corresponding enthusiasm. There were, in fact, several minor incidents impeding the implementation of the 1954 Agreement. More serious was the fact that we had not been allowed to take material to start the construction of the trade agency in Gartok in western Tibet, nor were we given facilities to rebuild the agency in Gyantse, washed away by floods in the Tsangpo.

The Prime Minister drove up the spectacularly picturesque road from Gangtok, which passes the beautiful Changu lake and in the upper reaches above the tree line, passes a riot of flowering rhododendron bushes. The first night we camped in Sherathang at an altitude of 12,000 ft, which was at the end of the motorable road and just below the Nathula Pass. The next morning we walked across Nathula and incidentally saw the first Tibetan chorten (or stone pyramid, found on all passes carrying Tibetan prayer flags on poles held up by a pyramid of loose stones). The Tibetan custom is to throw a stone as they pass the chorten on the left while looking away. This is supposed to propitiate the mountain gods and ensure safe passage and success of one's mission.

When we crossed Nathula we were met by a Chinese Colonel, with a detachment of mounted soldiers of the People's Liberation Army, and they escorted the party down to Yatung. It was raining and for most of the long ride we faced a blistering cold wind which pierced through our anoraks. It was a relief to reach the Kargyu monastery, which lies half way down the trek to Yatung. On the Dalai Lama's instructions, a special room, opened only for His Holiness, had been prepared for the Prime Minister to rest. The Chinese Colonel tried to dissuade the party from making the halt but Nehru insisted on doing so. The Chinese Colonel outraged Tibetan sensitivity by lighting a cigarette in the monastery. Nehru, cold and a little weary, was also anxious to smoke but, after pulling out his cigarette case, as if by some divine prompting, stopped and put it back in his pocket. In the Tibetan mind this confirmed what Dalai Lama had indicated that Nehru was a Rimpoche, an incarnate Lama himself.

On arrival in Yatung, the Prime Minister and party were received by Surkhang Shape (a senior member of the Tibetan Kashag) representing the Dalai Lama, and General Tan-Kuan Sen commanding the Chinese forces in Tibet. In the evening the Chinese hosted a dinner in honour of the Prime Minister and Mrs Gandhi. The entire party stayed in the extensive complex of the Indian Trade Agency, where Captain and Mrs Johorey of the Indian Frontier Administrative Service played thoughtful hosts. Major Chibber, the Consul General who had come down from Lhasa, briefed the Prime Minister during the evening. The next morning Nehru noticed the names of various Indian Army units engraved on the high rocks overlooking Yatung. After the British had established their control over lower Tibet, Indian army detachments were assigned garrison duties and before each unit left, it carved its regimental insignia for perpetuity. (I daresay stone masons have by now been commissioned by the Chinese to erase these offending souvenirs of imperialism!)

Before continuing the ride towards the Bhutan border, the Prime Minister and Mrs Gandhi walked down the main street, which was lined by shops owned by Indians. Their welcome was fulsome but it was plain that careful steps had been taken to exclude ordinary Tibetans from coming near Nehru. When Mrs Gandhi, on her own, detoured into some side-streets and started to distribute toffees and sweets to the children, she saw the Chinese soldiers pushing away the Tibetans, sometimes by mild baton charges. The Yatung transit must have been the first eyewitness image in Nehru's mind of the harsh repression under way in Tibet. Later in the morning, with the PLA units as escort, we rode east up to the bridge on the Amo Chu, which formed the boundary between Tibet and Bhutan. One noticed that a Chinese photographer was discreetly photographing each one in the party as we went across the bridge in single file.

Once across the bridge, Prime Minister Nehru and Mrs Gandhi were received by the Bhutanese Prime Minister Jigme Dorji and other senior officers. We were now on friendly ground and the welcome was not just correct but spontaneous. There were still four more days before we reached Paro. Typically, everyday the trek would be divided into three segments: we set forth after an early breakfast; the first halt would be around 11 o'clock in a forest clearing for coffee and relaxation after a tiring ride-cum-walk; the second halt would be for lunch, and the third around tea time in a place where there would be an overnight halt and a hot dinner. Nehru and his daughter never seemed to mind the primitive standards of comfort and toilet arrangements because of the exhilaration of the surrounding mountains and forests, but everyone was truly grateful for the collapsible chairs which Jigme Dorji had thoughtfully brought for the party. At one halt, after an afternoon shower, we saw what everyone in the party thought was the first sight of an almost complete rainbow above the neighbouring mountain peak. We passed by a field that was a carpet of edelweiss flowers. With her Swiss schooling Mrs Gandhi told everyone that in Switzerland edelweiss was much cherished: it was found only in isolation and that too on inaccessible high rocks. She collected a handful and distributed them to members of the party.

For the fortunate few who were in the senior party, every evening was a kind of long informal seminar led by Pandit Nehru. It ranged over flora and fauna to politics. He articulated the anxieties in his mind on the future of India-China relations, the prospect for the Buddhist way of life in Tibet and whether it could survive with the forced pace of modernization and alien ideological imposition. I had taken maps of the route and the adjacent areas with me. These would be spread on the ground or on the folding dining table and the Prime Minister tried to locate the ranges, peaks and passes that we had crossed, or which were visible.

On the sixth day, as we descended from the middle level heights, Paro came in view. As a contrast to the mountainous terrain we had traversed, Paro was in a flat valley with lush ripening paddy fields. It was dominated by an impressive Dzong (a fort-cum-administrative headquarters across the Paro River). The Taktsang monastery—the so-called 'Tigers' nest'—hanging, as it were, from a sheer precipice, was visible on the distant mountain. We were told it was in this monastery that Guru Padmasambhava had spent many months in meditation while in Bhutan. No shops could be seen, which confirmed that barter was still the basis of exchange. Bhutan was evidently still at the stage before the wheel had been discovered. (I confirmed later that no local inhabitant had seen a bicycle.) In these idyllic pastoral surroundings, thriving under the benign protection of the Buddha, it was understandable that Bhutan wanted nothing more than to be left alone.

FORMAL AND INFORMAL ENCOUNTERS IN PARO

We entered Paro led by masked dancers and serenaded by Bhutanese horns and drums. We were all on horseback and were led through a flag-bedecked pathway to a large Bhutanese-style mansion in the middle of a walled enclosure, the VIP guest-house.

The programme of the week's stay was a mix of great formality and relaxed informality. The first engagement on the following morning after our arrival was the formal call by the Prime Minister and Mrs Gandhi on the King and the Queen. Being duly briefed in advance, the Indian Prime Minister and the accompanying officals were all formally attired in *shervanis* and *churidars*. His Majesty Jigme Wangchuk and Her Majesty Ashi Kesang invited the guests to sit beside them and the two delegations ranged themselves in strict seniority on opposite sides. The Bhutanese were in ceremonial *khos*, with everyone wrapped in long shawls in colours specific to their rank and they all carried a short sword in a gold and silver scabbard. The return call, when the King and his entourage came to the guest-house, was equally formal. The more significant talks took place informally between the King and the Prime Minister at dinner meetings, social functions, sports meets, and picnics, where the conversations progressively loosened the formality of the visit.

That the monarch was not distant from his people came through when the King himself took part in the archery competition and personally pulled in a tug-of-war match. To underline the importance of the visit as an unusual gesture, the most sacred giant thangkha (perhaps 100 x 60 ft) was unveiled in the courtyard of the Palace. To set eyes on it guaranteed the blessings of the Buddha and the indulgence of Guru Padmasambhava.

One day a picnic was arranged at a spot next to the Paro River, a few kilometres away. The entire party proceeded on horseback in a slow dignified walk. Nehru got impatient and the imp in him decided to gallop away ahead of the entire Bhutanese and Indian party! On two occasions, the Prime Minister decided to dress in a Bhutanese *kho,* and wear the embroidered knee length boots presented to him by the King. The first occasion was for the formal dinner and this won such enthusiastic admiration that the next day he put it on again for the archery meet. I cherish a signed photograph of Nehru in full Bhutanese dress, inscribed, in Hindi, *Jagat ko.* Mrs Gandhi also appeared in a *baku*—Sikkimese style ladies' dress with a fine weave and a multi-coloured apron, and this pleased Her Majesty, whose mother was of the Sikkim royal family. These seemingly unimportant non-political details went towards breaking down the lurking reserve, and created the climate of confidence essential to facilitate the substantive purpose of the mission.

DIPLOMACY OF COURTESY AND COUNSEL

Nehru had sensed the anxieties troubling Bhutan. While the ordinary Bhutanese were still content with the traditional way of life and oblivious to the world beyond the mountains, the

King, the Prime Minister, and a few senior officers were gravely perplexed at the challenge of adjustments for a small country, sandwiched between two large ones, both with alien philosophies of governance. They were aware of the fate that had befallen the theocratic polity of Tibet. The Bhutanese decision makers were fearful lest the Khampa revolt spill over across the frontier and the Chinese intrude in hot pursuit of real or fictitious insurgents. There was some solace, but not real comfort, that no political or ideological propaganda had been directed against Bhutan, but they were not confident of Bhutan's own capacity to contain possible contingencies in the future. The Bhutanese officials were by no means sanguine about the contagion of democracy and socialism coming from India. The border with India was open, unpoliced and freely accessible; without the knowledge of the Indian authorities, there could be disaffected elements taking refuge in southern Bhutan. Traditional Bhutanese polity also suspected the spread of an alien religion—Hinduism—with its own culture and caste structure, which had come with the Nepalese who continued to infiltrate the southern slopes of Bhutan. In the face of all these anxieties, Bhutan's overriding concern was how to manage its independence and preserve its identity without being lured or deflected either from the north or the south.

The Bhutanese are naturally reticent and were in awe of Nehru, who had already established a reputation as an international statesman. But the very fact that Nehru had decided to come to Bhutan, notwithstanding the long and arduous journey, was recognized as proof of friendship. After all no VIP of even approaching rank had ever braved the passes of the Himalayas or the malarial jungles of the south. Nehru never even hinted that his visit was a favour; his manner throughout spoke volumes about his interest and respect for the country and its institutions. The Bhutanese King was much younger, but Nehru was consciously on guard against being overbearing or intellectually patronizing.

Having put the Bhutanese at ease, discreetly the Prime Minister told the King that India only wanted to be a trustworthy friend and Bhutan had the right to determine its own pace of change. Apa Pant and I were in attendance and Jigme Dorji was supporting the King. Nehru confided to the King that China was again showing expansionist propensities and the Tibetans were unhappy at the disrespect for their autonomy and institutions. Bhutan would be well-advised to accept the inevitability of change intruding into Bhutan's historic isolation. To preserve the distinct personality of Bhutan, it was prudent to plan for controlled modernization. He urged more focus on education by opening schools and sending young boys of promise to study in India. Bhutan also required access to technical know-how and improved medical care. He commended Bhutan for protecting its rich wealth of forests but he suggested that there was scope for improvement in agricultural productivity. Nehru described at length India's own plans of development: even though its problems and politics were on a different scale, he said, the goals were similar—the greater welfare of the ordinary people. Bhutan could eventually harness its hydel potential to great advantage and by selling the surplus to adjoining states of India increase its revenues and ease the incidence of poverty.

Nehru emphasized that in order to facilitate even gradual steps to development, it was imperative to start building modern communications. In this context, the idea of a direct road from India was mooted but Nehru added that to build a motorable highway from the Indian border, through a series of intervening mountain ridges, to the Bhutanese's capital would require a major engineering effort and considerable time. The King seemed to appreciate the logic and the implications. [The Phuntsholing-Thimpu road was entrusted for survey to the Indian Border Roads Organization in the following year (1959) and the entire length of the road to Thimpu and Paro was opened in 1965. Since then other transverse motorable roads linking different valleys in Bhutan have been completed.]

The Prime Minister also urged the devolution of executive responsibilities but left it to the King to decide on whether and how far to democratize the political structure. Following Nehru's visit, King Jigme Wangchuk (and even more his successor, the present King) started the process of decentralization in decision-making. The Prime Minister was careful not to urge any military cooperation or treaty with India on the Nepalese model, but suggested that Bhutanese cadets could be trained in the academies in India. The idea of an military training mission came later. Nehru hinted that advisers on administration and police organizations could be made available by India. The whole approach of the Prime Minister was one of shared concern and transparent sympathy, not of frightening Bhutan into friendship. The Prime Minister was aware there were elements within Bhutanese officialdom who had strong reservations about coming too close to India and consequently alarming or irritating the Chinese in Tibet. The Indian Prime Minister gave no grounds to aggravate any such suspicions.

Nehru was greatly touched by the welcome and the transparent simplicity and confidence of the people as he saw them at work and at play. Mrs Gandhi told me that her father had not been so relaxed for years. Before starting on the return journey, the two held a giant tea-party-cum-public meeting. By public pronouncement, all residents of Paro and the neighbouring valleys were invited. (The Bhutanese always carry a cup in the kangaroo-like fold in their *khos* and so the impossibility of providing crockery was no impediment.) Nehru and Mrs Gandhi personally served tea and biscuits to several hundred people who sat in long rows. A raised platform was improvised for the Prime Minister to address the people and the King himself acted as the interpreter.

Nehru spoke what was uppermost in his mind to the Bhutanese people on the following lines:

> Some may think that since India is a great and powerful country and Bhutan a small one, the former might wish to exercise power and pressure on Bhutan. It is essential that I make clear that our wish is that you should remain an independent country, choosing your own way of life and taking the path of progress according to your will. At the same time we two should live with mutual goodwill as members of the same Himalayan family. The freedom of both Bhutan and India should be safeguarded so that none from outside could do harm to us.[1]

These words carried conviction because they were uttered on Bhutanese soil and translated by the King. They strengthened the cumulative impact of Nehru's informal and friendly style

[1]G.N. Mehra, *Bhutan: The Land of the Peaceful Dragon*, New Delhi: Vikas, 1974.

for a whole week of, transparent sincerity. The most wary Bhutanese officials were impressed. But it is to the late King the major credit must go for the courage of responding to this promise of trust and cooperation with India, and as a follow-up, soon afterwards authorizing the construction of a direct land route and initiating other measures to develop Bhutan's economic and social potential.

THE AFTERMATH OF NEHRU'S VISIT

The India-China crisis erupted in March-April 1959—a little over six months after the Nehru's visit. Bhutan observed a discreet silence on the India-China altercations. Bhutan, however, did not raise any objections when the Indian Prime Minister stated in Parliament that an attack on Bhutan would be considered an attack on India and quietly banned trade with Tibet. After the Dalai Lama escaped from Lhasa and took refuge in India, several thousand Tibetans fled from their homes and monasteries; a sizeable number wanted to come through the passes into Bhutan. In the beginning Bhutan tried to prevent the entry of the fleeing Tibetans, but later, on humanitarian and religious ground, about 6,000 Tibetans were allowed in, though they were discouraged from settling in Bhutan. China for its part made a point of not alarming Bhutan, but in Bhutanese minds was the knowledge that the Ching dynasty had claimed that Bhutan (and Sikkim and Nepal) were tributaries of China. One suspected, and this was confirmed subsequently, during the Sino-Indian discussion on the Boundary Question in 1960, China did not accept India's prerogative to represent Bhutan and Sikkim.

The running anxiety during the 1960s for Bhutan was to steer its external relations with China by giving neither provocation nor the impression of getting into a bear hug of dependence with India. Both could jeopardize its autonomy. But in 1961 a Chinese map revealed that there have been divergences with Bhutan's own definition of its territorial limits. India was anxious that in the spirit of Article II of the 1949 Treaty, Bhutan should not deal directly with China. There were differences in the interpretation of the clause. India felt Bhutan was obliged to act according to the advice tendered, but Bhutan asserted that, having received the advice, it was not obliged to follow it. These diplomatic exchanges had continued for years. In India there were fears of Chinese military action (on the lines of the 1962 War) and it was important that Bhutan should not be out of step with India. Yet it was also clear that something of the confidence generated by the Nehru visit had frayed after Nehru passed away.

Soon after I returned from a posting in Peking in 1966, although Bhutan was not part of my responsibility I was sent by the Cabinet on a secret mission to urge Bhutan to permit India to protest against the occupation of some isolated Bhutanese enclaves in western Tibet. I spoke to His Majestry, and Bhutan agreed to announce that India had been requested to take up the question with China. I believe it was the last occasion when Bhutan made public that India was asked to act on its behalf in the spirit of the treaty. It created general satisfaction in the ministry that Bhutan was abiding by the spirit of the treaty, as no one knew that we had actually urged Bhutan not to protest directly to China. I thought this was a rare occasion of secrecy being maintained and so saving embarrassment to Bhutan. (But months later the US Consul General in Calcutta on a visit to Delhi betrayed that he knew about my visit. The CIA must have had its informants even in Bhutan!) China of course asserted that the matter concerned China and Bhutan and that the Indian government had no right whatever to intervene. That Bhutan initially upheld our interpretation of the treaty was, I believe, only because the King and the Royal family had had developed great confidence in Nehru and thus in me personally.

We have been fortunate in posting some exceptionally sensitive envoys to Thimpu who, along with their wives, have truly enhanced confidence in relations with India. But alas, as with Nepal, we have also, had ambassadors adopting superior big-brotherly attitudes and creating a chasm in our relations, which then took years to heal. There is no mission, in my view, in India's entire diplomatic network, where the personalities of the ambassador and his wife make such a crucial difference as in the capitals of our contiguous small neighbours.

Even before, and more so after the motorable access into the interior was completed, Bhutan embarked on planned but controlled development. With the spread of education and the availability of technical manpower and revenues generated from the sale of surplus power from the Chuka hydel project to India, there is a visible improvement in the social and economic standards of living of the people. After Paro developed an airfield and Bhutan launched its own airline, the country has benefited from elite tourism but always kept on a restricted scale.

The 1960s and early 1970s were years of anxiety in the internal politics of Bhutan. In 1964 Jigme Dorji, the Prime Minister, who under the King's direction, was shrewdly managing the internal and external policies was assassinated and this created suspicions of conspiracy even against the established monarchical order. His Majesty King Jigme Wangchuk himself suffered a massive heart attack and then in 1972 passed away. These developments led to serious internal dissensions. Fortunately the young Prince, then aged 17, after he assumed the throne, managed Bhutan's affairs with great sagacity and succeeded in preserving its institutions and its autonomy.

Shaken from its introverted insulation, in the last 30 years Bhutan has pursued the old goal of autonomy, but adjusting to the changed international circumstance by gradually seeking greater recognition with a higher international profile and simultaneous diversification of economic support. In the late 1960s, with India's prior knowledge, Bhutan joined the Colombo Plan, which permitted the training of young Bhutanese in Commonwealth countries. The next step was to become a member of the Universal Postal Union. (Bhutan's beautiful postage stamps, printed in Switzerland, have become philatelic collectors' pieces and a source of substantial foreign exchange earnings.) The major support for Bhutan's five-year plans has continued to come from India, but Bhutan has been given liberal discretion in determining its own priorities. In the course of the years, India's aid has been supplemented by significant contributions from the UNDP, and bilateral assistance from countries like Australia, New Zealand, Switzerland, etc. What is interesting is that Bhutan has refrained from appealing to the big powers for aid.

By the 1970s India too gradually 'modernized' its own

attitude to Bhutan by accepting, indeed supporting, the search for direct international contacts for the country. In 1970-1 India proposed Bhutan's membership of the UN. Initially some countries were lukewarm and considered it ill-conceived magnanimity, but we persisted and in the second attempt were successful in having Bhutan seated in the UN. Thereafter in addition to the mission in Delhi, Bhutan has opened a Permanent Mission in New York and thus can have direct diplomatic dealings with all member nations. A third mission was opened by Bhutan in Dhaka and now there are also missions in Thailand, Kuwait, and in Geneva. Bhutan remains careful not to allow its capital to become the venue for great power politics by allowing resident missions of the big five or other important countries. The Chinese have welcomed Bhutan's international presence. Since 1984 several rounds of direct talks between Bhutan and China have been held, alternating between Thimpu and Beijing. After the twelfth round, an agreement between Bhutan and China was signed in Beijing in December 1998. What needs to be underlined is that Bhutan's sovereignty and independence today is as secure as when it had chosen to isolate itself from international contacts.

WHAT IF NEHRU HAD NOT VISITED BHUTAN WHEN HE DID?

Nehru's visit provides a rare example of how to successfully husband diplomacy between unequal neighbours in the twentieth/twenty-first century. In retrospect, the significance of the visit cannot be underestimated. It was the last time that any Indian dignitary went to Bhutan through Tibet. In the encounters, a lesser personality than Nehru could not have blended transparent sympathy and understanding with non-domineering counsel. A more coercive diplomatic style might well have ended in polite nods but hesitant follow-up, and delayed the strengthening of connections to the South (India). If Prime Minister Nehru had not succeeded in confidence-building and encouraged the graduated opening of communications, it is possible that the road into Thimpu may not even have started for many years. Bhutan would have perforce remained largely economically dependent on the Tibet connection. The process of internal development and political emancipation would have stultified, or would not have preserved Bhutan's cultural and religious personality.

As an intellectual exercise, it bears speculation as to what might have been if Nehru had not gone to Bhutan when he did or had not been so consummate in his diplomatic mission. One possibility is that after being lured into a Chinese embrace, using the comparatively easier access through the Chumbi Valley, Bhutan would have been 'Tibetanized'. Bhutan's autonomy, faith and lifestyle would have been eroded and its monasteries kept as tourist attractions. The sponsorship for its international personality might have come from China and this might well have created great alarm in political decision-making circles in India and ended in a stalemate, frustrating Bhutan's own aspirations for a dignified autonomy.

Alternatively there could have been a variant of the ups and downs of political relations between India and Nepal. India has the advantage of closer religious and cultural affinities with Nepal than with Bhutan. In the 1960s and 1970s Nepal started playing its own variant of non-alignment between its two big neighbours. Nepal distanced itself from India with the plea that Nepal should be accepted as a 'Zone of Peace'. Mutual confidence has oscillated between presumed friendship and anti-Indian populism. Diplomacy between Nepal and India has suffered from insensitivity on both sides.

Another speculative contingency is that Bhutan might also have been 'Sikkimized'. Sikkim's autonomy anxieties led to impetuous manoeuvrings by members of the royal family, combined with exaggerated expectations of 'international' rescue, which ended in the integration of Sikkim with India and the supersession of the 1950 Treaty. (Bhutan has always been afraid of the Nepalese minority being fanned into disaffection as happened in Sikkim but India has refrained from involvement in the problem.)

A fourth contingency was confidentially mooted when India was benumbed after the defeat by China in 1962. Worried about another attack by China along the north-eastern border and the inability of India to defend Bhutan, the suggestion was to quietly facilitate Bhutan being authorizated for the installation of US missiles in the country. Bhutan would have had the same kind of umbrella protection as Taiwan does, except there are no waters separating Bhutan from China's ground forces. The suggestion was not seriously pursued but had it been, the chances are, there would have been a re-enactment of the 1950 scenario, when apprehensive of US intensions, the Chinese forces overwhelmed the established frontier—in this case the Himalaya (in 1950 it was the river Yalu).

All these alternatives would have been departures from Bhutan's consistent desire to nurture its independent polity and personality. Everyone of these contingencies would have had disastrous consequences and are dreadful even to contemplate. As it happens, today Bhutan is internationally respected and incidentally India's relations with Bhutan are firmer than with any other of its neighbours.

Bhutan has wisely hastened slowly and so preserved its independence. It remains mindful of India's interests and observes the spirit of consultations to preserve the full measure of mutual trust. Although it is sometimes pejoratively so described, Bhutan has not become a satellite of India and, as far as I can tell, India has generally refrained from exercising unwarranted pressure on Bhutan. On many occasions, such as at the time of the Soviet intervention in Afghanistan or the recognition of the Vietnam-sponsored Heng Samrin government in Kampuchea, Bhutan, in fact, voted differently from India. Bhutan has, also understandably, shown a special sensitivity for the disabilities of landlocked countries and has not hesitated to affirm the rights of small countries to their own nationalism when they happen to be neighbour of a big country. Bhutan is now an active member of the SAARC and remains vigilant in safeguarding its particular interests in South Asia.

CHAPTER 2

Diplomatic Advocacy in a Crisis of Mutual Misperceptions

Negotiating the India-China Boundary Question – 1960

THE BACKDROP: THE DELUSION OF THE BOND OF ANTI-IMPERIALISM

The India-China war of 1962 should never have taken place; nor for that matter should there have been nationwide hypnotic euphoria of 'Hindi-Chini bhai bhai'. That was no doubt promoted by Nehru, but was echoed with seeming sincerity by Chou En-lai. The second was a folly of wishful idealism and the first was the resort to punitiveness in international politics. But as is now well recognized, both were manifestations of gross misjudgements with disastrous consequences, which took years of diplomacy to rectify. If the clock could be turned back, India and China in their sagacity and self-interest would have acted differently and, by now, may conceivably have resolved the problem of their common frontier. Many countries in the course of history have made comparable mistakes. Barbara Tuchman in her *The March of Folly* has analysed four cases where 'nations acted against their own self-interest' and suffered ignominiously. One example she describes with painstaking historical accuracy is how England lost America in the eighteenth century; another, how, in our own time, America betrayed herself in Vietnam. The whole tragic story of Sino-Indian relations illustrates the costs of not being diplomatically sensitive to 'sovereign otherness'.

The principal factors behind the mutual misunderstanding can be illustrated by the intellectual make-up of two great personalities of the twentieth century—Nehru and Chou En-lai. Nehru came to power with three quarters of a lifetime of opposition to imperialism, a commitment to democracy, the Fabian approach to restructuring society and a not forgotten revulsion at Western complacency at the rise of fascism. After distilling lessons learnt from European history and the more recent damage and suffering from the two World Wars, he wanted India to stay detached from bloc politics and promote true internationalism for peace. On top of these imprints on his mind, was grafted the inspiration from Gandhi of scrupulous adherence to truth, transparency and non-belligerence, and that the means shaped the ends. Nehru was fully persuaded that the nationalism of the newly independent countries in their own enlightened interest must give priority to development, guard against militarism, and rely on diplomacy and cooperation. Chou En-lai, also of aristocratic lineage, had received a different kind of intellectual baptism. He had been a disciplined member of the Communist Party of China and was committed to a militant universalistic ideology; embedded in his memory was betrayal by Stalin's Russia (1927), the experience of twenty years of civil war, the isolation in the Yenan caves, negotiations with KMT in Chungking and failure in the patriotic search for unity to fight the Japanese invaders. Chou En-lai's experience was of war as well as statecraft, which justified the advancing of national interest by improvization, including postponing the resolution of problems considered not 'ripe for solution'. He followed Mao-tse-Tung in the Long March across barren fringes of China. China which has never accepted any other nation to be its equal, has inherent faith in its destiny that sooner or later it is bound to regain the 'Mandate of Heaven'. For the Chinese Communist Party (as one of the pamphlets in the Sino-Soviet polemics in 1964-5) said, 'Peaceful Co-existence was temporary tactics: it was not an article of faith.'

When the People's Republic was proclaimed on 1 October 1949, India had almost finalized drafting its Constitution. India rejected allegiance to the Crown in England but accepted it as a symbol of the association for continued membership of the Commonwealth. The Constitution adopted the model of parliamentary democracy as functioning in the United Kingdom. It guaranteed fundamental rights of speech, faith and the legitimacy of political opposition where people could change their rulers periodically. This was a far cry from authoritarian centralism behind the Communist Party of China.

Both India and China drew strength from their ancient civilizations, but their historical experiences were different. India had suffered many invasions but had 'absorbed' the intruders, indigenized and respected foreign religions; it rejoiced in linguistic and cultural diversity and consequently came to respect the plurality of countries and civilizations. China, on the other hand, had developed in isolated splendour, producing a built-in confidence in its civilizational superiority over the non-Han world. Those who spoke alien languages were treated either as tributaries or looked down as barbarians. In spite of these differences, Nehru sincerely believed that the parallel struggles in recent times against domination, exploitation, and humiliation at the hands of European powers would overcome the differences of their national personalities.

This is not a comprehensive survey of half a century of Sino-Indian relations. It is primarily a case study of the phase when I was a privileged witness on the fringes and, following higher level decisions, was asked to lead the official team for discussions on the Sino-Indian Boundary Question. My professional association with China started at the end of 1956 when I was posted to the Eastern Division as a Deputy Secretary in which post I continued for nearly five years. My previous background was of Europe, with German and French as my languages. As an illustration of the quirks of administration, when I was pitchforked into this division I had never even been to Calcutta. The priority of my attention was to help establish a single line administration for NEFA and constitute the Indian Frontier Administrative Service. As time went by, after 1959 China became the dominant pre-occupation of my desk and all the others had to be neglected and eventually shed.

India was quick to recognize the Peoples Republic of China in 1949 and, defying American displeasure, plead earnestly for it to replace the Kuomintang in the UN. On the other side, when in 1950 China embarked on the military intervention in Tibet it showed no sensitivity towards Tibetan aspirations and did not observe the courtesy of informing India of its intervention. Nehru, in response to the Parliamentary alarm at the smothering of Tibet, declared 'Maps or no maps, the

McMahon line is our border'. India persisted with its principled, even if unrequited friendliness towards new China. During the Korean War (1950-3) and the Geneva Conference on Indo-China (1954) India lived up to its claim of supporting emergent Asia, even though Communist China had described India as 'the running dog of the imperialists'. In the agreement of 1954, India readily surrendered the inherited privileges in Tibet and recognized it as an autonomous region of China. The cumulative impact of unilateral friendliness seems to have led to the confirmation that India was indeed independent and commanded respect not only in the Third World but internationally. Chou En-lai visited Delhi in 1954 on the way back from Geneva. This resulted in the joint affirmation of the famous five Principles of Co-existence.

Differences in the Indian and Chinese socio-political ideologies were always evident but for Nehru, the international idealist, there was sufficient common interest around anti-imperialism that such divergence would not become conflictual. Non-alignment was an earnest of India's bonafides of non-hostility: differences when they surfaced were minimized or suppressed by New Delhi. For example, in a letter written immediately after the 1954 agreement that in the middle sector of the Sino-Indian boundary though described as border passes, did not mean they were along the boundary. This ambiguity was deliberately overlooked as well the possible implications.

One can be certain that when making the pledge of non-aggression and mutual respect, neither the Indian nor the Chinese Prime Minister had any inkling that the differences in their respective notions of the common frontier carried explosive potential and would make a mockery of their commitments to friendship. When Nehru introduced China to the Afro-Asian community in Bandung, he was hoping to demonstrate the credibility of the new nationalisms. The earnest efforts to assuage the fears of communist China in Burma and South-East Asia were well-intentioned and seemed to have been welcomed by China. (Only later was Nehru criticized for having been patronizing towards Chou En-lai in Bandung.) There was not the slightest touch of harboured affront or reserve when Chou En-lai paid three visits to India in the winter of 1956-7; both rejoiced in manifestations of friendliness with millions shouting 'Hindi-Chini bhai bhai'. Even if Chou En-lai had nationalistic reservations, they were secretly nurtured. Nehru could be forgiven for taking at face value Chou's disclaimer that the erroneous maps to which Nehru drew attention were only old KMT maps and that resolving such problems to mutual satisfaction after modern surveys would not present difficulties.

In hindsight, the People's Republic may well have been irked at India being considered the natural leader of the non-aligned and Afro-Asian nations. In 1955 even Churchill hailed Nehru as the 'Light of Asia' and so underlined India's then international standing despite our past record of sturdy anti-imperialism. Therefore it may well have been considered a good tactical investment by China if only temporarily.

The Chinese must have seen the official map of India issued by the Surveyor General in 1954 and could not possibly have been oblivious of India's notions of the 'boundary'. While the charge of Nehru's naiveté in not persisting with the enquiry of suspected major differences on the common frontier, China too was less than straightforward. Chou may well have been playing the game of skirting an unpleasant issue. (Ambassador Pannikar had also, in internal discussions, advised against raising the border question when it was urged by Sir G.S. Bajpai, the former Secretary-General, prior to the discussions on the Tibet region.) As it happened even while the manifestation of good relations between the two governments was publicized, small and seemingly needless impediments were encountered in Tibet in the implementation of the 1954 agreement, but they were discreetly minimized. For example, one of our first notes on intrusions in western Tibet naively complained that perhaps it was only through oversight that visas had not been obtained.

My own desk-bound introduction to China was enriched by first hand experience: in 1957 when as a Deputy Secretary, I was asked to accompany Vice-President Dr S. Radhakrishnan, deputizing for President Rajendra Prasad he undertook a tour of Cambodia, Laos, North and South Vietnam, China and Mongolia. The important focus of the visit was ten days in China. The stay in Peking, in my view, was the high noon of India-China friendship. The Vice-President and I were put up next to Mao's Library in the compound of Zhong-nan-hai where the members of the Politburo had their residences. In some other respects greater honours were accorded to the Vice-President than even to the Prime Minister two years earlier. (I do not know of any other Head of State or dignitary being so accommodated in Zhong-nan-hai before or afterwards.) Mao personally played host to the Vice-President. Kalidas's *Shakuntala* was performed for him, which must have required months of choreographic rehearsals. The Vice-President was touched by these and other special gestures, but in his address to the National People's Congress, disregarding the advice of Ambassador R.K. Nehru, after paying tribute to the triumphs of the People's Republic he was very forthright. Having heard how the Hundred Flowers experiment of free expression of criticism had been recently wound up, he said the people should be more openly associated with government; otherwise, he warned, 'with raw courage' they could threaten the achievements and stability of the Republic. It was unusual to make such criticism in Communistic China, but my point in mentioning this is that Dr Radhakrishnan was so respected as a philosopher statesman that there was no dilution in the warmth or expressions of friendship towards him personally or for India.

There was, therefore, some baffled concern when the Embassy in Peking reported at the end of September 1957, that the *People's Daily* had announced the completion of the Aksai Chin highway. Perhaps deliberately, the announcement was delayed until after the Vice-President's visit and we were saved an embarrassment. Non-provocative caution had ruled out aerial reconnaissance. Winter was approaching and it was only in June 1958 that two patrol parties were sent out to the extreme north and south in order to confirm that the highway cut across areas notified as Indian. Subsequently, I discovered an old report written in 1955 by our Trade Agent for Western Tibet—one Laxman Singh Jangpangi, who had informed the ministry of the construction of such a road being under way. Laxman Singh Jangpangi is one of the unsung heroes of India's relations with Tibet. A Garhwali who started his career as a Lower Division Clerk and slowly climbed the official ladder, he knew Tibetan and had a lifetime of familiarity with the trans-Himalayan middle sector. He wintered in Almora but every summer, living under canvas, trudged from one trade market to the next where Indian products and salt were sold in exchange for Tibetan wool. The 1955 report of the road was overlooked or deliberately suppressed in the mood of cultivating China. I am glad that on my recommendation, Laxman Singh Jangpangi was awarded the Padma Shri.

The 1954 agreement had agreed to a Trade Agency being established in Gartok but, one way or another, the Chinese authorities in Tibet obstructed the construction of a building to house the proposed agency. (In Yatung and Gyantse, the British had built large compounds for housing an extensive establishment.)

Going back to the Sinkiang Highway, of the two patrols sent in the summer 1958, one returned but the southern one failed to do so. In October 1958, a formal enquiry was made by the Foreign Secretary to the Chinese Ambassador. The Chinese reply was evasive and reiterated that modern surveys had not been completed. This compounded the impressions from other bits of evidence. In the Barahoti discussions, held in the 1957 summer in Delhi, there was no transparency on the Sino-Indian boundary. The Joint Secretary, B.K. Acharya, had led the talks (I was a member), but such suspicions as were aroused were suppressed on the grounds that the West could exploit them.

Yet the dichotomy of affirmation of friendship on the one hand and ambivalence on the boundary and impediments in the full implementation of the 1954 agreement on the other, led Nehru himself to address a letter to the Chinese Premier on 8 December 1958. The thrust of the letter was that while India remained committed to cultivate China's friendship. India had publicly made clear its notions of the boundary, but we wanted confirmation that there was no major disputation of India's territorial limits. The Prime Minister kept the despatch of the letter secret as it could give grist to the critics of his foreign policy and undermine the confidence that, though democratic at home, India had come to enjoy the friendship and trust of both major Communist powers.

We in the ministry felt concerned, at the beginning of January 1959, but there was no sense of a crisis looming ahead. Indirect proof of this complacency was that casual leave was readily granted to me. In the last 10 days of January 1959, three middle level officers—Air Commodore Goyal, Lt. Col. Khanna and myself—and Shobha Kanwar decided to go skiing in Gulmarg. There were then no functioning hotels during the winter and, in any case, we could not afford to stay in Nedou's, even if it had opened. At an altitude of over 9,000 ft. the night temperature were known to drop to –25 ^{0}c and living in a hut with an old fashioned wood stove was going to be tough. We were going to ski mostly on the hillocks of the Gulmarg golf course and occasionally climb up to Khilanmarg with non-skid skins fixed on our skis. The Prime Minister somehow heard about our plans, probably because of Shobha Kanwar, who often helped with German and French in the Prime Minister's house. He knew I was at a sensitive desk, but instead of forbidding the ten days absence he asked me to take along Rajiv Gandhi in the party. Rajiv was then on his annual vacation from the Doon School. We could scarcely refuse but were fearful of the responsibility as none of us was sufficiently proficient to teach a total novice (who, as it turned out, was recklessly daredevilish). But the future Prime Minister was an easy and cooperative member of the party and no major mishap occurred.

A reply dated 23 January from Chou En-lai to Nehru's letter of 8 December had been received while I was on leave in Kashmir. In this letter, the Chinese side for the first time affirmed in writing that the Sino-Indian border was not settled but he still did not indicate China's own definition of the limits of the country. On 22 March Nehru wrote back giving fuller historical evidence to support the line which had been openly delineated in the 1954 map issued by the Survey of India.

Soon after my return, B.K. Acharya, a senior ICS officer, who had been head of the Eastern Division since 1957, proceeded on leave prior to taking up his appointment as Ambassador to Czechoslovakia. I mention these extraneous details to convey that normal administrative processes in that period, were continuing.

THE CRISIS IN LHASA, MARCH 1959

Through 1958 we had been receiving reports about the growing Khampa disaffection in eastern Tibet and the tension between the Dalai Lama and his cabinet (Kashag) on the one side and the Chinese authorities in Tibet on the other, but the dimensions of the dramatic developments were not recognized in the Ministry of External Affairs. In fact, on 10 March, the critical day in Lhasa, Nehru in a public speech in Calcutta was speaking of a 'clash of wills' rather than a 'clash of arms' in Tibet, but there was a telegram on my desk that Lhasa was very tense with vast crowds surrounding the Norbolinka Palace determined to prevent the Dalai Lama from attending a cultural programme being staged in the Chinese military camp. The Tibetan faithfuls were apprehensive that the Dalai Lama would be abducted by the Chinese military. (The tension in Lhasa during 1958-9 facing the Dalai Lama, the Kashag, the Tibetan populace and the Chinese authorities, all engaged in separate political calculations, is described in detail by Tsering Shakya in *Dragon in the Land of the Snows*.) On 17/18 March itself we in the ministry knew from a telegram from the Consul General Chibber that the Dalai Lama, in disguise, along with some members of the Kashag had escaped from the Palace. The Chinese apparently only got to know of this a few days later. On 23 March, they started a crackdown operation in Lhasa and brutally suppressed the protesting crowds. Dalai Lama's immediate destination was not known but we had reason to believe it would be the Indian frontier. In the long trek, Dalai Lama was escorted by the Khampas and guided through territories where the People's Liberation Army then had no control.

Way back in 1952, the Chinese Premier had told Ambassador Pannikar that should the contingency arise of the Dalai Lama seeking asylum in India, it would be understandable if it was not refused. (When Nehru visited China in 1954, K.P. Singh, a Nepalese leader who later was to become Prime Minister, was in asylum in Peking.) However in 1956-7 when the Dalai Lama and Panchen Lama were in India, following the celebration of 2500th anniversary of the birth of the Buddha, Chou En-lai also paid several visits to India. Nehru, assisted by T.N. Kaul, then head of the division in of the ministry, had exercised strong pressure to dissuade Dalai Lama from staying back in India. It was looked upon as grossly embarrassing to the developing friendship between India and China. But in 1959 when the Dalai Lama was fleeing Tibet, Nehru was aware that the hope of Tibet being allowed to enjoy the autonomy promised in the

17-Point Agreement of 1951 between the Chinese authorities and Tibetan representatives and reiterated in the Nehru-Chou meetings in 1956-7, had been belied. Nehru got some inkling of the disaffection prevailing in Tibet from the denial of permission to go to Lhasa and from his personal impressions when he crossed the Chumbi Valley on the way to and back from Bhutan in September 1958. There was also a tinge of guilt in his mind at having disallowed the Dalai Lama to stay on in India, even temporarily, in February 1957. With Nehru's basic sympathy for the peaceful Tibetan people, an assurance was extended that this time the Dalai Lama would not be denied entry or stay in India.

Perhaps I was the first to receive an advance copy of the message on 31 March that the Dalai Lama and party had crossed through the Bumla Pass in the Kameng frontier division. I was dining with a Political Officer in the US Embassy and arrived late for dinner, but I did not then know that an operative in the pay of the CIA, who was in the Dalai Lama's party, had been in direct wireless touch with the American Embassy.

It proved a great advantage that NEFA was beyond the 'Inner line' and still under the External Affairs Ministry. With a wholly different rationale from that of the British administration in quarantining the tribal areas, Nehru did not want the tribal culture overwhelmed or 'commercialized' by the intrusion of people from the plains with the establishment of the usual administrative infrastructure.

The Dalai Lama and his entourage stopped at the Tawang monastery which also belongs to the Yellow Hat Sect of Mahayana Buddhism and so held the Dalai Lama in special reverence. The party was advised to stay a fortnight in the divisional headquarters in Bomdila. This period of rest and recuperation allowed time for the government in Delhi to make preparations for his semi-permanent residence. The Home Minister, Govind Ballabh Pant, persuaded G.D. Birla to vacate and make available the Birla House in Mussoorie. At one stage it was suggested that I should go to Bomdila to be with the Dalai Lama, but since I was at the hub of administrative responsibilities as well as handling a battery of questions in Parliament, the suggestion was summarily dropped. The Foreign Secretary, in fact, asked the Prime Minister if the Joint

Secretary who had recently demitted charge but was still in India, should be recalled but apparently Nehru thought as I was familiar with the problem, I could be left to do the best there was. And so by chance, in the biggest crisis for our Foreign Policy since Independence, the operational responsibility fell on my shoulders as a Deputy Secretary (the equivalent of a senior First Secretary). P.N. Menon who had served as Consul General in Lhasa and at the time was the 'spokesman' of the External Affairs Ministry, was chosen to proceed to Bomdila as Liasion Officer with the Dalai Lama. He continued in that capacity for several months. With a very sparse administrative infrastructure, the burden for the Political Officer having a VIP and his entourage on his hands was not easy, but we were fortunate in having an extremely able and tactful incumbent in Harmander Singh (later awarded the Padma Shri), who belonged to the recently constituted Indian Frontier Administrative Service.

DALAI LAMA GIVEN NON-POLITICAL ASYLUM

The Dalai Lama's arrival in India was broadcast round the world. In the climate of the Cold War, it was billed as the greatest escape of the century and the ultimate indictment of the communist system. Scores of journalists, some very well known, converged on the little town of Tejpur on the banks of Brahmaputra, the nearest point from which the Dalai Lama would emerge from the Inner Line. Everyone wanted the first, if not the exclusive, story on the reasons for his break with the Chinese communists and the details of his adventurous trek across the barren Tibetan plateau. However impatient during his two-week wait, the Dalai Lama remained inaccessible and this was exasperating for the international media. One of them filed a report that, in a chartered aircraft, he had flown over the place where the Dalai Lama was staying and he went on to concoct a story about his activities. The *Express* of London managed to bring out Heinrich Harrer to supplement its reporter who had arrived earlier. (During the war, Harrer along with another Austrian named Aufschneiter had escaped from a prisoner of war camp in Dehradun and after overcoming many hazards, including being nearly caught by Indian police patrols, eventually reached Lhasa. He became the teacher of the young Dalai Lama and subsequently wrote the best-seller, *Seven Years in Tibet*. It was hoped that he at least would be able to get a private interview with his old pupil.)

Conditions in Tejpur were quite inadequate, indeed harsh, for the invasion by members of the international press corps. There were no hotels and only one inspection bungalow and a small mission compound; the heat and humidity were exasperating. The correspondents complained collectively to the Ministry of External Affairs and sent a garland of old newspaper cuttings to the Prime Minister. It was decided to send Samar (Tinoo) Sen, who had been the spokesman of the ministry and was then working as Joint Secretary In-charge of the European Division, to improve the facilities for the journalists congregated and sweating in Tejpur.

It was only too obvious that Dalai Lama, when he came out of the NEFA, would have to satisfy international curiosity about his political story as well as the physically arduous journey. The world wanted to know whether he would become an anti-communist crusader, but India had its own interest in not being buffeted away from its foreign policy approaches. I took the draft of a statement to the Prime Minister at his house around 10.30 at night and he edited it personally. I transmitted the final version to P.N. Menon for submission to the Dalai Lama as a suggestion from the Government of India. It has long been suspected that Nehru took the initiative and was personally responsible for denouncing China and its policies in Tibet. I suppose I was the only person who knew of Nehru's semantic inputs. The statement categorically affirmed that the Dalai Lama had come into exile of his own free will because his hopes of autonomy for Tibet, as promised, had not been respected. The statement sought to reflect the Dalai Lama's sentiments but moderated possible embarrassment for India. Dalai Lama emerged from his sanctuary of the Inner Line on 14 April. Sonam, the interpreter we had deputed, read the statement, which was distributed by Samar Sen and later by the ministry. Since no questions were allowed, it left the press angry and frustrated.

Accompanied by P.N. Menon, the Dalai Lama and his entourage were brought by a special train to Dehradun. Despite all efforts to enforce security and prevent further contact with the press, Marilyn Silverstone, one of the many photo journalists who had rushed to Tejpur, somehow succeeded in boarding the train. This began her special reverence for His Holiness. She stayed on in India and incidentally struck a friendship with Frank Moraes, the highly respected editor of *The Times of India*.

I was deputed to receive the Dalai Lama on behalf of the Government of India on his arrival at Birla House in Mussoorie. M.G. Kaul, then Home Secretary of UP, S.P. Varma the Inspector General of Police, and a lady representing the Birla family formed the small reception committee. This was my first contact with Dalai Lama but ever since he always meets me with a smile and a hug of recognition. I went back to Delhi the next day and reported to the Prime Minister and the Foreign Secretary. On 22 April both the Prime Minister and Foreign Secretary proceeded to Mussoorie. With the Prime Minister and head of the Foreign Office away, I knew I would be besieged with enquiries from diplomats and the international media. The Prime Minister jocularly said to me at the airport 'Now you are in sole charge'. The Prime Minister's conversation with the Dalai Lama lasted four hours. The Dalai Lama recounted the developments in Lhasa prior to his escape. Nehru expressed his understanding and sympathy for the Dalai Lama and the agony of Tibet but, as one learnt from the record and subsequent conversations, he made it clear that during the stay in India, Dalai Lama was not to contemplate functioning like the head of a government-in-exile.

While both the decision-making principals were away, I decided to prepare the draft of statement the Prime Minister was due to make in Parliament on Monday, 27 April. Normally Nehru was in the habit of speaking extempore from points scribbled as notes; unlike his successors, he seldom asked for the draft of a statement. My draft was in fact used extensively. The statement defined the triple elements in India's policy: national security; friendship with China; and the autonomy of Tibet under Chinese suzerainty. Nehru resisted demands for more active support for Tibet's aspirations and informed the Lok Sabha that he would not like the Dalai Lama to create an embarrassment to India's cherished relations with China. He did not, however, conceal his sympathy for the Dalai Lama and the suffering of Tibet.

While in the West there was political interest in the Dalai Lama's escape, in India it reflected a civilizational attribute. Hinduism had a tradition of accepting a plurality of faiths and worship wherein everybody's God deserved to be respected with spiritual reverence. The Dalai Lama in Mahayana Buddhism ideology was an incarnate Bodhisattva and so for Hindus, as much as for Buddhists, there was a spiritual dimension to the respect he commanded. The strong reactions in Parliament cut across party affiliations. Many in the Congress ranks were critical of restrictions being placed on the Dalai Lama's freedom by the Indian government. All press contacts including even with Heinrich Harrer were refused. If I remember correctly, *Time* magazine had a cover story showing Dalai Lama behind Indian barbed wires—the implications being that the flight was from one political prison to another. It was obvious to thoughtful observers that Nehru was walking a tight rope weighing public and parliamentary opinion and yet trying not to be pushed into unfriendliness with China. India had accepted that Tibet was a part of China and we were pledged to non-interference.

CHINA BLUNDERS IN NAMING NEHRU

China was grossly embarrassed at the worldwide publicity of Dalai Lama's escape and the condemnation of the suppression in Tibet; it made India a scapegoat in its defence. Only a high level decision could have decided that Nehru's speech of 27 April was fully reproduced in the *Peoples Daily* of (Renmin Ribau) Peking and subsequently all the cadres were advised to study it. On 6 May, the *Peoples Daily* published a two-page article, 'Nehru's Philosophy and the Revolt in Tibet', with obvious take-off on Nehru's speech. There was a similar thrust of argument running through the note presented on 16 May by Pan-tzu-Li, the Chinese Ambassador in Delhi, to the Foreign Secretary. It ended with a barely concealed threat: 'Friends, You too cannot afford two enemies. Is that not so?' It has long been suspected that the *Peoples Daily* article was drafted by Chou En-lai. My own suspicion is that the mix of the third person and the second person—unusual for a diplomatic note—may have emanated from Chairman Mao himself.

The substance of the Chinese defence-cum-counter-attack contained the suggestion that the Dalai Lama had been abducted by certain 'Indian elements'; that Dalai Lama was 'held under duress'; that the 'so-called revolt was only the work of a few upper strata reactionaries'; that the revolt was 'engineered by imperialists and foreign reactionaries'; that India like China had imperialist enemies—hinting at the West, etc. References were also made to India's expansionist designs. (Though not verifiable for obvious reasons, the broad fact was that two-thirds of Tibet and 80 per cent of the people were sympathetic to and supportive of the Dalai Lama.) The line of argument advanced by China was consistent with the programmed explanation that disaffection in one-party states, however widespread, came from a minority; the 'people' never revolted, only a handful of 'reactionaries' did.

The *Peoples Daily* article and the Chinese note, in my view, were proof of gross misconceptions of nationalism of India. It overlooked the decade old efforts by Nehru in personally husbanding faith in friendship with China. It betrayed a total lack of political understanding of the functioning of a parliamentary system and the democratic polity of India. There were, no doubt, people of Tibetan stock in and around Kalimpong who could be described as 'bourgeois reactionaries' and who were sympathetic to and even abetting the armed insurrection in Tibet, but these were also truly loyal to the Buddhist faith and the way of life of Tibet. It was undeservedly flattering of India's operational capabilities if it was seriously believed that the Tibetan exiles, even with the assumed help of intelligence agencies, could reach all over Tibet or conspire to abduct the Dalai Lama and stimulate an extensive and sustained insurrection. It was patent that despite reforms and developmental investment, the People's Republic had failed to win over Tibet. The Chinese leadership, including Mao-tse-Tung and Chou En-lai, had had several meetings with Nehru and must have been aware of his principled and unrequited support for the seating of the People's Republic in the UN, unconditionally surrendering the privileges inherited in Tibet, and in leading the Indian people in proclaiming 'Hindi-Chini bhai bhai'. It was a politically insensitive mistake to accuse Nehru as connected with the revolt in Tibet. It was no secret that even after Dalai Lama had been given asylum but in the face of strong public demands, Nehru was putting great political restraints on the Tibetan leader.

Anyone with a superficial understanding of India even from a distance could also recognize that Nehru was the pride, the unmatched darling, of the Indian people. Chou En-lai at least had personal experience of Nehru's position in India. The editorial comment accusing or linking Nehru with the revolt in Tibet shocked every section of opinion in India. The accusation, in fact, crystallized into a deeply felt sense that China had been indulging in deliberate deception and conscious betrayal of Nehru. The implied threat in the diplomatic note angered Nehru personally; it made a mockery of the spirit of the *panchsheel*. In my view, not the Nehru-Chou meeting in 1960 as some critics have argued, but this accusation of Nehru by name was the fatal turning point in Sino-Indian relations. If the Chinese had made all those accusations of abetting the disaffection in Tibet but without naming Nehru and had waited a while, even if some small incidents had occurred on the border, Nehru would have 'managed' to keep relations from further deterioration. In May 1959, for the first time since he became Prime Minister in 1947, Nehru was put on the defensive. Democratic public opinion went into a reaction and refused to endorse his sagacity and restraint.

Even the cumulative effect of the reactions should, Nehru thought, not be allowed to do irreparable damage to relations with China or compel a modification of his cherished hope of keeping India non-aligned. It is this anxiety that is the backdrop of the curt rejection of President Ayub's offer publicly extended in April 1959 of joint defence of the subcontinent against the threat of China. To Nehru the idea of India finding common ground against China with an ally of the West in the containment strategy was unthinkable. Alas in about two years time, without Pakistan repudiating its military links with the United States, China and Pakistan would begin exploring meaningful functional cooperation (including territorial adjustments on Kashmir's northern border). The history of the subcontinent may have taken a different course if Ayub's offer had at least been courteously examined.

The aggravation of Indian opinion was reflected outside

Parliament. The eminent political leader, Jayaprakash Narayan, who commanded respect next only to Nehru, speaking to the Indian Council of World Affairs said something to the effect that even if it was a lost cause, he would plead for the independence of Tibet. Although Nehru persisted with efforts of not allowing the total destruction of the fabric of China-India relations, he was in no position to moderate Indian opinion after the insulting misjudgements of his transparently friendly efforts.

There was some internal professional dissent: giving asylum to the Dalai Lama was a needless damage to our foreign policy, T.N. Kaul, then Ambassador to Iran and once an ardent advocate of India-China friendship suggested to me that we should push the Dalai Lama back into Tibet. I said that the Prime Minister was not allowing the Dalai Lama to use India as a political base for anti-Chinese activity but I did not think he would be able, politically speaking, to compel him to return as we had done in 1957.

For me from March 1959 onwards was a long hot summer and a very busy winter. I was at the centre of growing responsibilities, which could not easily be deflected. In June K.L. Mehta became Joint Secretary and head of the Eastern Division. After some months, I was allowed to transfer responsibilities for Bhutan, Sikkim, and Nepal to Rikhi Jaipal against a new post of Deputy Secretary and I was left to concentrate on work connected with China and Tibet, directly under the Foreign Secretary.

NEHRU APPROVES LETTING IN TIBETANS AND SAVES THE NUCLEUS OF A CIVILIZATION

The Prime Minister had been initially hesitant to encourage the flood of Tibetans who followed the Dalai Lama, but the stories of their desperate plight made him decide that no one who arrived on our borders should be turned away. Thousands of Tibetans in small parties began to stream in across our borders and we had to improvize their feeding, shelter, and minimal medical facilities at halts in out of the way places in NEFA. After a few weeks, a camp was established in Misamari near Tejpur, the most convenient location for holding incoming refugees. For Tibetans accustomed to living on the high plateau, the hot plains of Assam took a heavy toll but they were relieved to be in a safe habitat. Until the camp was established, I was sending wireless messages to prepare different staging posts for incoming Tibetan parties. I remember one day sending 80 messages for these kinds of logistics. Eventually B.N. Nanda, a retired official from the old Commonwealth Relations Department, was made responsible for establishing and running the camp.

We also had to create an institutional infrastructure to receive and distribute the gifts that had started pouring in spontaneously from all over the world and make sure that they were not pilfered or sold in the market. A Central Tibetan Relief Committee under the Chairmanship of Sucheta Kripalani—later the Chief Minister of UP—was established with Kalyan Singh Gupta as Secretary and I was regularly liaising with this Committee. It is to the credit of Sucheta Kripalani's leadership that no complaint ever came of money or supplies being illegitimately diverted. Nehru recognized that vast numbers of Tibetans (eventually totalling about 1,00,000), were going to be in India for a long stay. The Prime Minister asked the different ministries and Chief Ministers to help locate land for Tibetan colonies where refugees could start making Tibetan artefacts and become self-supporting.

Many who came were escaping from monasteries and brought Tibetan religious manuscripts and valuable Tibetan *thankas*. Fairly early in the refugee reception, it was decided to separate the monks and send them to the camp in Buxar. For a while the abandoned Second World War military barracks became the nucleus of Tibetan monasteries in-exile. Nehru approved the establishment of Tibetan language schools, being financed by the central government, so that the Tibetan children could continue to be instructed in their own language. It has seldom been recognized that through such cultural sensitivity, Nehru was responsible for saving the authentic nucleus of the Tibetan civilization. If after 40 years of exile, there are Tibetan scholars, monks as well as young children speaking the language and cherishing faith in Buddhism, it is due to Nehru. Though living in exile, the Tibetans are earning and praying in dignity in Dharmshala, Mussoorie, Dehradun, Darjeeling, and Karnataka.

PARLIAMENTARY ANXIETIES

It was not the Tibetan refugees, for long my main preoccupation, but the continuing political crisis in relations with China, that was my main cause for anxiety. In the summer and autumn of 1959, a succession of unexpected incidents accentuated our anxieties. Longju, Migyitun, and Khinzemene in the Eastern Sector were small intrusions but more serious was the clash near the Kongka Pass in the Western Sector, where the Indian patrol sent to locate the southern extremity of the Chinese intrusions was captured, and Karan Singh the leader and six members of the patrol, killed. The parliamentary interest aroused after the Dalai Lama's arrival never slackened during the year. Newspaper reports of every incident, sometimes actual and sometimes distorted, were printed under banner headlines. Each report led to an immediate demand for an adjournment motion in one or both Houses. Typically the motion for urgent discussion would be filed in the Speaker's office at 11 a.m. and under parliamentary practice, it required priority attention at the end of the question hour at noon—the so-called zero hour. A copy of the adjournment motion would reach Seshan, the Private Secretary of the Prime Minister at 11.15 a.m. and he would promptly telephone to me in South Block, *Phir aa gaya hai* (it has come again). I would rush to Parliament House, reach Seshan's office at about 11.25, and grasp the thrust of the member's alarm, dictate a couple of paragraphs on the basis of what I could remember on the specific point to one of the Prime Minister's own stenographers who would bring it back to me by 11.55 so that I would be ready to put it in the Prime Minister's hands at midday. I would add some details and background verbally. On an average, when Parliament was in session, I would be in the official's box of one or the other House four days in a week. No junior minister was ever asked to handle questions if they related to China. Nehru would walk across from the Lok Sabha to the Rajya Sabha or vice versa to give short reactions and say why the adjournment motion should not be taken up. This could go on for half an hour. The Prime Minister got irritated that I was not available to brief him during his walk across the Central Hall. I explained that I had to run around the long outer gallery, about 60-80 yards, which took many minutes, since officials were not allowed in the Central Hall. He was so exasperated in not having me verbally brief him when he himself was rushing from one House to the other that, on his instructions, as a unique exception, I was issued a Central Hall pass by the Parliament Secretariat so that I could walk with him. Apart from such adjournment motions, there were starred, unstarred, and short-notice questions and, of course in every session each House had one- or two-day debates on foreign policy focusing on China. During sessions about three-quarters of my day was taken up by parliamentary work. Nehru paid scrupulous deference to Parliament and it was surprising that the Chinese never noted its significance. In late August and early September, Nehru had made extensive statements that in the Western Sector, the border was vague but this did not imply that over that vast area China had stronger historical connections. However, national anxiety was heightened when the *Times of India* carried banner headline—as if it was not known before—that the Sinkiang Highway cut across Indian territory on the Aksai Chin plateau.

On 8 September 1959 came Chou En-lai's reply to Nehru's letter of 22 March. In this letter, for the first time, the Chinese Prime Minister categorically affirmed the claim in support of their line as delineated on the 1956 Chinese maps. The tentativeness and disarming vagueness of the earlier correspondence was not reiterated. The Chinese maps to which Nehru had drawn attention and Chou En-lai had almost brushed aside as based on KMT surveys, were now claimed as correct, even while continuing to argue that the whole border required formal delimitation. The letter shocked sober opinion even in the Communist Party.

Parliamentary suspicions had deepened after the border clashes. The mistrust was almost amounting to anger at the government for its systematic suppression of information pertaining to problems with China. After Chou En-lai's latest letter, in the face of distrust and suspicions of secrecy, Nehru (a democrat at heart) announced that all notes and papers exchanged in the previous five years which pertained to relations with China would be released in official 'White Papers'. The decision was spontaneously taken, without reflection and without internal consultations and, in effect, it compromised confidentiality, which is an essential ingredient of diplomacy and inter-governmental exchange. (Woodrow Wilson, in his idealism, had urged 'open covenants openly arrived at', but this had never been followed in diplomatic intercourse.) The commitment that every diplomatic document exchanged would be made public inhibited our relations with China for years.

Nehru had discouraged a Tibetan government-in-exile, but sensing the mounting anger against China, the Dalai Lama started speaking out politically. Even so, the Government of India refused to plead for Tibet in the UN General Assembly. However, under relentless and repeated parliamentary pressure following Chou En-lai's letters, Nehru reaffirmed that India's borders were clear, traditionally confirmed, and no major disputation about their alignment could be countenanced. Earlier Nehru was categorical about the Eastern Sector (generally referring to it as McMahon Line). S. Gopal, the Director of the Historical Division, returned from London having studied the India Office Archives and other evidence, and asserted that evidence on the Western Sector (and Aksai Chin) also had strength and merit, and Nehru stopped referring to Ladakh with the earlier lack of confidence such as 'not a blade of grass grows there'.

Around November 1959, the Chinese may have belatedly recognized the strong feeling aroused in India and decided to undertake measured damage control and defuse the growing hostility against China. In this spirit, the proposal for a 20 km. withdrawal by both countries, all along the line of administrative control was made but the public position had already hardened, especially after reports of casualties and torture of Indians captured at the Kongka Pass. But even temporary withdrawal from what was affirmed as our own territory would have outraged public and parliamentary opinion. The Indian reply to the Chinese proposal, which reflected this political mood, emanated from the Foreign Secretary's able mind. In the Western Sector, our reply suggested that both sides withdraw beyond the line claimed by the other country. This would have involved China vacating several thousand miles of occupied Indian territory, but a much smaller area by India. Our note implied that there was no need to apply the same principle in the Eastern Sector, as it would have meant Indian withdrawal from the whole of NEFA where there was no comparable problem.

When the withdrawal proposed by China evoked an unsatisfactory response, a long soberly worded note came from the Chinese in December urging the desirability of a reasonable settlement. As another friendly gesture, Chou En-lai suggested a summit meeting either in Delhi, Peking, or Rangoon. Indeed U Nu, the Burmese Premier, offered to go to Peking to explore the potential for mediation. Well intentioned, U Nu overlooked the mood in India. In the face of parliamentary opinion, any such step of mediation or a summit meeting would look too much like appeasement, unless China first offered to withdraw from Indian territory. Nehru himself was mentally prepared to let China continue to use the Aksai Chin Highway on lease from India, but by this time, even mighty Nehru had to take note of the collective sensitivity of Parliament, notwithstanding the fact that his own Congress party commanded a comfortable numerical majority. Where national honour was perceived as having been slighted, whips could not be used. Nehru was on the defensive.

It was in this stalemated tension that over Christmas 1959 I made bold to write a confidential paper, arguing that the problem of India-China was more than a territorial dispute; it had revealed political differences and civilizational divergence. In the parliamentary frenzy serious deeper issues had been obscured and should be now considered. We had to be concerned, for example, at China's attitude towards Sikkim, Bhutan, and even Nepal, all strategically important for India. It was a five or six page note reflecting on the prospect of a possible Prime Ministerial meeting which may have to be accepted some time in the future. I marked the paper to the Foreign Secretary and though I had plenty of occasions, never mentioned it to the Prime Minister himself. I had hoped that the Foreign Secretary would forward it with his own comments to the Prime Minister and provoke him into reflecting on the issues raised. No reaction came. The paper lay on the Foreign Secretary's table for months. Finally it was returned to me, without comment or a date, in June 1960—after the Prime Ministerial meetings—but just before the official team was set to leave for the first meeting in Peking. I may have exceeded my brief but, on the other hand, I felt it was my duty to put my thoughts and anxieties on paper. It was a busy time for all of us dealing with China but in retrospect I regret I did not nudge the Foreign Secretary with an enquiry and suggest putting it to the Prime Minister.

NEHRU DECIDES TO 'TALK' TO CHOU EN-LAI

In the middle of February 1960, Nehru modified his earlier hesitation about not meeting with the Chinese Premier, and decided to invite Chou to Delhi in April. This may have been influenced by the passing visit of Khrushchev, but more likely he did not want to be inconsistent with his own approach towards diplomatic methods in conflict amelioration. However, when the budget session started, strong fears were again voiced of a climb down in the offing and so assurances had to be reiterated by Nehru that there would be no dilution of the commitment about the national territory.

With Chou En-lai's visit in the offing, Gopal and I made a list of a possible 108 'items', which we thought, could come up in the Prime Ministerial discussions. Some 60 issues on this list required assembling historical evidence that could be disputed, and these were assigned for preparation of briefs under Gopal's direction to the officers in his division. Roughly 40 items had political implications and so remained my personal responsibility. I had no one to whom I could devolve my share of the work. Preparing briefs, some only of half a page or little more, but many requiring longer elaboration, needed study to marshal the background into cogent arguments, and reference to the 'Top Secret' files. I knew I should not take secret files home, but daylight hours were mostly taken with meetings and parliamentary business and so for much of March, I slept in the office on a sofa which fortunately had no side rests. Late at night was the only time for concentrated study. One of my personal assistants agreed to stay till 11 p.m. I dare say, I must have been the only officer at work virtually through the night but the exhilaration of responsibility gets sharpened during a crisis. I did not advertise my nocturnal sojourn in the office—I used to go home in the morning for bath and breakfast—but word spread through the Central Registry which along with cipher bureau worked 24 hours. I was rewarded with nods of appreciation of the Prime Minister and senior colleagues. As a mark of recognition and encouragement, Nehru asked Mrs Gandhi to ring up my wife and asked her to bring the children to see the giant pandas and play in the garden of Teen Murti House.

By May 1959, I had completed three years at headquarters and although I had only twelve years service, I was approaching the zone for promotion to the junior selection grade. In the spring chain of postings, the Foreign Service Board in the normal course approved my appointment as Consul-General, Saigon, the head of the post accredited to the Government of South Vietnam. I knew I was in a post of critical responsibility and in the thick of a serious crisis and so I never dropped any hints about the due promotion. At that time there was only one post equivalent to that of a Counsellor and that was earmarked for the spokesman and Director of External Publicity. Foreign Secretary Dutt was a conservative administrator, and against the proliferation of ranks and posts but a year later—on the eve of Chou En-lai's visit—without any request from me, he took the initiative and as a special case, a post of Director was created and I was put in independent charge of the Northern Division dealing with China. It was evident that I would be expected to stay on for some more time and of course I took it as a mark of confidence.

On the eve of Chou En-lai's arrival there were intensified apprehensions in the Opposition benches and even amongst Congress supporters and outside observers that Nehru might surreptitiously compromise on India's territorial integrity. He had, after all, gone back on his refusal of a meeting with the Chinese Premier without the latter's prior withdrawal and so public demonstrations led by the Jan Sangh were organized with placards reading 'No surrender of Indian territory', 'Down with Chinese Imperialism', etc.

To questions about the rationale of the change of attitude Nehru in a kind of verbal sophistry, sought to make a distinction between 'talks' and 'negotiations'. Nehru was no doubt shaken by China's affirming once disowned cartographical claims and the bitter reactions to the Kongka Pass and other incidents, but his faith in reasoned friendliness between newly independent countries had remained unshaken. The Nehru mindset probably also harboured some hope that India's unwavering friendship, the articulated strength of nationalism in India, and the weight of evidence being marshalled, the Chinese Premier may show a willingness for accommodation like agreeing to lease territory around the highway in the Western Sector. However, even in his mind no retraction from the notified and affirmed frontiers of India was seen as politically feasible. On the other side, one could vaguely divine that Chou En-lai in persisting with the idea of a summit meeting may well have had serious expectation of stronger compulsion to defuse the tension and therefore a commitment could be clinched which would improve the climate and bring about a sort of truce against further accidental conflicts. He may have expected that he could persuade Nehru to limit patrolling along the zigzag line of control. In brief the two governments remained at cross-purposes and neither fully understood the other, and yet both, for separate reasons, did not want to aggravate the deterioration of relations.

INDIA-CHINA REMAIN AT CROSS PURPOSES IN TALKS, APRIL 1960

Chou En-lai, accompanied by Foreign Minister Chen Yi and a large delegation, arrived in three special aircraft on 19 April and received a correct but not effusive welcome. The size of the Chinese delegation and the proposed duration of a one-week stay was indicative of serious purposefulness of the visitors: India had expected that the stay would be for two days only. There were in fact, seven meetings, all one-to-one between the two Prime Ministers with Chieh acting as interpreter for Chou En-lai and Paranjpe for Nehru. The meetings were held in the sanctuary of the Teen Murti House, the Prime Minister's residence, which enabled control of access to the press or unauthorized personnel. Gopal and I generally sat downstairs in M.O. Matthai's office sipping interminable cups of tea, coffee, or glasses of *nimbu pani* but none of us, much less the Foreign Secretary, was ever summoned during the meetings. I do not believe our fat briefing folder was ever used. I cannot help feeling that it was a mistake for Nehru to decide to meet on a one-to-one basis. We could provide details and even send slips with suggestions. Sitting behind the principals may or may not be necessary in offering timely correctives to any inadvertent slips, but attending summit level talks would give a first-hand flavour for officials to follow-up and subsequent internal discussions. It was for the Foreign Secretary to make the suggestion but he refrained from doing so.

Chou En-lai was an ace diplomat, in total command of details and able to weave these into a plausible conceptual framework. Nehru understood international affairs in depth and combined it with the transparent sincerity of an idealist, but did not have the matching capacity of marshalling facts. My guess is that the reason why Nehru did not have any advisers sitting in the room with him was not intellectual arrogance but because Chou En-lai was accompanied by his Foreign Minister in addition to a platoon of officials and experts. If Nehru were to have anyone with him, it would have had to be one if not more of the senior ministers. For different reasons Nehru probably hesitated to have G.B. Pant, the Home Minister, or Morarji Desai, the Finance Minister with him because he suspected they were not quite on the same wavelength in Foreign Policy approaches. Having Krishna Menon would have only aroused public criticism. However, these senior ministers did have pre-arranged separate meetings with Chou and Chen-Yi and got a flavour of their strong views. (Note-taking officials were allowed to be present at these meetings.) Krishna Menon took the initiative to call on the Chinese dignitaries with or without the Prime Minister's approval, but this created some internal comment. Anyway, we never saw any records of Krishna Menon's meetings.

The overriding political fact was that the Prime Minister of India was boxed in by Parliament and the aroused public opinion in the country. It should be emphasized that in April 1960 there was not the remotest apprehension of a major conflict ahead between the armed forces of China and India. Nor to my knowledge was there, at the time, a single person in Parliament or outside, not even in the Left parties, suggesting that India should make an accommodation on the basis of the recognition of the Indian control in the East in exchange for India accepting Chinese control of Aksai Chin. In any case no such offer was made during the talks from the Chinese side. It is only in retrospective sagacity that some analysts and observers, foreign and Indian, who have suggested that April 1960 was the moment to offer a barter deal of *de jure* recognition of the Eastern Sector (McMahon line) and in return for conceding broadly the Chinese claims in the Western Sector. Amongst them are not only detached observers but even some career officers, but most of them were removed physically or intellectually from the scene of the action. Incidentally, although throwing the Chinese out was being constantly parroted, I do not recall anyone inside or outside government daring to even speculate on the hazards of military operations aimed at evicting the Chinese from Aksai Chin.

Much of the presentation and argumentation between the Prime Ministers was really a reiteration of what was contained in their respective letters to each other. After the meetings, Nehru would briefly summarize the conversations to the Foreign Secretary where Gopal and I would be present, and periodically to the Cabinet Committee. I would be first to receive the transcript as dictated by Paranjpe to stenographers immediately after the conclusion of each session even if it was a late evening session. A separate copy was sent to the Foreign Secretary.

The transcript of the last but one meeting was brought to my flat in the Diplomatic Enclave around 5.30 in the morning. With no substantive progress in the talks before the meeting was concluded, Chou En-lai put forward Six Points which he hoped could be endorsed by both the Prime Ministers. At the meeting Nehru raised no objection as they seemed innocuous and unobjectionable. When I read them I was alarmed as I thought it would go against Nehru's pledge to Parliament and could be politically embarrassing for him. Superficially nothing could be more trite and platitudinous than the first of these six principles which stated, 'There exists a dispute with regard to the boundary between the two sides.' The second affirmed that 'there is a line of actual control up to which each side exercises administrative jurisdiction'. The other four points were equally plausible and concluded with the unexceptionable hope that there should be tranquillity on the border. (Incidentally I have long suspected that it is the imaginative extrapolation from these Six Points which is the basis of the supposition that Chou En-lai formally offered a settlement by the exchange of NEFA for Aksai Chin.)

The devil was in the implications of those Six Points. I read and reread the transcript, dressed quickly and around 7 o'clock rushed to the Foreign Secretary's house on Race Course Road (at present the PM's residence) and mentioned to him that in the light of the Prime Minister's categorical and repeated commitments to Parliament, we cannot accept that 'there is a dispute'. The Foreign Secretary did not wholly share my alarm and since he was not yet dressed for office, told me to go to see the Prime Minister and mention my interpretations and fears. I went to Teen Murti House where the Prime Minister had finished breakfast and was meeting the daily gathering of visitors. He asked me to accompany him to the South Block but as I did not want to leave my car behind I followed him. In his office I stuttered my anxiety that since we had argued that the Chinese had unlawfully come into what we had notified as Indian territory, a distinction has to be made between a 'dispute' and a 'claim'. Before I could explain myself fully, he showed his characteristic impatience and said, 'It is obviously a dispute; otherwise why am I talking to Chou En-lai and wasting his time and mine?' Nehru assumed the familiar visage of anger when someone made a foolish suggestion. I was probably not very coherent. Anyway there was not much time and he and I both proceeded separately to the house of the Home Minister, Govind Ballabh Pant, where the Foreign Affairs Committee of the Cabinet was meeting at 9.15 a.m. for a final review. Nehru summarized the gist of the conversation to his colleagues and got the approval of the line to be taken, which was broadly consistent with our previous stand. He did not specifically dwell on the Six Points. From this meeting, Nehru was going straight back to his residence for the seventh and final meeting with Chou En-lai. I was naturally silent during the Cabinet discussions. (Even the Cabinet Secretary and Foreign Secretary did not normally speak unless asked a question.) However, as the Prime Minister was getting into his car in the portico, somewhat impetuously—as it was in front of other ministers and the senior secretaries—I again made bold to mention to the Prime Minister that consistent with past pronouncements, we cannot subscribe to the idea of a dispute mentioned in the Six Points. If we accept them then we cannot charge the violation of our frontier. The Prime Minister heard me and said nothing and got into his car.

As soon as I got back to my office in South Block, I was summoned by the Foreign Secretary and was roundly admonished for daring to advise the Prime Minister and that too in the presence of his Cabinet colleagues. Mr Dutt said something to the effect that I was young for this responsibility but must not outrage discipline. However, in the drive back from Maulana Azad Road to Teen Murti House, Panditji must have reflected on what I had repeatedly sought to urge. Anyway as soon as the last meeting with the Chinese Premier started, Nehru referred to the Six Points and told Chou En-lai that he could not subscribe to them as an agreed statement. Nehru's not acquiescing of the Six Points in the penultimate session and his repudiating in the agreement in the final session is confirmed in the official records of the visit. The meeting went over familiar ground with a politeness characteristic of both statesmen.

I mention this episode not just because in my concept of civil servant ethics, I strongly believe that we have an obligation to volunteer advice and dissent even if not asked (and of course once decisions are taken to implement them faithfully or resign in protest), but in this case, in my view, a great political pitfall lay ahead for the Prime Minister. Had he endorsed the statement, our case, as put forward in Nehru's own letters, indeed the coherence of our stand would have been totally compromised and he would have been embarrassed at reneging on his repeated pledges to Parliament. Right or wrong, the Government of India had taken the position that our boundary, though traditional, was clear beyond any major dispute. In passing it is worth mentioning that for fifty plus years China has jibbed and protested on the remotest legal implications of Taiwan, not being *de facto* considered even temporarily as part of mainland sovereignty. Similarly, India has challenged any suggestion that there was a dispute (not just a problem) about Kashmir.

Because of Nehru's refusal to subscribe to the Six Points, Chou En-lai affirmed them unilaterally and this was done by his calling a Press Conference in Rashtrapati Bhavan at 10.30

in the evening. (The Chinese dignitaries had other engagements during the day and Chou En-lai and party were due to leave for Kathmandu the next morning.) I sneaked into the Press Conference, which lasted till after midnight. There were many questions from the foreign and Indian journalists. Chou En-lai demonstrated his urbanity and was confident and plausible. He declared that questions asked and his own replies would be published verbatim in *The Peking Review*. In reply to a question he said China respected India's relations with Bhutan and Sikkim, but when finally the transcript of the Press Conference was printed, careful scrutiny showed that the adjective 'proper' had been inserted. (The implication was that China would respect the relations between India and Bhutan and Sikkim, which China considered 'proper'.) As it happened, we had kept a tape recording of the Press Conference. All this has no present political importance but it is, nevertheless, significant for historical veracity. Neville Maxwell may have been unaware of this background and so in his book *India's China War* he attributes the decision to hold the Press Conference to the Chinese Premier's habit of accessibility to the press! The Indian Prime Minister's reactions to the press enquiries at the airport after seeing off the Chinese party and his statement in Parliament and Chou En-lai's critical comments in Kathmandu were important but they are on public record and require no elaboration.

JOINT COMMUNIQUÉ COMMISSIONING OFFICIALS

Although there was no joint statement on the substantive issues and no consensus on the Six Points but, as generally happens after all high-level meetings, total failure is seldom blandly announced and a sort of ongoing effort is agreed. In this spirit, both Prime Ministers agreed that the dialogue should continue. An extract of the agreed text of the communiqué reads as follows:

> The two Prime Ministers, therefore, agreed that officials of the two governments should meet and examine, check and study all historical documents, records, accounts, maps and other material relevant to the boundary question, *on which each side relied in support of its stand, and draw up a report for submission to the two governments*. This report

would list the points on which there was agreement and the points on which there was disagreement or which should be examined more fully and clarified. This report should prove helpful towards further consideration of these problems by the two governments.

During the period of further examination of the factual material, every effort should be made by the parties to avoid friction and clashes in the border areas.

The communiqué was to give the impression that the process of exploring each other's views was continuing. The joint communiqué was drafted somewhat hurriedly after the last meeting of the Prime Ministers by the Foreign Secretary (I was not involved in it). Three years history with honest, even if unrealistic, idealism on the one hand and misconceived prevarications on the other, followed by a cascades of provocative Chinese statements on extraneous events in Tibet, some strong political fallout in India had left no room for meaningful negotiations, at least not for officials. A little reflection would have made it clear that the assignment was virtually impossible not only because of the chasm of differences but because, at least the Indian side, was hemmed in by imposed political constraints. The essence of the Chinese case was that a boundary line had no validity if it was not jointly surveyed, described, or negotiated—in other words, formally delimited; for India, the traditional limits were declared as clear and publicly affirmed in an official map. This assertion had not only been conveyed diplomatically but was affirmed openly to a democratically elected Parliament. Old delineations like the Macdonald McCartney line lying further west, or the Ardagh line further east in the Western Sector, were by implication to be quietly disowned. The significant phrase was that officers were to furnish evidence *on which each side relied in support of its stand.* Maxwell does not even quote this crucial phrase of the communiqué.

Some post-hoc analysts give the impression that the official teams had the latitude of negotiators. Superficially the officials were being instructed to proceed on a search for objective historical research in a scholarly exercise. Almost every analyst has missed the point that the Indian side were advocates in defence of a specified delineation already established and communicated in the Prime Minister's letters. The latter left not an iota of discretion for give or take, or the remotest loophole for concession on a particular pocket, even if the Indian evidence was flawed or absent. The Chinese were not answerable to an accountable government, responsible to a vigilant legislature. Indeed the Chinese had a negative vested interest—that a boundary did not exist, and was not clear as it had not been formally delimited (and by unspoken implication that none was therefore violated in secrecy). I do not believe that this was understood when the communiqué was drafted.

The other point, wholly extraneous but which made the task of the Indian team even more complicated, was the coincidence with a Supreme Court judgement over Berubari, an enclave in East Pakistan. An India-Pakistan agreement had been reached to exchange pockets in adverse possession but on an appeal from West Bengal, the judgement declared that, regardless of 'additions' to India, any part once considered Indian on the day the Constitution was promulgated (26 January 1950) could not be surrendered without a constitutional amendment. In the mood of the country, the Indian case against China was thus legally and politically complicated as had never been foreseen in the previous decade. In the early 1950s, the various lines proposed in the past—the Ardagh line, the McCartney line—were probably considered. The line adopted was not the maximalist line but when the original delineation was conveyed by the Ministry of External Affairs (possibly in the early 1950s) to the Surveyor General for incorporation in the 1954 map, there was no anticipation of the kind of political or legal hostage or a diplomatic complication for India.

Our boundary does have broadly the powerful logic of human geography and historical evolution. As administrative control became more effective and assertive, lineal cartographic boundaries came to be embodied in treaties. Where mountains lie astride two countries (like France and Spain on either side of the Pyrenees), the watershed has come to delineate the limits and became the lineal boundary. However, at high altitudes like in the Himalayas, over long stretch of history, the truth is that it was a kind of frontier zone of gradual blending of ethnic stock, economic activity, and cultural identity. This is patently true as regards Tibetan, Indian, and Nepalese ethnicity. At the western end, the Karakoram range is indisputably within India but Aksai Chin is a barren uninhabited plateau. Though not as clear as in the Eastern and Middle Sector, our delineation upholds the watershed principle as the frontier follows the Kuen-lun range. Historically the Chinese from Sinkiang even had even less contact with this area than the Ladakh and the Dogra rulers. Indeed the Chinese had no historical familiarity with the whole of southern Tibet and the high Himalayas. Francis Watson, in *Frontiers of China*, provides a possible clue. He avers that China's historical notions of natural frontiers reflect a preference for looking down on a neighbour from the frontier. This would explain why the Ching dynasty and even the 1954 map of the People's Republic showed Nepal, Bhutan, Sikkim, northern Burma, half of Vietnam and of course NEFA (Arunachal) as part of the domains of China. In hindsight in 1947-54, we should have recognized that trans-Himalaya was a frontier or border zone and should not have been cornered into the constitutional rigidity of a linear definition. In the Western Sector, moreover, there was no resident population and/or strategic significance. This is hindsight wisdom applicable to both India and China.

Indian Officials had a Politically Hazardous Assignment

The full political and legal complexity were not fully grasped when officials were commissioned to marshal evidence 'in support of the stand of the two sides'. In any case it was going to be a tough exercise covering the entire length of our northern boundary and furnishing evidence in all its aspects. There was a deadline of four months to complete 'a joint report'. As far as I know, this assignment was unprecedented in its scope and intensity. It was quite unlike the China-America talks in the 1950s and 1960s when negotiators met conveniently at irregular intervals in Geneva and Warsaw and the familiar positions were reiterated and the delegates dispersed after brief meetings. The official talks on the India-China boundary question in 1960 were different; it was commissioned when we no longer affirmed fraternal friendship. Yet, at least in external relations in the mind of the Prime Minister, we were not enemies. An unforeseen political chasm in the relations had been catalysed by developments in Tibet, which gave gravity to the territorial dispute, but when the official talks were launched, both teams were anxious to prove their viewpoints and the strength of their respective cases to the other side. I repeat that neither side at the time expected that the crisis would end in a conflict. Both sides, however, had to show serious purposefulness knowing that the West and the Communists, as well as the 'friendly' neighbours and the bigger group of the non-aligned, were watching. The full implications only began to be obvious as we started preparing for the talks in Peking, scheduled to start in early June.

It was decided, presumably by the Foreign Secretary with the approval of the Prime Minister, that I should lead the official team. Our delegation for the first session was small. S. Gopal was the deputy leader and he had exceptional ability and grasp of the historical evidence and dimensions of the crisis. In addition there was Murty, who aside from being a historian was a Chinese speaker and had served as Assistant Political Officer in Tawang. G.N. Rao, an extremely able Research Officer from the Historical Division, had lectured at a post-graduate college. Paranjpe was our interpreter. The powers that be decided not to include Krishna Rao from the Legal Division, presumably because of the suspicion that he had strong affiliations to Krishna Menon and may have been a discordant member of the team, and so we had to improvise the legal arguments without any professional competence. Dr Gopalachari, Gopal's deputy in the Historical Division, was left behind to provide expertise available in the ministry. [He joined the second (Delhi) session.]

It was going to be a challenge to muster telling evidence covering 50,000 sq. miles. We would also require intellectual agility to scrutinize and expose flaws and promptly demolish the evidence that could be brought forward by the Chinese side. We had no illusions about the enormity of the task or the uncertainties ahead but I was confident that we had an exceptionally able and dedicated set of colleagues who would work cooperatively as a team.

Having heard of some post-hoc dispute on the veracity of some points in the negotiations on the Tibet region held in Peking in 1953-4 and wanting to avoid similar risks, I suggested to the Foreign Secretary that I would like to keep verbatim record, at least for our own information, of the entire proceedings and so I urged him to permit me to take three stenographers with our delegation. Mr Dutt instinctively wanted to limit extravagance and foreign travel to the barest minimum. (In five years as Foreign Secretary he probably did not go abroad even five times, and not once to the UN or the USA.) He agreed to permit only one stenographer to go with us. Luckily Roy, one of my own personal assistants and therefore familiar with the subject and exceptionally intelligent and fast, was agreeable to accompany us. Ambassador Parthasarthy in Peking agreed to make available stenographers from the Embassy, so that we managed to implement my determination to keep a complete transcript of every meeting. It is gratifying that no dispute has ever arisen of what, in fact, was said during the talks. We had trunkloads of material to take with us and so from Hong Kong to Peking, we travelled by train even though that required forty-eight hours. The Ambassador placed one of the buildings, which had been the residence and office of the Military Attaché, for our exclusive use.

A preliminary problem was the extent to which the Ambassador should intervene during the course of our talks. When the Chinese refused to acknowledge the legitimacy of the northern borders of Sikkim, Bhutan and the northern part of Jammu & Kashmir, the Ambassador wanted to take up the question to reinforce our right to do so with Chen Yi the Chinese Foreign Minister. But Chang-wen-Chin, who was the Director of the First Asian Division and my opposite number, was known to enjoy the confidence of the Chinese Prime Minister himself and the Foreign Minister, and it was realized that ambassadorial intervention would not be useful. I reported to Delhi after every meeting by telegram, but as a security precaution, I only dictated in the open garden, which was fortunately not unpleasant in the summer evenings. We kept Ambassador Parthasarthy informed, but the official delegation functioned autonomously of the Embassy. The pace was so intense that after the first week, I realized that even asking instructions or guidance from the ministry was inviting frustration. A reply was unlikely to come in time and in the meanwhile we would remain paralysed. After consultations amongst ourselves, we decided to take the risk of determining our own negotiating strategy.

We met every other day, three times a week. The average duration of meetings was four hours, frequently more, and the last meeting in Delhi went on for nine hours. The summary of the two reports—ours and Chinese—are bulky as can be seen from the photographs of the signing. The report was printed hurriedly to be ready at the beginning of the budget session of Parliament. An English edition was brought out by China in 1962. (I may have the only copy signed by my opposite number, Chang-wen-Chin, which he gave me at my request when I was posted in Peking in 1964.) The verbatim record, 3,000 pages of foolscape has also been printed but is available only for reference in the ministry.

SALIENT POINTS OF THE INDIAN SUMMARY

Summarizing in detail the arguments would be tedious and only repeat the contents of the Official Reports. I would however like to draw attention to some points, which have not received the attention they merit either because they are concealed in our 'officialese' or because their significance has been inadequately grasped.

(1) After the discussions in the first few meetings, we somehow managed to agree on a procedure, which gave the resemblance of a common agenda and yet allowed both sides to pursue their preferred thrusts. The Indian side could concentrate on the factual evidence under the agenda heading 'Tradition and Custom: Agreements and Administrative Jurisdiction'; the Chinese followed suit, but reverted whenever possible to their thesis on the imperative of formal delimitation. Consistent with their approach, the Chinese wanted all items to be discussed together for the entire length of the boundary but, considering the nature of the evidence, we preferred to do so in three sectors—Eastern (east of Bhutan coinciding with the McMahon line), Middle (west of Nepal along the Himalayas) and Western (south of Kuen Lun covering the Aksai Chin plateau up to Pangong Lake).

(2) Following the protracted difficulty of harmonizing the two

approaches for a common agenda, from the Indian side I argued that we must try to define the actual area, for which the two delegations must provide supporting factual evidence. This could best be done by each side furnishing to the other side a map (on the same or comparable scale) of what was considered to be the extent of its sovereign domain. Where the two alignments overlapped would define the geographical limits of the area we had to cover. We suggested that following UN practice, the maps exchanged should be on the 1:1000000 scale. The Chinese were initially reluctant to provide any map.

This provided the first point of confrontation between the delegations. I said they could draw the line according to their understanding, 'as far as Delhi if they so desire', but every country must have some notion of its limits. This discussion straddled several meetings and then I hinted that without such a definition, we could scarcely proceed further. With this gentle ultimatum, after a 'coffee' break, allowing for a higher level decision, the Chinese finally agreed to give us a map but it was on 1:5000000 scale—much smaller than our suggestion. I asked the leader of the Chinese delegation to sign it for authenticity and correspondingly I had the privilege to certify our northern frontier on a 1:70 miles scale (which was roughly comparable) and gave it to the Chinese side. That evening, walking in the garden of our house, Gopal and I felt that we had probably scored an important point in favour of our case; in effect the Chinese have accepted that boundaries can come into existence even if they are considered not 'formally delimited'.

(3) The exercise of furnishing evidence began with the precise, point to point, description of the boundary according to our delineation. We had agreed that both sides would have the option to seek clarification on evidence furnished by the other where it was considered obscure. The Indian description, it will be seen from the report, was more precise and detailed. The description compiled by G.N. Rao was precise but I or Gopal were in no position to verify it. (It was subsequently discovered that it did not always tally on the ground with the

watershed principle.) The Chinese gave a much vaguer description and were unable to answer the many questions put by my colleagues. This confirmed that the Chinese were not really familiar with the southern limits of what was considered China. (This is understandable as they had not really controlled the southern extremities of Tibet and Sinkiang.)

(4) At the third and final session at Rangoon, starting in November 1960, having added up the items of evidence furnished by the two sides in the Peking and Delhi sessions, we tabled a comparative statement. (We overlooked the fact that we considered many Chinese items, which were 'negative', irrelevant or imprecise). The items furnished by India added to 650, while the total for China was only 245. The Chinese objected to the inclusion of this rather embarrassing statistical comparison, but eventually Chang-wen-Chin let the table stand by a semantic change: substituting 'comparison' with the phrase, 'enabling this compilation'.

(5) Refuting the argument that China had used Aksai Chin to construct the highway from Sinkiang to Western Tibet and that even after years of completion of the highway India was not aware of its existence, we argued that trespass does not give legitimate title: indeed international law did not demand the continued occupation of territory if the title could be established.

(6) We adopted a novel method of approximating to the injunction of listing points of agreement and disagreement. In the third session, we exchanged the summaries on each item as drafted by the respective delegations and allowed the other side to scrutinize the text and check that it was faithful to the evidence furnished in the substantive discussions and no new evidence was being brought in at the summarizing stage. This way the two reports with a common forwarding letter, approximated to the injunction to list jointly the points of agreement and disagreement.

(7) The 'conclusion' remains the most important part of the Indian case. While much of the detailed evidence was the work of my historian colleagues—and they did an

exceptionally competent and commendable job—I had taken upon myself to thread together the overall summation underlining the salient features of our case and the weakness of Chinese argumentation. I had to take great care not to be caught in the trap of 'negotiations' or conceding that the lack of formal delimitation meant that India's frontier as delineated officially, carried no legality.

Before leaving Delhi, somewhat hurriedly, I had prepared the draft of the concluding chapter of the Indian report. The rough draft, about 80 pages in typed sheets (and eventually 50 pages in print) was ready only on the eve of our departure for the third session which with approval was to be held in Rangoon. I took the rough draft to the Prime Minister for approval. Although it was my doing, I requested Gopal to come with me. Sitting in the upstairs small sitting room of Teen Murti House, as it happened, next to the original Tang Dynasty horse presented to him by Chou En-lai during the 1956-7 visit, Nehru spent nearly two hours carefully going through the draft. He asked a few questions, made some serious and not so serious comments, but in the end approved the draft and the thrust of the argument. This gave me a great deal of confidence as I had come close to making some bold policy enunciation with political undertones. Surprisingly, many points have escaped the notice of the critics. Let me briefly highlight some of these points:

(1) The conclusion brings out our conceptual theory on the evolution of international boundaries. The process took diverse forms: *delineation* on agreed maps; *definition* going by specific coordinates; *description* by listing recognizable features; *demarcation* with markers or pillars on the ground. *Formal delimitation* was optional and could follow by adopting one or more of these methods. Boundary treaties were features only of the last 200 years of history but boundaries and state maps go back thousands of years, during which they came to command respect and acceptance. Boundaries, we argued, evolved through what one could call the process of *historical delimitation of frontiers*. A cursory scrutiny of boundaries around the world shows that, unless artificially altered by force or agreement, they

came into existence around natural features like mountain barriers, watersheds, rivers, etc. The Indian alignment was based on the Himalayas, respected and crystallized more precisely by the drainage divide along the crest of the highest range. It was pointed out that China's recent agreements with Burma and Nepal confirmed our contention that not only did geography shape history and cultural and ethnic divisions, but these evolved into 'traditional' lineal boundaries. China had agreed with Burma that there was a 'traditional' line running along a watershed, which in turn, coincided with the line described as the McMahon line. The line drawn in 1914, was therefore not an imposed arc but ran along the natural traditional divide between Tibet in the north and the Indian and Burmese principalities to the south of the water parting. This triple coincidence proved the fundamentals of India's contention.

(2) There is a whole section in the conclusion in which, as untutored lawyers, I argued that even if all the evidence furnished by India were set aside, the items tabled by China in their implications, could be sufficient to substantiate the Indian alignment. This exposed the weakness and contradictions of the Chinese evidence but this of course irritated the Chinese delegation.

(3) In the Eastern Sector, the only item which the Chinese had brought forth pertained to small pockets just adjoining the Himalayan watershed, but nothing to cover the entire area which cartographically runs along the edge of the foothills and adds up to a claim of 33,000 sq. miles.

Our evidence in the Western Sector was comparatively meagre. This was a barren uninhibited area and, over long stretch of history, left as a no man's land. However, the evidence to prove that it was traditionally considered part of Sinkiang, as asserted by China, was non-existent. In fact, during the nineteenth century, for a time, the Dogra rulers of Kashmir had maintained administrative posts there through the bitter winters. We underscored that there was total absence of historical control by China south of the Kuen Luen range and no proof, until trespass and the invasion of 1950, in support of the Chinese claim.

In the face of this assertion, the Chinese side produced two items to prove the pre-1950 title. They were (i) an item to show administrative control of Sinkiang in what we call Aksai Chin, (ii) a map of the 'Northern Warlord' dated 1927 showing jurisdiction and control over the area claimed. Taking great risks, my colleagues questioned the authenticity and functioning of the administrative unit and the publication of the map. The Chinese side was forced to admit that the administrative structure was 'proposed' but had never actually been established and that the map was a secret one. (All the maps printed in our Atlas of the Northern Frontier had been published in India, China, or some other country.)

(4) Politically the most difficult part of the talks was to face (and skirt) the question of the historical status of Tibet. We knew that between 1911 (when the Manchu Empire collapsed) and 1950, China had not even an Amban in Lhasa, and Tibet was functioning independently. But in 1954 India had recognized Tibet as part of China and at least until 1960 India-China relations were in a period of friendship or at worst diplomatic crisis, but not expecting a conflict. When asserting our territorial limits, we did not want to appear to be repudiating a negotiated agreement or to revert to claims of the British imperialists. On the other hand, it was essential that we uphold the validity of the Simla Agreement and specifically that the McMahon line legally confirmed the watershed boundary. Whether Tibet was independent or not was avoided, but for our purpose we asserted that Tibet had enjoyed treaty-making rights in 1914 and subsequently. The participation of Lonchen Shatra as Tibetan plenipotentiary along with Ivan Chen, the Chinese representative in the Simla parleys in 1914, was recognition of China's acceptance of Tibet's full powers to participate in the meeting and initial the McMahon map. In effect, we argued, that regardless of the international status of Tibet, it continued to be recognized by the government in Nanking that it had treaty-making rights and was exercising these in dealing with the British India in 1914s, and the 1920s, 1930s and 1940s. There was acquiescence or consent of the then

government of China. We pointed out that to deny Tibet's right to sign the McMahon line agreement would negate almost all evidence tabled during the discussions as there were practically no non-Tibetan corroboration to their claims.

(5) The argument which goes to the heart of the Sino-Indian crisis was that, while Indian diplomacy had been consistently transparent and credulous in the quest of China's friendship, including India's notion of the common frontier, China's own diplomatic practice was evasive, ambivalent and deliberately misleading. (True to Nehru's approach in not damaging relations with China, I carefully avoided a pejorative word like deception.) I recalled that China never tires of public protest at the slightest suspicion derogatory to China's political and territorial sovereignty. There must have been more than a thousand protests whenever there was the remotest implication that Taiwan was not a part of China. The North East Frontier Agency is mentioned in the Indian Constitution; Nehru's first statement regarding the border in the Eastern Sector was made in Parliament as early as in 1950; the Survey of India issued its first post-independence official map in 1954; Nehru took the initiative in drawing attention to erroneous Chinese maps in 1956 and in subsequent letters as well as in many official notes, protested even small violations of the proclaimed India delineation.

The relevant section in the conclusion is on pp. 274-6. It is politically the most charged part of the report. I would not have dared to include it if Nehru had not seen the statement in draft. Some extracts merit reproduction:

> If the alignment now claimed by China was even then regarded as the correct one, then to have kept undisclosed a claim of this magnitude was seriously misleading and contrary to the spirit of mutual confidence and respect for territorial integrity explicitly affirmed in the *Panchsheel*. Peaceful relations between sovereign nations are based on the assumption of the most honourable motives and intentions. India had reason to believe that China had accepted and acquiesced in the traditional Indian alignment and was only now creating a major boundary question and not that China had sought to deceive India until September

1959 and then for the first time openly disclosed her claims to Indian territory.

. . . The entire record of Sino-Indian relations since 1947 is a standing testimony of India's determination to promote friendship with China and to live in trust along the common border.

As far as I am aware, this was the first time that, on behalf of India, it was stated that China was not observing the famous *Panchsheel.* Krishna Menon would have been outraged had he seen this draft. The Foreign Secretary, a more cautious official, might have advised omitting the section, but the Prime Minister did not object to this formulation. It provided the basis for contending that China was stopped from pressing its claim.

Chang-wen-Chin was quick to grasp the damaging implications of the formulation as I had discreetly suggested that 'we preferred to believe it was a recent claim rather than that Chou En-lai was deceiving Nehru'. He challenged it as drafted but in the procedure agreed before hand, he was precluded from demanding its erasure.

(6) The last sentence of the conclusion comes as close as it was possible to get in implying that the Chinese were on Indian territory and should withdraw. 'The facts, therefore, demand respect for this boundary defined by Nature, confirmed by history and sanctioned by the laws of nation.'

In all honesty our evidence was uneven but objectively and comparatively strong. The positive support for the Chinese claim of jurisdiction or control even using Tibetan sources was truly meagre (except about the Tawang area which had traditional connection with the Drepung monastery in Lhasa). For us, superiority in the quality of the Indian claim was more than a matter of intellectual satisfaction, as a flaw in the Indian case could have been of great embarrassment in the surcharged atmosphere of democratically governed India. However, considering the way the crisis had developed, we could have no illusions of bringing about any difference in the ground realities, much less bringing about a Chinese withdrawal.

Two copies of the report were signed by S. Gopal and myself and by Chang-wen-Chin and Yang-kung-Su on 12 December 1960. We saw the Chinese delegation off and only then realized it had a longer secret tail of supporting officials whom we had not seen in the conference room. For the sake of prestige, the number of Chinese coming to meetings never exceeded our small delegation, which always paraded in full strength.

NERVOUSNESS AND EXHILIRATION AT COMPLETING THE ASSIGNMENT

The six-month long intensive 'negotiations' were for us a challenge of frightening dimensions. We found ourselves having to prove the geographic reach of the country as defined in Article 1 of the Constitution. No greater burden could fall on a citizen or an official. Our Parliament was going to scrutinize the result of our labours with a toothpick and if we had failed it could have embarrassed Jawaharlal Nehru, the much-loved Prime Minister. This oppressed me with a terrible burden of responsibility. We had to prove positively the legitimacy of the claim to 50,000 sq. miles of India, which had never been examined in anything like this detail in 1950 or in 1954, when the first map was published.

All members of the Indian team, in different degrees and ways were taut and nervous. I, for one, started smoking during these long sessions. Gopal did not smoke but he was all the time fidgeting with matches, waiting to light my cigarettes. Murty in Peking increased his rice intake to almost one kg a meal and in front of our eyes became grotesquely rotund. (Not surprisingly he died at a comparatively young age of a heart attack, after he had married a Canadian.) It should be added that though we were tense, so were the Chinese; yet we maintained friendly personal equations. When we got off the negotiating table, we were tolerably relaxed. Both sides entertained each other frequently not only in our respective diplomatic missions but in restaurants in the capitals. We took the Chinese team to Moti Mahal and the Chinese entertained us in famous Szechuan and Peking duck restaurants. Chang-wen-Chin and all his colleagues even came to dinner in my small flat in Chanakyapuri in Delhi. (Chinese diplomats had never before partaken of hospitality which was not 'official'.)

In the third and final session in Rangoon, U Nu thought this crisis in Sino-Indian relations over a territorial dispute could be overcome with goodwill, and that the problem was amenable to resolution by friendly informality. He arranged that both teams should be in cheek by jowl proximity for some days. (He did not understand the gulf of political rigidity under which we Indians were labouring.) He sent both teams for a few days to Taung Gye, a hill station in the Shan States. In a second attempt at relaxed informality, he persuaded us to go on a day-long river cruise on the Irrawady. Barrington, the last Anglo-Burmese ICS officer, who was Foreign Secretary, at my suggestion, took me out for a round of golf but since he did not want to be seen fraternizing only with Indians, he invited Chang-wen-Chin also. Chang did not swing a golf club but walked with us for 18 holes.

We could only come prepared with points or statements for the initial presentation of the afternoon and thereafter had to improvize. The greatest handicap was because I did not know Chinese and had to respond immediately after Chieh, the Chinese interpreter, had finished translating the statements by the leader or the deputy of the Chinese team. To relieve the tension, at one stage, I parodied a German marching song about the Watch on the Rhine. My improvisation went as follows:

Zum Lein
Zum Indische Lein
Fest steht und treu
Die Wacht am McMahon Line

No one from our side or the Chinese side followed German but I thought I detected a small trace of a smile on the face of Chang-wen-Chin. In the coffee break, I asked him, point blank, whether he knew German and he honestly disclosed that around 1928 he had spent two years at Heidelberg University. Then I said, 'You must also know English', and he did not deny it. He had thus the advantage of having a few minutes to mentally think his replies while Paranjpe was reproducing in Chinese what one of us had said in English. Later I found a book entitled *The Last Chance in China*, which gave Chang-wen-Chin's distinguished Manchu ancestry and mentioned that in

1943 he was the English language interpreter of Chou En-lai in negotiations with the Chang-kai-Shek in Chungking. He continued, however, to use the interpreter in working sessions. However, it did give us both occasional opportunities to get into a huddle on some little semantic problem to facilitate progress.

There was a brief suggestion that the Chinese text would be authentic, but this was overcome when we hinted that we would have to wait for finalization until we got an authentic translation in Hindi of the voluminous report. The English text was then readily accepted as a good practical neutral language.

The real unsung heroes were four stenographers whom the Foreign Secretary had permitted me to take to Rangoon. In barely one week, the four copy-typed the equivalent of 600 printed pages, thumping away on pre-electronic machines for almost twenty hours a day. Any correction required retyping the whole page. (We were told to hurry as the Burmese government wanted the Indian delegation to vacate the rooms in the hotel for a huge Chinese delegation expected a few days later.) Some of us stayed up till the small hours of the morning to sustain the morale of our typist heroes, who had tea and their meals next to the typewriters. No one could have done the job, preparing two original texts except persons from the subcontinent, at least so I reported to Pandit Nehru on our return. On my suggestion, the Prime Minister came to his office on Christmas day 1960 for a photograph with all the delegation. Everyone, including the typists, got a copy. A special monetary reward was also sanctioned, but only after a lapse of months.

We felt satisfied that we could accomplish the assignment within six months. (We had got the two Prime Ministers' approval to extend the time limit prescribed by two months.) In our joint submission to the two Prime Ministers, we recorded an honest expression that, notwithstanding difficulties, we worked in harmony and in a spirit of cordiality and co-operation. We went on to express the hope that the report would prove helpful to further consideration of the boundary question by the two governments, but this was a formality rather than an expectation. Frankly in the heart of hearts of the Indian side, perhaps also of our Chinese counterparts, we did not believe that the official talks and report could lead to an acceptable denouement. The Sino-Indian boundary had become a major political problem. We were, privately surprised at the coherence and consistency of our advocacy and the comparative superiority in the quality of our evidence. The officers of the Historical Division had done a remarkable job in collecting relevant material from diverse sources—India Office Archives, photostat maps from the Berlin museum, records from hill districts, diaries of many travellers—and these details were brought forth in an impressive compilation. This was all done within six months and, in part, while we were simultaneously engaged in arguing our case to our Chinese opposite numbers. It may not be too boastful to claim that our anticipation of the Chinese case was better than their insights into ours. S. Gopal and my other colleagues were more knowledgeable, scholarly, and intellectually sharp witted. We were gratified that objective observers within India and even elsewhere thought India had vindicated its case.

The Prime Minister with appreciative mention of S. Gopal and myself, commended the report. Pandit Govind Ballabh Pant, the Home Minister, had followed the problem from our telegrams from Peking more assiduously than any other minister or even the Prime Minister. I have been told by his son, K.C. Pant, that at the moment when the senior Pantji suffered his fatal stroke, he was preparing his reply to the debate on the President's address in the Rajya Sabha and actually dictating a fulsome tribute to the work of our team.

It was a matter of gratification that though tensions and anxieties about the border persisted, during the six months of the talks, even without a formal agreement for stopping patrolling, the Sino-Indian boundary had remained quiet. Not a single border incident had occurred like those in the previous and subsequent periods.

SCHOLARS AND ANALYSTS STARTED THEIR STUDY ONLY AFTER THE OFFICIAL REPORT

It is worth recalling that, Nehru had publicly disputed the Chinese cartographic claims in 1950 when the PLA marched into Tibet. Not a single substantive academic analysis was published for the ten years thereafter. The first book on the

Sino-Indian boundary, authored by S.K. Mukherjee, came out in 1962, after the publication of our Report. Alastair Lamb, commissioned by Chatham House, wrote a short book in 1963 on the China-India Border; Fisher, Rose and Huttenback brought out an objective study also in 1963; but the book which made a worldwide impact was Neville Maxwell's *India's China War*. This only came out in 1970. Maxwell's book is well researched but almost deliberately partisan and stops with the end of the 1962 conflict. His thesis, in brief, is that the war was due to India's provocations and intervention in Tibet. He certainly did great damage to India. He carried a subjective bias. From Nehru's statements and conversations there was sincerity and transparency of purpose while china was evasive and secretive in 1956-7. Even if there were incidents and provocation but not an 'attack'. Maxwell concludes the book in 1962 and one suspects the Chinese even in hindsight, would prefer to disown the punitivness in relations with India and with Vietnam (1979). Four decades have passed and no one now accuses India, or the CIA, of such malevolence, but Tibet has not yet been fully stabilized. Most studies have taken the Officials' Report as the benchmark of reference on the issue. Though not as prolific as Sino-American relations or US-Soviet relations and the Cold War, the Sino-Indian relations have become a minor academic industry. Scores of books, hundreds of articles have appeared on the subject, and all after our Report. Some are semi-official, some deliberately biased, and others truly well-researched and objective (which does not mean they are supportive of India). One book, which I came across recently called 'protracted contest' by Garver, shows great scholarship and comprehensive research but alas reveals a pro-Chinese tilt. I was struck by the author's subjectivity in reference to the 1960 talks and the 1965 India-Pakistan conflict where I was involved as a close observer. (At the end of the paper I list some of the books which I have consulted.)

Most academics, in my view, have failed to capture the political climate in which the events unfolded. Though the studies are written with the benefit of hindsight and rely on newspaper records, parliamentary speeches, editorials in English language papers, they do not fully reflect the mood of the country. Maxwell was a witness and does quote extensively, but his bias comes through unmistakably. He seemed to fancy himself as a latter day Edgar Snow with a vested interest as a spokesman for China covering up her flaws and diplomatic omissions. Indian reactions range from democratic outrage and negotiating rigidity at what was perceived as unwarranted accusations, a lack of transparency, etc. Though not an exact parallel, this can be compared to British public and governmental rejection of diplomacy and compromise after the Falklands were occupied by Argentina in 1982. Nehru too, like Mrs Thatcher, was responding to public opinion but even after three years, Nehru refused, perhaps unrealistically, to contemplate and order preparations for the possibility of a major military invasion. Maxwell was witness to the working of democracy but shows insufficient understanding of India.

The most interesting study is by Xuecheng, entitled *The Sino-Indian Relations*. The author acknowledges his gratitude to me by name. His institution, the Institute of Asia-Pacific Studies of the Chinese Academy of Social Sciences, probably sent him to Austin Texas because it was known that I went there each year to teach in the autumn semester. We had several long discussions and I agreed to answer his questions frankly but I find no impact of my arguments, instead only some avoidable misperceptions on the Indian as well as the Chinese side in the book. The study looks to me as a semi-official articulation of the familiar official Chinese position. I would commend a comparatively balanced monograph by two colleagues, C.V. Ranganathan and V.K. Khanna, which came out in 1999, but to my mind the Chapter 'Way Ahead' borders on the wishful. They place too much store by VIP visits and essentially temporary agreements, which raised platitudinous hopes but only covered up inner ambitions and anxieties. Those surfaced after the Pokharan explosion and the continuing supply of nuclear know-how to Pakistan. No author, including the Indians, seems to have grasped that for the Indian officials it was an exercise in advocacy in defence of the position already taken by the government when the crisis was precipitated by Chinese insensitivity to India's political ethos. Our report was not an objective collective Ph.D. thesis. We were representing the will and consensus of India as reflected by the democratically elected government at the time but we managed to marshal material that no academic historian had done until the crisis broke.

In May 1961, having completed two years more than the normal period of headquarters posting, I was transferred to take up appointment as the minister in Bonn. I was, therefore, only a distant observer to the tragic developments that followed the approval of the so-called Forward Policy in June 1961 which culminated in the India-China War in the autumn of 1962. Right up to September 1962, Nehru, Krishna Menon and other decision makers (including some military commanders) did not anticipate the dimensions of the military conflict starting around Thagla ridge. That was followed by the massive invasion along a 2,000-mile front, beginning on 20 October 1962 and in a second phase in November. Finally the unilateral ceasefire came on 21 November 1962. The story has been told many times. In Germany I was frequently questioned about the developments but I had only speculative insights on the military operations. The India-China war, as stated earlier, remains a gross example of compounding misperceptions on both sides. Mao and Chou En-lai and the political and military staff officers in Peking discussed (and grossly misjudged) Nehru for allegedly being unfriendly towards China and so planning a punitive Chinese operation, the decision makers in India were wholly innocent of the danger. Michael Breecher in his biography of Nehru puts his finger, quite accurately on attitudinal prism of the decision makers. Alas politically and psychologically the conflict proved fatal for Jawaharlal Nehru.

Yaacov Vertzberger's study of the conflict is illuminating in trying to grasp the roots of the related misperceptions. Steven Hoffmann followed the problem of India and China crisis for more than 20 years and published his study only in 1990 with documented objectivity.

PERSONAL REFLECTIONS ON INDIA-CHINA RELATIONS

Let me mention some developments in my own experience which flowed from the chance of being involved in dealing with China and leading the official team in 1960:

(1) While we were in the Delhi session of the talks in September 1960, Nehru went to Pakistan to sign the Indus Treaty. I had made bold to suggest on a file, and verbally to the Prime Minister, that he might moot to President Ayub that, while India and Pakistan disputed the future of Kashmir, the two countries could agree on the 'boundaries of the State of Jammu & Kashmir'. (China was not accepting our right to describe the boundary west of the Karakoram Pass as it was under Pakistani control.) There is a photograph of Nehru, Gopal and myself walking up and down on the tarmac just before he took off for Karachi in full view of all the dignitaries who had come to see the Prime Minister off: at that time he was actually discussing this idea. Until then, no agreement between China and Pakistan had even been broached, much less concluded. At this time Nehru was more favourably inclined towards Pakistan than when he had summarily dismissed the suggestion of talks on Joint Defence of the subcontinent. Nehru was intrigued with my idea and did mention it to Ayub and, I believe, it was not rejected out of hand. (I did not specifically suggest using a pre-war or our own map of 1954 but either way it would have included Aksai Chin in India.) It bears speculation that if we had followed up on the conversation, Aksai Chin and part of the northern territory of what, at one time, was considered part of Kashmir state might not have been alienated in the subsequent Pakistan-China agreement when talks got under way. Pakistan might have hesitated to affirm claim to parts of Hunza and Raksam valleys in the north but it would have been committed to Aksai Chin being part of Kashmir. The question really fell in the domain of the Pakistan division of our ministry, and in 1960 no one even remotely contemplated the possibility of China befriending Pakistan while the latter remained a Western ally. China-Pakistan talks on the northern part of J & K State actually got started in early 1962 and the agreement ceding what at one time was considered part of J & K was concluded in 1963.

(2) Incidentally on 27 October 1962, the *People's Daily* brought out another article 'More on Nehru's Philosophy', an

aggressive attack more vicious than in May 1959, accusing Nehru of having ambitions to build an empire to satisfy the Indian bourgeois and Western imperialists. Nehru was accused of 'frantic hostility towards China' and lacking in empathy for the Indian people. The article was timed to meet international criticism of the wanton armed action against India launched on 20 October. In the light of current Sino-US relations, it appears ironical. Considering the record of Nehru's faith and advocacy for trust and friendship with China and swinging Indian opinion in that direction, this comment was rubbing salt on India's wounds and showed either total ignorance or callous disregard.

(3) In the autumn of 1963, apparently on Nehru's instructions, I was prematurely transferred from Germany to take over as head of the Embassy in Peking. Parthasarthy, the Ambassador, had been withdrawn and Counsellor P.K. Banerjee had been in-charge since end of 1961. I spent several weeks on 'consultations' during which I visited some border areas that had been the arena of conflict the previous year. The Prime Minister summoned me several times to brief and instruct me on my prospective assignment. It was apparent to me that he really wanted to think aloud on the bitter implications of the 1962 conflict and the future relations with China. When I reached Peking, it was the darkest period in our relations. Though courtesy was shown to me I had very infrequent access to the Chinese Foreign Ministry. Other diplomatic colleagues gave me some deference as one who had experience of negotiating with China, but at Chinese functions I was lonely in the diplomatic crowd!

(4) There were many pinpricks and the secret was to take them cheerfully in one's stride without showing irritation or exasperation. One had to be careful and warn colleagues not to break the strict rules forbidding the photographing of old women with bound feet, or going outside the limits of the city and the western hills. There were more serious hazards of not falling for intelligence agency traps like being tempted by anonymous letters to meet in out-of-the-way *hutungs* (streets) or restaurants.

(5) In May 1964 when Panditji died, Chou En-lai came to sign the condolence book at the Indian Embassy. As he was leaving, he said to me, 'Nehru was my friend and I greatly regret his passing away' or words to that effect. These remarks do not fit in with other comments attributed to Chou En-lai suggesting that Nehru was arrogant or patronizing. One got some premonition of the changed official Chinese attitude when the Chinese Foreign Office refused to give us copies of the photographs taken in the Indian Embassy of Chou En-lai signing the book as it would be a reminder of his paying tribute to the late Indian Prime Minister.

TWO ULTIMATA DURING INDIA-PAK WAR IN 1965

Even though I was in the diplomatic doghouse in Peking, I truly relished my posting and consider it to be the most instructive periods of my career. It coincided with the open polemics between the Soviet Union and China. I also got a close view of the developments in Sino-Pakistan relations. The high point or perhaps the lowest point was the India-Pakistan war in August-September 1965. Soon after the conflict began, Chinese statements and editorials started accusing India of 'aggression' in Kashmir and against Pakistan. This became the refrain in the banquet speeches in honour of visiting dignitaries and I made a kind of innovation in diplomatic practice that if the accusation was unmistakably to India (and not vague or ambivalent), I would get up and walk out. I would generally not wait for the end of the speech but would get up at the paragraph thus giving time to signal my colleague if present or the military attaché at a distant table to follow me. Knowing my practice, the Chinese hosts started playing games with me such as not distributing English translations of the speech to my table or jamming my car so that the chauffeur could not extricate the vehicle and my wife and I would freeze on the steps of the National People's Hall.

The culmination came on 16 and 19 September, when I was summoned in the middle of the night and handed out what were a time-bound ultimata. India was accused of building bunkers across the Sikkim/Tibet border and thefts of yaks and sheep and was given a deadline of three days to remove, return, and comply with their demands. It was obvious that China had pledged contingent support to Pakistan when earlier in the year Ayub and Bhutto had come visiting Peking after Pakistan had started planning Operation Gibraltar. The India-Pakistan war had not gone as well as Pakistan had hoped. The tribal intrusions had not ignited into a 'prairie fire' of revolt in the Valley; the Pakistan army attack in the Chamb Sector invited a diversionary counter-attack by the Indian army towards Lahore and Sialkot. Pakistan must then have requested simultaneous pressure from China, specially to protect East Pakistan. When not summoned to the Foreign Ministry, each night for a whole fortnight I was telephoned between 1 a.m. and 3 a.m. (In jocular tone, I told friends in the Diplomatic Corps of my discovery of a 'nightclub' in Peking and gave them the address of the Waijiaobu, the Foreign Office, identifiable, I told them, by big red-painted gates!) The Waijiaobu got known as Mr Mehta's nightclub.

The Chinese, in giving the ultimata, wanted us to assume that China may declare war or at least precipitate incidents, which could pin our forces down and forestall reinforcements to the western front. Conceivably it could have led to a break in diplomatic relations and so, as a contingency precaution, I ordered the secret records to be sifted and most ciphers destroyed; I offered to let anyone who so wanted, to feel free to send his family back to India. There was tension, but no one responded to the offer. The morale of the embassy was very high.

After the first ultimatum, the Government of India notified that we would be agreeable to impartial examination to prove the trumped up nature of the charge. On 22 September 1965, the day when the second ultimatum was due to expire, I sent, unasked, what I consider the most risky and the most important telegram of my career. (I sometimes conceitedly compare it to Kennan's 'long telegram' from Moscow in 1946, which eventually led to the Policy of Containment.) I analysed Sino-Pak relations and made bold to predict that China would, in fact, climb down when the deadline of the second ultimatum expired. China, I argued, was prepared to oblige Pakistan by trying to frighten India, but except when it perceived a threat to its own security and integrity, it was not going to get militarily involved for the fulfilment of another country's national ambitions. None of my colleagues in the embassy encouraged me. One had to muster intellectual and moral courage to imply that the threat to India could be ignored. It transpired that my analysis was contrary to the consensus in the ministry as well as amongst the defence authorities who were nervous at the possibility of a second front along Sikkim or NEFA. Apparently mine was the only correct prediction given in writing in advance of the expiry of the deadline. If I had been proved wrong, it would have or should have been the end of my career. The Prime Minister Lal Bahadur Shastri seemed to recognize the risk I ran, and recorded his approbation on 24 September itself and when I met him, he expressed appreciation that I had volunteered the prophecy.

After walking out on the National Day banquet on 30 September in the presence of Chairman Mao and all other leaders, I flew out to Delhi for consultations and called on various authorities including the Foreign Affairs Committee of the Cabinet and on General Chaudhuri, the Chief of the Army Staff. I argued that China's hostility though deep, would not manifest itself in a repeat of the 1962 operations against India. China would, in my view, embark on the diplomatic, economic, and political attrition of India.

Since 1976, slowly our relations have normalized but even so there have been ups and downs. Many Indian strategists and intellectuals have argued the possibility of a repeat of 1962. In 1965 one Cabinet Minister even gave me a rough date. However, I stand by my judgement that unless we made a grossly serious provocation, China will not militarily attack India. China's ambitions are to match the super powers, and a regional operation would be a provocation and a complication. China remains politically ambitious but militarily prudent.

PUBLIC CLAMOUR FOLLOWING THE RAGHUNATH-VIJAY INCIDENT, 1967

Even though I had volunteered to stay beyond the normal term, a few months into my second term in May 1966, I was transferred back to start the Policy Planning Division in the ministry. The division was conceived as a 'think tank' to be kept informed by receiving telegrams distributed to territorial divisions, but it had no day-to-day responsibilities. In 1967, however, when the Cultural Revolution was raging in China, the Foreign Secretary, C.S. Jha, asked me to become 'operational' in handling the Raghunath-Vijay incident. For the sake of brevity, I will not describe the wholly ludicrous charges which led to K. Raghunath being dubbed a spy and 'bloodied' when he was about to leave China and Vijay, his newly arrived successor, being declared *persona non grata*. Public and parliamentary opinion, including of the Communist Party of India, were outraged. The Chinese Chargé d'Affaires was in my room when I received a telephone message that a Jan Sangh led large protest demonstration had broken through the police cordon and was surrounding the Chinese Embassy. I was the one to first convey this information to the head of the Chinese Embassy who got visibly flushed and nervous. However, I assured him that I would personally make sure of his safe return to his embassy. It took some time to muster a police escort but finally to assuage his anxiety, I with one of my personal assistants, travelled in his car, leaning forward to take the impact of any brickbats which may be thrown if the Chinese envoy was recognized. Vast crowds were still milling along Shanti Path frontage of the Chinese Embassy, so we went to the gate no. 5 which is roughly opposite 'Mansarover', the residence of Maharaja Karan Singh of Kashmir where it was comparatively dark. At that time the compound wall was barely 4 ft high and there were no sharp steel spikes as it does now. I asked the Chinese Chargé d'Affaires to jump over the wall (the gate was locked). Once in the safety of his own mission, colour and confidence returned to his mien. He then asked me to come inside and see the hurts and the damage inflicted by the Indian 'hooligans'. This, of course, I refused, as I was not going to risk being a witness against my own countrymen. Police reports, which had been transmitted to my office, feared that some Chinese officials who had come out of the embassy and 'fought' the attacking crowd may have been injured. Chinese diplomats round the world were then trying to prove to the Red Guards, in the face of humiliations being infected on the ministers, that they too were fearlessly militant.

I went straight to Parliament to report to the Prime Minister where the Cabinet had been in session and waiting my report for almost an hour. Only later that evening were we certain that the injuries sustained by the Chinese were not fatally serious but some were taken to the Willingdon (now Rammanohar Lohia) Hospital. I visited the injured the next morning and was assured that they were being well looked after and found that the embassy was fully satisfied with the medical attention the Chinese personnel had received. Following the public protest and 'attack' against the Chinese Embassy, our Embassy in Peking was surrounded, where our Chargé d'Affaires Ram Sathe, my successor and all the Indian-based personnel had been assembled. The Chinese servants employed by the mission were stopped from providing essential supplies like milk for the children and vegetables for meals. I called the Chinese chargé, and demanded immediate normalization within twenty-four hours. After the notice period expired and with no relaxation of interrupted supplies as previously planned, we arranged to stop Indian servants and supplies reaching the Chinese compound. A day following our retaliatory steps, the quarantine of our embassy in Peking was lifted and we did likewise. Measured retaliation worked as planned.

However, the mood of anger in India was not assuaged and the feeling persisted that national honour had to be redeemed. The humiliation of 1962 had not been forgotten. Some MPs, including C.P. Dange of the CPI, suggested that diplomatic relations should be suspended. I was against such a step knowing that it was the young Red Guards and not the Chinese Foreign Office who were in control and that once relations were broken it may take a long time to restore them. As a retaliatory measure, we too had declared one of the Chinese Embassy officers as a spy and a second one as *persona non grata*, but this was insufficient to mollify Indian opinion.

We refused the request to let China send a plane to evacuate the injured embassy personnel and their families unless reciprocally the China allowed us to fly an Indian aircraft starting from Hong Kong on a similar mission. This was not acceptable to China. But a few days later around 4 p.m. the Chinese Embassy informed us of the call sign of an aircraft which would approach from East Pakistan the following morning. I promptly informed the Chinese, simultaneously by all possible means including a direct *en clair* telegram to the Foreign Ministry, that India had as much sovereignty over its air space as the Chinese had over theirs and no aircraft could come into our airspace without prior authorization. I also conveyed this by telephone to Ram Sathe in English but thereafter I asked my friend and colleague Ashok Bhadkamkar, whose room was nearby, to repeat my message in Marathi but the moment he started in Marathi, the telephone went dead. It again got connected when we resumed speaking in English. I was then confident that the Chinese had got our message! However, as a precaution, I also alerted Air Headquarters to make sure that a flight from a fighter squadron was ready to be airborne to compel any incoming Chinese plane to land at Allahabad. It should not be allowed to reach Delhi. Late that evening the Defence Minister, Sardar Swaran Singh telephoned agitatedly and firmly told me that without due authorization I was risking provoking a grave incident, possibly war. I told the minister that there was no time late in the afternoon, to get the many required approvals but I was confident there was no such danger. The aircraft could be, or so it could be claimed may have already have taken off. We could not let China unilaterally violate our air space when a reciprocal suggestion had been turned down. In point of fact, after our warnings no aircraft came. (I wish I would live to the day when there is freedom of information in the People's Republic and, like with the KGB records, the Chinese archives become accessible and we could get a flavour of the decision-making at the Peking end when they were debating whether or not to cancel the despatch of the relief aircraft. However, before that there would have to be fuller access to our own old secret records!)

Though we had stopped a unilateral Chinese rescue mission, we still had the problem of 'regaining our honour' without closing down our embassy. This was finally achieved a few days later by taking charge of the person declared a spy after he got out of the car of the Chargé d'Affaires at Palam Airport. (From our intelligence sources and the scrutiny of the passenger list, we had found out that the 'spy' along with the one declared *persona non grata* and some others from the Chinese Embassy were booked to fly to Kathmandu the following morning.) The person declared *persona non grata* was allowed to go through with minimal formalities as for other outgoing diplomats. After all the other commercial passengers had boarded, the 'spy' was escorted to the plane in full public view with two tall uniformed policemen one on either side. I was myself discreetly at Palam. By prior arrangement a photograph was taken when the 'spy' was crossing the tarmac. When this photograph appeared the following day on the front page of Delhi newspapers, India's honour stood upheld! There was no further demand to suspend diplomatic relations with China! India's dignity had been demonstrably vindicated and the crisis was resolved!

THE SPRING OF NORMALIZATION, 1976-1979

In 1976 when I was Foreign Secretary, Mrs Gandhi approved the reupgrading of our mission in Peking to the ambassadorial level. Shri K.R. Narayanan, who later became our President, took over as Ambassador in July 1976. This was the signal for quietly burying the commitment not to normalize relations until Indian territory occupied by China had been vacated.

In 1979 I accompanied A.B.Vajpayee, then Foreign Minister on a visit to Peking, the first high level one since that of Dr Radhakrishnan in 1957. The Soviet Union was seriously apprehensive at the moves by India to improve relations with China. On arrival in the Chinese capital and prior to the welcoming banquet, I called on Vice-Minister, Han-nien-Lung, whom I had known before and told him that we would be deeply concerned if the Soviet Union was criticized in our Foreign Minister's presence. (As part of the efforts to befriend the USA, Deng Hsio-Ping in his just concluded American tour had lost no opportunity to denounce the USSR.) Because of our timely request, the Soviet Union was not mentioned in the banquet speech and so we could live up to our assurances that the old steady relations with the USSR were not being jeopardized and we could demonstrate the efficacy of beneficial bilateralism with our biggest neighbour.

We had made clear in advance that the Foreign Minister was not going to bring up the boundary question, which had remained basically quiescent since 1962. (A 1967 incident on the Sikkim border was an aberration traceable to Red Guard militancy.) However, on all other issues, Vajpayee's conversations in Peking were an unqualified success. On 17 February China invaded Vietnam and Deng-Hsio-Ping, in reply to question by a press correspondent, said that the operations would be brief, like the attack on India in 1962. The Indian Foreign Minister after leaving Peking and visiting Shanghai, was then in Hangchow. Our relations with Vietnam were friendly so following Deng's insulting reference to operations against India, the Indian Foreign Minister decided to cut short his visit and left China a day earlier than scheduled, omitting the stop in Canton. Deng should have anticipated India's sensitivity but the timing was wholly independent of relations with India. The Chinese attack on Vietnam, in my view, was precipitated because China had confidentially learnt that the USSR was about to sign an agreement with the pro-Vietnam, pro-Soviet Heng Samrin government in Kampuchea. The Chinese action was an attempt—as it happened, a disastrously unsuccessful one—at the pre-emption of Soviet involvement in South-East Asia which China considered her own sphere of influence. The pro-Soviet and anti-government lobbies in India were quick to appropriate the stigma of the Chinese attack as a calculated insult on India.

Vajpayee's success was indicated by China stopping mention of Kashmir or Sikkim in public statements at least while the Janata government was in power. The Chinese were also as good as their word in not giving any more arms aid to Naga rebels. Vajpayee's visit was indeed symbolic of a new spring in Sino-Indian relations.

ENCOUNTERING MY NEGOTIATING ADVERSARY AFTER 23 YEARS

In 1983 Chang-wen-Chin was Ambassador in Washington and Chieh, his interpreter in 1960, was his no. 2. (Later Chieh went on to London as Ambassador and finally became Under Secretary-General at the UN headquarters.) I had not met Chang-wen-Chin since 1966 but I knew of his historic role in fetching Kissinger on his secret mission in 1971 and in the subsequent Sino-American normalization. I met Chieh by accident at Professor J.K. Galbraith's annual commencement party in June 1983. Chieh must have informed his chief of my presence and my planned visit to Washington. Chang-wen-Chin called me to a friendly one-to-one lunch at the Chinese Embassy. We went over our discussions more than twenty years earlier. With the license of irresponsibility, I told him that it was an avoidable mistake to have bracketed Nehru by name with the revolt in Tibet: there might have been a chance to arrest the further deterioration and perhaps enable re-normalization if the *People's Daily* article had simply criticized India in ideological terms. He did not demur to my somewhat unsolicited hindsight criticism. The tenor of our conversations was warm and informal.

I was then on my way to take up an appointment as Visiting Professor in the LBJ School at the University of Texas at Austin. At my suggestion, he seemed to be agreeable in principle to come to Austin-Texas if invited by the Dean or the University President. The university authorities warmly encouraged my suggestion and so I wrote to the Ambassador Chang and he agreed to visit the university. This created quite a sensation, including in the State House (Governor's residence) when the first official visit to Texas by the Ambassador of the People's Republic of China, was to be at the suggestion of a former Indian diplomat! The LBJ School invited him to deliver a lecture in a big University Hall on China's Foreign Policy. Only the two of us were on the podium in front of a very large audience. In introducing him, after recalling his distinguished career, I said that the only reason I found myself sitting next to the Ambassador was because for six months, in 1960 I had sat opposite him in adversarial discussions and diplomacy. It was a tribute to his self-confidence to have come at my suggestion to attend functions in his honour at the university.

The last episode neatly winds up my own story of the ups and downs in involvement with China. I acknowledge to a sense of immense gratitude and the privilege of a career in the Indian Foreign Service in which, chance brought China into my horoscope. It included exceptional opportunities, terrible responsibilities and frightening intellectual agony. Aside from what has been described here, three significant episodes are almost unparalleled in the annals of diplomacy but each is symbolic in itself.

As mentioned, the Vice-President S. Radhakrishnan and I were put up in a house in Zhongnanhai. Going by the map in the biography of Li Zhisui (Mao's personal physician), the house in which we stayed was called Chrysanthemum Fragrance, but the important point was that it was within the exclusive forbidden part adjoining the Forbidden City. That was rare enough. But I have a copy of a group photograph take outside Mao's library apparently called Harmony Hall. On either side of Mao-tse-Tung and Radhakrishnan are eight weather beaten veterans of the Long March who in 1957 were alive and members of the Politburo. Bahadur Singh, our Counsellor, and I happen to be standing behind Chairman Mao-tse-Tung. (The only other two Indian survivors of that distinguished group who are still around are K. Natwar Singh (then a language training officer attached to the embassy, and now the Foreign Minister) and Paranjpe, till then the most experienced Chinese language interpreter in the world. I cannot help wondering whether there are any other such souvenirs of trust and confidence in India with the rulers of China. It was the high noon of India-China relations.

At the other extreme, as mentioned earlier, was when I was given an ultimatum during the India-Pakistan War of 1965. Neville Chamberlain gave an ultimatum to Hitler on 1 September 1939 when Germany attacked Poland, but these are rare in modern times. (The Japanese never gave one before the attack on Pearl Harbor.) The purpose of the Chinese ultimatum was to frighten India and to insult the Indian Chargé d'Affaires. A Vice-Director, Yang-kang-Su, fairly junior in the hierarchy was authorized to serve it. It was expected that I would be shocked and rush back to transmit the threat. Anyway Yang was in no position to answer my request for clarifications. Finally I put it to him, 'was I to understand that if India could not meet these absurd demands, the People's Republic of China would go to war with the Republic of India?' The Vice-Director was flustered and got up, and, at 2.30 a.m. or thereabouts, said in all seriousness that he had another appointment! He extended his hand to say goodbye and I pulled my hand behind my back somewhat dramatically and walked out. Diplomacy has its own methods of registering protests against outrageous international demands.

The third unique incident flowed out of the humiliation and actual injuries to my friend and colleague, Raghunath. Until now, to avoid embarrassment to China, I have never recounted the incident. By personally escorting the Chinese Chargé d'Affaires, I ran the risk of brickbats from the protesting fellow countrymen landing on my face sitting in the Chinese Embassy car. It must be a rarity in the annals of diplomacy to make the head of another mission jump surreptitiously and in an undignified manner into his own mission. To my mind it has broader significance. In keeping with the code of diplomacy, even in the face of unprovoked outrage, a receiving country is under obligation to physically protect (and restore) an envoy to the immunity of his mission. I cannot think of any similar incident, which brings out both the hazard as well as the obligations of diplomacy. It also illustrates that even in the face of populist anger and other pressures, one must not lightly sever established diplomatic links.

LANTERN AT THE STERN: RETROSPECT ON SINO-INDIAN RELATIONS

The marathon talks in 1960 that were entrusted to my leadership were only a chapter in the ongoing story of India-China relations. Some supplementary reflections that too, twenty-two years after retirement, may be permissible to throw further light on the broader scope of India-China political relations.

These fifty years and more of India-China relations were an avoidable tragedy but I believe we understand each other better now. There were not, then, or subsequently, any great differences on the importance of bilateral relations with China but one has to ask: has the experience curbed the inclination to wishfulness? We still do not know if we are on the same timescale of history insulated against both euphoria and false fears. After the early telescoped phases beginning with one-sided rationality (1949-54) followed by faith in a common bond of Afro-Asian anti-imperialism (1954-8), the unexpected deterioration traceable to opaqueness in the comprehension on both sides ending in armed conflict (1959-62), and a long period of political hostility and diplomatic attrition (1962-75), can we be certain that the restoration of rational normalcy (1976 onwards) is immune to intellectual and political shocks? Functional bilateral cooperation is now being proclaimed by both governments. High level visits (Foreign Ministers, Defence Ministers, Prime Ministers, and Presidents) have been exchanged. Even the Army Chiefs have visited China. A lot of words, speeches, communiques and statements, the rituals of modern diplomacy, have been uttered or written, but they are not necessarily a reliable compass immune to volcanic disruption in the future. Even friends of China were inwardly surprised at the insensitivity to India's security concern in the continuing supply of nuclear material and know-how to Pakistan and the aggressive condemnation of India's nuclear explosions which overlooked that India has as much (or as little) right to an independent nuclear deterrent as does China. One cannot help but conclude that we have yet to fully and unsentimentally understand the 'otherness' of China. China is able to wait out strategically and improvise tactically. This stumps democracies like India (and the USA), which have no comparable patience or sustained policy spread over decades, leave alone centuries. China's historical self-confidence is unique but we do not know whether it will be able to master the consequences of science, technology, and political awareness which in the modern world empowers people beyond national control as seen in the Tiananmen square protest of 1989.

Nehru's failures were not of naiveté but of idealism without the yeast of statecraft. His conceptual vision had some flaws of wishfulness and suffered aberrations because of Partition, disappointment with power politics, and the UN being influenced by great-power rivalry. The fact however remains that the world at the beginning of the twenty-first century approximates more closely to Nehru's vision than that of Mao or any other statesman of the time. As Nehru expected, the international society has become pluralist and ideologically agnostic: security and strength, as he prophesied, depends on economic and social progress and not just on military capability. He alone focused on the importance of international technological gallop and its grafting into people's aspirations and to democratic self-governance.

In relation to China, in my view, virtue and prophecy were

on India's side. The two Asian giants working in harmony through the decades could conceivably have been the principled guarantors of liberation and peace, but both had their separate political navigational courses and the flush of their friendship obscured their differences. The divergence in their nationalism was prised open rather unexpectedly, but the old mindsets in Indian decision-making had no understanding of how the Forward Policy of 'filling the vacuum' would be considered provocative and provide an opportunity to show that there was only one colossus to bestride the Asian stage. In the wake of the humiliation of national defeat, some minds are still obsessed with the fear of a repetition of 1962 and some think this time it could be nuclear. Sagacity has come a long way to put present relations on a more level field for diplomacy.

Just as China never bothered to understand the working of democracy, India never followed carefully the impact of domestic debate inside China. Mao's ideological militancy after the Lushan plenum in 1959 and the ascendancy of the Left, the serious crisis of food shortages in 1961-2 following the failure of the Great Leap Forward with 30 million deaths, the virulence of the Cultural Revolution in 1966, all had foreign policy linkages but these were not woven into Indian perceptions. (Such aberrations could not occur, as Amartya Sen has repeatedly argued, in a democracy.) Mao's call 'to make revolution and bombard the party headquarters' led to a nightmare of Red Guard-created chaos. However, India underestimated China's capacity of recovery and the significance of the Deng-Hsio-Ping takeover when he launched full throttle to repudiate the constraints of leftist economic dogma. India for long simply jogged along with its mixed-economy and the Hindu rate of growth.

Over these decades, India and China have been more or less friendly; the two countries were destined to be rivals but not long-term military enemies. As the two biggest developing countries, they had and have competitive leadership ambitions but both are apt to overlook that size is a handicap in modern times and with universalization, political awareness were bound to arise, unless diplomacy was truly sensitive of hegemonic propensities. These population giants could be tempted to detach themselves from the fraternity of the poor and the small and manoeuvre to belong to the club of great powers. Both China and India are keener on the quest of nuclear capability than on persisting with the diplomacy of equality and persuasion.

The search for a new axis with China (and/or Russia) against the United States is again harking back to wield the capacity of international blackmail. The truth is that both countries have their own need of economic cooperation, trade, technology and investment with America. India does not now consider the USA as malevolently inclined and is not apprehensive of America's power as it did in 1950s, through the Cold War years, but China certainly is fearful and determined to outstrip the lead of the sole hyper-power. With its spectacular economic progress and trade surplus, China has developed an unexpected great bargaining power. In my view India and China cannot now unite in a partnership of common purpose against the sole super power.

It is also worth remembering that the triggers to the ups and downs in Sino-Indian relations were always extraneous developments, not bilateral problems. It was the independent attitude of India on Korea (1950), and on Indo-China (1954) that catalysed bilateral friendship in 1954. It was the revolt in Tibet, not the Sino-Indian boundary question, that led to the downturn and crisis in 1959. The border has remained basically quiescent since 1962. When we re-upgraded our relations in 1976, no one objected that we were overlooking the parliamentary resolution, still on the statute book, that laid down as a precondition the recovery of all occupied Indian territory. Mrs Gandhi could have started the process of a border settlement when she came back to power in 1980. Rajiv Gandhi missed an even greater opportunity in 1985 when he had a three-fourths majority in the Lok Sabha. Alas Rajiv Gandhi deferred his visit to Beijing until 1988 by which time India was enfeebled by intervention in Sri Lanka and had lost its standing in Nepal and Bangladesh. Confidence building agreements and exchanges of maps were of cosmetic and of hypothetical significance only: internal political hurdles in India had to be overcome in advance for a full boundary settlement. But while a settlement will improve, it will not automatically or permanently transform relations or make them immune to deterioration. It will not eliminate the long-term challenge to bilateral diplomacy. We have to recognize that the stage when China needed India's support is long past.

China now outmatches Japan, Russia, and the European Union. It would like to keep this group of permanent members of the Security Council restricted to this number and would discreetly oppose India becoming the sixth member, even though it may have greater hesitation in opposing a bigger enlargement of the Security Council. China will try not to dilute its relationship with Pakistan even if relations with India improve. There is a new element of hesitation that the Muslim (Uighur) population in Sinkiang may be getting moral and material support from Islamic fundamentalists who have their epicentre in Pakistan. China has its own Achilles heel: liberalization has been possible because of political authoritarianism under party control, but in the twenty-first century, political democracy may demand greater respect for human rights, and democracy cannot forever be denied.

India is no more in the same league and standing as China, but it has an advantage with its established democracy. It is breaking out, alas little too slowly, from its socialist hypnosis. It could, I believe, regain its international respect as being more in tune with the future but for that it must be wary of not going the way of the Soviet Union—a flabby over-militarized giant unable to hold a nation of diversity together. The road map we are following at present points only in the direction of continued invigoration of economic dynamism, improving governance, and assuaging peoples' cynicism. Internationally India must not simply pay homage but successfully demonstrate or rather re-demonstrate the original Nehruvian approach of unselfish respect for the equality and legitimacy of all nationalisms. It must with transparency respect enlightened international principles such as adherence to the universal declaration on Human Rights.

India-China relations have greater complexity than was realized by Nehru. To stabilize them will be a long haul. It will demand patience, sagacity, diplomatic skill, and above all, an unwavering faith, and not tactical adjustments or euphoria round the declaration in proclaiming the principles of peaceful coexistence.

BIBLIOGRAPHY

Ali, S. Mahmud, *Cold War in the High Himalayas: The USA, China and South Asia in the 1950s*, Surrey: The Curzon Press, 1999.

Bajpai, S.C., *The Northern Frontier of India—Central and Western Sector*, Bombay: Allied Publishers, 1970.

Bhattachrjea, Mira Sinha, *China, the World and India*, New Delhi: Samskriti, 2001.

Bhutani, Sudarshan, *A Clash of Political Cultures: Sino-Indian Relations (1957-62)*, New Delhi: Roli Books, 2004.

FitzGerald, C.P., *The Chinese View of Their Place in the World*, London: Oxford University Press, 1965.

Garver, John W., *Protracted Contest Sino-India Rivalry in Twentieth Century*, New Delhi: Oxford University Press, 2001.

Government of India, *Report of the Officials of China on the Boundary Question*, New Delhi: Ministry of External Affairs, 1961.

Heinrich, Harrer, *Seven Years in Tibet*, London: HarperCollins, 1997.

Hoffmann, Steven A., *India and the China Crisis*, Berkeley: University of California Press, 1990.

Huck, Arthur, *The Security of China—Chinese Approaches to Problems of War and Strategy*, London: Chatto & Windus Ltd., 1970.

Lall, John, *Aksaichin and Sino-Indian Conflict*, Bombay: Allied Publishers, 1989.

Lamb, Alastair, *Tibet, China, and India 1914-1950: A History of Imperial Dioplomacy*, Hertingfordbury: Roxford Books, 1989.

Liu, Xuecheng, *The Sino-Indian Border Dispute and Sino-Indian Relations*, Lanham, Maryland: University Press of America Inc, 1994.

MacFarquhar, Roderick, *The Politics of China 1949-1989*, Cambridge: Cambridge University Press, 1993.

Maxwell, Nevile, *India's China War*, Bombay: Jaico Publishing House, 1970.

Mehra, Parshotam, *An Agreed Frontier-Ladakh and India's Northern-most Borders 1946-1947*, New Delhi: Oxford University Press, 1992.

Mullik, B.N., *The Chinese Betrayal*, Bombay: Allied Publishers, 1971.

Peoples' Republic of China, *The Sino-Indian Boundary Question*, Peking: Foreign Language Press, 1962.

Rahul, Ram, *The Himalayas as a Frontier*, New Delhi: Vikas Publishing House, 1978.

Ranganathan, C. and Vinod Khanna, *India and China: The Way Ahead after 'Mao's India War'*, New Delhi: Har-Anand, 2000.

Rao, Gondker Narayan, *The India-China Border—A Reappraisal*, Bombay: Asia Publishing House, 1968.

Sen, S.P., *The Sino-Indian Border Question—A Historical Review*, Calcutta: Institute of Historical Studies, 1971.

Shakya, Tsering, *The Dragon in the Land of Snows: A History of Modern Tibet Since 1947*, London: Pimlico, 1999.

Tsering, Shakya, *The Dragon in the Land of Snows*, London: Pimlico, 1999.

Verma, Shanti Prasad, *Struggle for the Himalayas*, Jullundur: University Press, 1965.

Vertzberger, Yaacov Y.I., *Misperceptions in Foreign Policy Making—The Sino-Indian Conflict 1959-1962*, Boulder, Colo: Westview Press Inc., 1984.

Vladimir, Yasenev, Yevgeny Stepanov, *China's Frontiers: Traditional Expansionism to Hegemonism Today*, Moscow: Novosti Press Agency, 1981.

Watson, Francis, *The Frontiers of China*, England: Chatto & Windus Ltd., 1966.

Zhisui, Dr. Li, *The Private Life of Chairman Mao*, New York: Random House, 1994.

CHAPTER 3

Diplomacy for Compensation for Indians

Negotiating with Idi Amin's Government - 1975

THE HISTORICAL BACKDROP

Throughout the nineteenth century and up to the First World War, India was the hub of the expanding British Empire. India had the experience and provided the structural administrative model for other British conquests. Until the colonial office and the colonial service came to be established, the governance of Kenya and Uganda were guided as much from Calcutta as from Whitehall. There were definite periods of intensified Indian migration to Africa, the first following the construction of the railway. The second phase came during the inter-War years and a third spurt took place after the Second World War. The cumulative outcome was that there were approximately 80,000 Indians, hereafter referred to as Asians, in Uganda, 215,000 in Kenya and some 110,000 in Tanganyika on the eve of the independence of these countries.

It was Mahatma Gandhi who launched the first non-violent protest against the racial discrimination and hierarchical social structure he found in South Africa. This lawyer from India was the first to demand equality and humanity for all races.

Thereafter Indian nationalism also became the beacon for a steady and uncompromising call for the end of European empires everywhere. India's identification with the newly independent colonies was so categorical that on 15 September 1953, Prime Minister Nehru declared in Parliament that 'Indians could expect no help from us if they seek special rights in Africa, which are not in the interest of Africa.'

*First published in *India Quarterly*, IIC Journal, New Delhi.

This idealistic internationalism, which virtually disowned concern for Indian kinsmen abroad, was going to be modified in subsequent decades, but as perceived at the time, it was consistent with the spirit of decolonization, non-alignment, and Afro-Asian solidarity. The fact remains that India initiated both the process that transformed the political map of the world (by which a hundred odd subject people became independent nations enjoying equal voting rights in the General Assembly of the United Nations) and the crusade against racial discrimination (which ended in the dismantling of apartheid in its bastion in South Africa).

The irony is that the pioneering role of India, which secured the fulfilment of diverse nationalisms, also brought about the nemesis of reverse racialism against the Indian emigrant communities. The 'winds of change' in Africa, which started with self-government for Ghana in 1957 and was followed by the transfer of power to Nigeria (1960), cascaded into the independence of Tanganyika (1961), Zanzibar (1962), Uganda (1962) and Kenya (1963). It was self-government in the British colonies that led to the loosening of the entrenched advantages of the Asian settlers. The processes began in East Africa where Indians had enjoyed near control of the economies of the countries.

In the face of reverse 'racialism' against Asians, the policy-makers in India faced a policy dilemma; whether to accept passively the right of the new countries to correct historical, political, and social inequities as emanating from the principles which India was the first to articulate—the right to self-government and to fashion internal policy for the welfare of the majority—or to protest its concern at the hardship to its ethnic kinsmen, and politely point to the decades of entrepreneurship and constructive contributions made by Indian settlers and plead for indulgence and, at least, fair compensation. It was a manifestation of the classic dilemma of diplomacy: whether to uphold fidelity to enlightened international principles even if it hurts internally, or to placate domestic opinion traceable to a narrow definition of 'national interest'. There was public resentment in India at the hardship inflicted on our kinsmen by independent Uganda, but whether it was due to consciousness of enlightened principles or just political inertia, India refrained from joining the chorus of international rage against Idi Amin. Anyway, it was this restraint which eventually paid off. India was the only country which got some compensation from Idi Amin.

Run Up to the Expulsion

The frontiers of Uganda, like that of many countries in Africa, had been drawn arbitrarily by concordats and treaties concluded between European powers in European capitals. Uganda embodied in its frontiers different tribes but, unlike Tanzania, they were not evenly balanced so that they could not be forged into a cohesive 'national' solidarity. In fact, before and after independence, tribalism vitiated the politics of Uganda. On the basis of an election held just prior to the transfer of power in 1962, Milton Obote formed the first government of the country. He ruled till 1971, when, during his absence from Kampala for the Commonwealth Prime Ministers' meeting in Singapore in January, General Amin, the Commander of the Army, staged a *coup d'état* and took control of the country. Obote was obliged to take refugee in Tanzania under the protection of his friend, President Nyerere.

To consolidate his position, Amin banned all political parties and elections. Initially he assembled an able technocratic cabinet and even drew talent from the Makerere University, but soon they all found themselves playing second fiddle to the army. To begin with, in 1971, Amin had also looked upon the Asians with favour, hoping thus to get their help in economic amelioration and so stabilizing his own position. To secure international legitimacy, he even tried to placate UK, France, and Germany and visited these countries without being invited. Yet, basically his was a military dictatorship that had no sanction except brute power. Following Amin's takeover and the smothering of democracy, internal economic conditions and the law and order situation continued to deteriorate and so dissatisfaction grew in Kampala as well as in the rural hinterland.

In his frustration, by 1972 Amin withdrew his earlier stance of friendliness towards the British and started blaming the legacy of imperialism for Uganda's subsisting problems. As a 'born again' Muslim, on his return from Haj, he converted churches into mosques and expelled all the Israelis and this further aggravated the economic dislocations and the rampant unemployment. (In 1973, he offered to lead the Arab armies against Israel in the Yom Kippur War.) In the process of jumping from one scapegoat to another, he purged the administration of experienced civil servants. The British had a dominant position in the economy, but subsequent to these haphazard and confused measures, the British (and the West) cut-off all aid and, wherever possible, withdrew investment and generally sought to ostracize Amin's Uganda.

India was not spared. As it happened, in 1972, President Giri was paying the first official visit to some countries in Africa. On the basis of photographs of crates containing presents being unloaded from the presidential aircraft at Dar-es-Salaam Airport, Amin charged India with supplying arms for an invasion to dethrone him. Such gimmicks did not help to consolidate Amin's domestic position. The police had already been emasculated of its trained commanders. The army alone was left as the base of his authority, but the army was exploiting the license to indulge in looting, murder and rape. A reign of terror plagued the country but it also posed a serious menace to Amin's regime.

'Economic War'—The Final Scapegoat

It was in this desperate domestic situation that in August 1972 Amin declared a war for 'economic liberation' from the stranglehold of the Asians. All non-citizens were notified to leave the country within ninety days. Indophobia, as Ali Mazuri calls it, was sufficiently widespread. It temporarily won acclaim as liberation from the exploitation by settler Asians who, he said, had turned the better part of Kampala into a smaller 'Bombay'.

At this stage, it may be pertinent to weave in a little background of the attitudes of the Asians themselves. The British government, to demonstrate its commitment to the old Empire and in the hope of retaining some prestige for the new Commonwealth, had promised the rights of British citizenship to the residents of their ex-colonies. But opinion in the UK, led by Enoch Powell and his Conservative supporters and the so-called Monday Club, had started raising the alarm of an impending invasion of the British isles by 400,000 'browns' and 'blacks', threatening to change the demographic complexion and destroying the social and cultural fabric of the ancient kingdom. It was in this context that the Labour government proposed and got passed the British Immigration Act (1968), regulating and restricting admission in the UK of persons of non-Caucasian descent. This precipitated a mini-rush by Asians to establish residence in the UK before the notified deadline. Asians became alive to the possibility of a nationalistic squeeze against them.

In the 1960s Amin's summary expulsion was not anticipated. However, after the British Immigration Act, some had started exploring the possibility of new locations and business opportunities abroad, but most middle-level Asians were reluctant or unable to move to unfamiliar pastures. They were fluent in Swahili, accustomed to local working conditions, and prospering where they were. Yet, as a re-insurance, they began straddling their nationality options. Not frequently in one family, there would be three different national passports. Most Asians decided to seize the option of retaining British nationality on the logic that the UK as the more powerful country with its commanding position in the Ugandan economy would have the will and capacity to accord them protection in an emergency. But a sizeable number took local (Ugandan) citizenship, and about 6,000 in Uganda took Indian passports.

Ironically, in retrospect as late as 1970, the Asians in East Africa had considered the economic climate in Uganda to be the least threatening to their future. In Kenya, restrictions were coming in, but the majority continued to thrive. Tanzania was the first to take radical steps when Asians in the rural areas were dislodged and later all properties, even in the towns, were summarily taken over. If any construction was more than ten years old, no compensation was admissible. But even Tanzania had not forcibly expelled the settled Asians. Amin's economic war, when it was declared in 1972, out-trumped Tanzania and of course, disregarded the consequences of the sudden departure of thousands who had provided the backbone to the economy, the retail trade, and the management of the industries in the country. Practical considerations were irrelevant in Amin's calculus! It was retaining power that was uppermost in his mind, and to that end expelling the Asians, as he calculated, would win him populist approval.

After Amin announced his decree, in the first month the British government reacted sharply but alternated between persuasion and threats, hoping that the decision could be rescinded. Geoffery Rippon, a minister in the British government, went to Kampala and appealed to Amin to at least stagger the eviction, but Amin remained adamant. In the address to the UN General Assembly, Douglas-Home, then British Foreign Secretary, appealed to the international fraternity to help share the 'burden' of rehabilitating the expelled Asians, but eventually the British government was reconciled to its own responsibility. Canada took a sizeable number, but the OAU (Organization of African Unity) was divided in its reactions. Mauritius, Tanzania, and Zambia were in a minority for condemning this kind of racist policy but most others muted their criticism of the violation of rights of settlers.

The Asians themselves were too fearful of Amin's brutal and arbitrary ways to protest or prevaricate in accepting the finality of the expulsion. Our High Commissioner in Kampala prepared forms in which details of the assets and self-estimated valuations were recorded before they left Kampala. Beyond helping in transportation, we instructed that as a humanitarian measure, ex-Ugandan Indian nationals should be exempt from custom duties not only on their personal belongings but also any 'stock-in-trade' which they brought with them and which could help them to launch their rehabilitation efforts. India, however, could not offer either cash or accommodation facilities; we simply advised them to rejoin their families in India.

The British government faced a far greater problem. The British High Commission had also kept the details of the assets abandoned by British nationals. India was asked to take some of the expelled, if only temporarily, and it agreed to do so but only if they had valid visa permits for eventual admission in the UK. Of the British passport holders, 23,000 availed of a special airlift to UK and about 5,000 came for a temporary stay in India. A Uganda Resettlement Board was set up in London to receive and disperse them in different counties; cash allowances were given for those who were destitute. The British government is reported to have spent 25 million pounds, which it hoped to be able to recover from Uganda at some future date.

PRELUDE TO THE NEGOTIATIONS

As mentioned, the eviction of Asians caused resentment and criticism in India but it was generally realized that we were helpless. In due course, the ugly episode slipped away from public attention in India. At the Non-Aligned Summit in Algiers in 1973, which Indira Gandhi as Prime Minister joined, Amin was also present as one of the Heads of State. The Ugandan President went to call on Indira Gandhi, and characteristically, was accompanied by a mixed ethnic entourage consisting of a Caucasian (British), a Sikh in a turban, a non-bearded Asian, and, of course, native born Ugandans. The Indian Prime Minister mildly reproved the Ugandan President for the harshness of the summary expulsions of Asians. Idi Amin, in response, whether meant seriously or not, promised that in due course he would pay 'full compensation'. No one took this at its face value because the economic situation of Uganda had patently deteriorated.

However, in October 1975, unexpectedly, a letter from Idi Amin was received by Indira Gandhi, requesting her to send her Foreign or Finance Minister to Kampala with a full delegation, including supporting officials, journalists, and broadcasters, where they would all be his guests. The details of the compensation for the assets of 'Indians' expelled would be amicably negotiated and based on mutual agreement, full compensation would be promptly paid. The Foreign Minister and the Finance Minister were reluctant to go and the suggestion informally went down the ladder of the governmental hierarchy. The Minister of State, the Foreign Secretary, the Economic Secretary, the Secretary in External Affairs dealing with economic questions were all sounded but all politely declined. Amin by this time was an international pariah. In any case, the probability of getting an acceptable quantum of compensation from a near-bankrupt country was rated so low that no politician or senior official wanted to risk public criticism at bringing back failure. The legal or moral arguments were obviously weak. The merits of the claim for compensation, had no sanction of precedent nor strong support of international opinion. Notwithstanding all this, the government could not refuse to respond to the offer of Amin.

I was then a junior Additional Secretary in the ministry. At that time I was superintending the Administration and Policy Planning divisions. The Foreign Secretary urged me to accept the assignment and do the best possible. I pointed out that my posting as High Commissioner in Tanzania from 1970-4, which gave me some background on East Africa's problems, would be an obvious irritant and a negotiating handicap. Obote, whom Amin had displaced, had been given political asylum in Dar-es-Salaam and I had occasion to meet him publicly with the Tanzanian President. Amin was known to have made viciously critical remarks about Julius Nyerere. The validity of my arguments could not be gainsaid, but since there was no other volunteer, I was told by the Foreign Secretary to proceed to Kampala. Civil service ethics demanded that one must accept an assignment if so ordered, but beyond being casually told 'to do the best possible', I was given no guidance or brief.

I am not a trained lawyer and the ministry's legal division had apparently no one versed in this aspect of international law. Anyway, no one from the division volunteered to come with me. From cursory information and quick consultations, I gathered that international compensation negotiations were highly complex, often contentious, and usually stretched over many years. Crucially, it required expertise on the evaluation of different kinds of assets, which was invariably disputed. In the end, I located Shri Ramachandran, who was then holding the post of Assistant Custodian of Enemy Property in a subordinate office of the Commerce Ministry located in Bombay. Ramachandran had started his career as a Lower Division Clerk about the time when Second World War started. He held a clerical job in the branch responsible for taking over of German and later Japanese assets when the British Indian government declared War in 1939 and 1941. By sheer dint of hard work and exceptional intelligence, he had risen from the ranks to his present position. He did not have legal training, but was the best expert I could find with some relevant experience. He proved an invaluable support to me in our negotiations on behalf of the expelled Indians from Uganda.

Reaching for Amin's Achilles Heel

Before proceeding to Kampala, I drafted and armed myself with a Letter of Introduction from the Prime Minister to President Idi Amin. It acknowledged the invitation, commended my nomination, and sought the President's indulgent encouragement to determine fair compensation for the distressed evictees. This letter was to be my entry for appeal to the Uganda President.

We were fortunate in having an unflappable and wise High Commissioner in H.K. Singh. Latterly promoted into the Indian Foreign Service, he was on his last post before retiring. On arrival in Kampala, the High Commissioner gave me a little more background to the despatch of the offer to compensate the 'Indian nationals'. The suggestion had apparently emanated from Obath-Offembi, one of the few surviving old civil servants, who had been elevated to the difficult responsibility of Finance Minister in Amin's government. With the world against Amin, the Finance Minister's lot was not a happy one; a opinion in the World Bank and the international aid-giving countries and institutions had become decisively unsympathetic to Uganda's economic expectations.

Apparently, Obath-Offembi had taken the initiative to tell the President that India's position was transparently weak but that her international standing was exceptionally high and unlike the British government and media, the country had been restrained in its public reactions, the Indians could be invited and disposed off with 50,000 pounds sterling. It would be a small price to restore Uganda's international standing and the result would be, he argued, that the President would be personally applauded round the world. The High Commissioner also told me that Obath-Offembi had hoped that by conducting the negotiations personally and so playing a publicly prominent role in enhancing Amin's own position, he would be saved from the apprehended dismissal and the fate which had overtaken so many of his erstwhile civil service colleagues. This projected scenario obviously appealed to Amin and so the offer was despatched to Indira Gandhi.

In Kampala, I called on the Foreign Minister and requested him to arrange an appointment for me to call on the President in order that I could personally deliver the Prime Minister's letter. I knew that the person who was going to guide the negotiations was Obath-Offembi, the Finance Minister, but the latter firmly refused to receive me. He was deeply offended that instead of a full-fledged Cabinet Minister, only a mid-senior level official (and not even the head of the Foreign Ministry) had been deputed by the Government of India. He maintained this boycott throughout my stay in the Ugandan capital. Fortunately, the Foreign Minister was able to secure the appointment for me to call on the President.

The date and place of my call was only intimated to us at the last minute. (Amin was so paranoiac about the threat to his life that, I was told, he never slept in the same house on two successive nights.) I knew my initial meeting with the President was crucial to the climate and the prospects of obtaining a reasonable amount in compensation, which could be defended in our Parliament. I presented the Prime Minister's letter to him. The President took about fifteen minutes to read the letter, which was a little more than one page in double spacing and all the while his thumb seemed to linger on every word. I waited patiently with a serious composure, but this gave me some indication of Amin's reading capabilities and his command over the English language! President Amin was obviously pleased to receive the letter from Prime Minister Gandhi. Trying to show off, he recalled that during Second World War, when he was with the King's African Rifles, he had fought with units of Indian army and even acted as an interpreter of Hindustani. To prove the point, he started counting in Hindustani—*ek, do, teen* (one, two, three)—but could go no further (I have never been able to confirm whether he was, in fact, with the 14th army on the Burma front).

I realized that it was my pitch with the President that would determine the attitude towards our negotiations. I told the President that his offer, if successful, could add an unparalleled precedent to international law and practice. No one in the past, had offered to pay cash compensation for individual assets nationalized by a government. The British government gave a sterling loan to enable Kenya to give compensation to the British landholders and it was disbursed gradually but, in fact, the money remained in London. Italy received no compensation for pre-war assets taken over when the Allies overran Libya,

Ethiopia, etc. I said I was aware that compensation negotiations are generally spread over years and disbursed in instalments, disregarding current values or inflation. I emphasized that the President's inclination to offer immediate cash to Indians would be setting a precedent, which will enthral the victims but embarrass many countries who have summarily expropriated private property.

The President looked visibly interested. I added that, we have noted that this offer to pay compensation was only to Indian passport holders, in striking contrast to the attitude towards those who chose British nationality. This was proof of his understanding and empathy towards the fraternity of the non-aligned. Idi Amin acknowledged that he had appreciated India's friendliness, and vaguely assured me that he would ensure that the negotiations were fair and conducted with despatch.

On the way home, the High Commissioner jocularly said that this interview may have been Amin's first introduction to international law. I said, not being a trained lawyer, I am not even sure whether my arguments were in accordance with compensation law and precedents, but I was trying to get on the wavelength of his wanting to improve his international image by humouring his vanity.

THE NEGOTIATING MARATHON

Before starting, we had to determine our own negotiating strategy. There were between 5,000 and 6,000 Indian passport holders who were affected by Amin's 'economic war'. We had about 2,000 claim forms registered with the Indian High Commission (each family must have filed a joint claim). It was estimated that the total claims of the 'Asians' must have been not less than several hundred million pounds. I was told that normally in such negotiations, even going by the original book value (rather than replacement worth) of the accepted assets, the settlement never exceeded 10 per cent of the estimated grand total.

I foresaw great difficulties and contentious headaches for the Government of India in assuming responsibilities for allocation and distribution of compensation to the affected individuals, especially as the amount would be a fraction of their claim. Therefore, I felt we had to avoid negotiating a round compromise figure by agreeing to some arbitrarily determined lump sum based on the percentage of the total values of the sequestered assets. (I assumed the Finance Minister in throwing up the round figure of 50,000 pounds, must have had some such strategy in mind.) From the very beginning, I was, therefore, determined that however tortuous, the negotiations themselves, it should lead to criteria agreed by both parties on every item on every claim and thereby facilitate disbursement by the Government of India without having to unilaterally determine the amount on each individual case. But this approach had to be sold to the Ugandan negotiating team. Since the Finance Minister had refused to receive me, I had to deal with the spokesman, the Permanent Secretary of the Finance Ministry, to urge that, in order to finalize decision on compensation and if it was admissible the quantum, the negotiating team should first jointly list the different categories of assets that figured in the claims.

After sample scrutiny of the forms, we made a list of nearly thirty such items. These included blocked bank accounts, safe deposit lockers, built-up homes, other landed properties, industrial plants and machinery, agricultural farms, Uganda government bonds, claims against insurance companies, social security dues, and non-fixed assets like cars, furniture, and heavy electrical appliances. We settled on principles for the admission and valuation of each of these items and the rate of amortization depending on the proven length of possession. By applying the criteria agreed in advance, we could jointly decide whether to accept or reject a claim, and if admitted, the amount admissable. The procedure suggested by me implied scrutinizing and taking individual decisions on, say, 10,000 items, as on each claim there would be typically six or eight items, sometimes more. Somehow the proposed basis was accepted by the Ugandans in the hope of disputing and rejecting most items in the claims.

In the discussion, especially on important items, I initially pitched at the optimal values but in further discussions, readily conceded to the Ugandans especially where it would be patently hard to determine the actual depreciated value or where one suspected there was deliberate exaggeration of the amount claimed. I was primarily interested in speed and maximization without controversy. For example, many claims had included motor vehicles of which a large number were Mercedes Benz and other such expensive cars. There was no method by which one could assess the condition of the vehicles at the time, even if they could be located after three years, and so I conceded that compensation for mobile assets such as vehicles, furniture, and appliances, could be summarily rejected.

The most important assets left behind were houses and properties. For most Indians, a personal home is the first item for the investment of savings. In India, I was told, houses for tax purposes are supposed to amortize in fifty years. The Ugandans were aware that Tanzania had decreed only ten years as the accepted life of a house. Familiar with the Tanzanian decision, I had no ground to resist accepting that the value of the house depreciated by 10 per cent every year from the date of its construction. In other words, even when the title was clearly established on scrutiny, no claim would be admitted if the house was built before 1962, the crucial year of the 'economic war' being 1972.

Accepting the Tanzanian precedent, unrealistic though it was, was our major concession and established the reputation that I was not unreasonably rigid. I really wanted to concentrate on items where the value could not be challenged. I decided to focus on the least controversial items, which were bank deposits and the amount only had to be tallied to the bank ledger. If the claim proved correct, there would be no ground to deny full reimbursement. To avoid controversy, I did not raise the question of interest on the amount, as it may have changed over time and could differ from bank to bank.

The Ugandan negotiating team represented almost all their ministries and must have numbered nearly twenty. Apart from the officials of the Finance and Foreign Affairs Ministries, there were officers from various departments like agriculture, industry, social welfare and also from the municipal bodies. On our side we were only four—myself, the High Commissioner, Ramachandran, and a stenographer from the High Commission. The negotiations took place in the new conference complex built by the Yugoslavs for the meeting of the Organization of African Unity during Obote's presidentship.

Considering the procedure which emanated from our side and was approved by the Ugandan Finance Minister, for nearly six weeks we were sitting across the table from 9 a.m. up to the small hours of the morning, at times averaging 17 to 18 hours a day, with breaks only for meals. To facilitate and expedite the negotiations, the Ugandan government offered that both teams would be the guests of the government for all meals while we were in session. The Ugandan civil servants welcomed this luxury as it meant good food from a hotel and included the service of beer and alcoholic drinks. Our team stuck to soft drinks and an occasional glass of beer, but Ramachandran would not take even a drop of alcohol. One could notice that after the meals many of our opposite numbers dozed, lost their concentration and let slip many claims which could have been challenged with more sober vigilance.

While Obath-Offembi refused to sit at the negotiating table, he was often present in an adjoining room and expected to be consulted for directions on all important items. He found various ways of harassing me in the hope of softening my negotiating stance. In the Kampala Hilton where we were put up on arrival as guests of the Ugandan government—in accordance with Amin's promise to Indira Gandhi—being merely an official, I would not be served breakfast at the time ordered, or when it came, there were no cereals or butter. I discovered this was 'under orders' and so I decided to move to stay with the High Commissioner and spent nearly a month in his architecturally elegant but small house. (Ramachandran moved to the house of one of the south Indian members of the mission.)

Obath-Offembi had other methods to tire us out. He insisted that we have no breaks for relaxation, even after the drudgery of scrutinizing claim after claim and item after item for weeks including Sundays. One day, I tried to take an afternoon off and wanted to play nine holes of golf. The minister, who kept in touch with his team, when informed, promptly sent a vehicle to the golf club and insisted that the High Commissioner and I get back to the conference table. On another occasion, when I tried to do some shopping, there was actually a minor explosion in the officially assigned vehicle, but happily, I was in the High Commissioner's car.

Overcoming Unexpected Hurdles

It was fortunate that I had decided to concentrate on bank deposits because there could be no dispute if the figures (without interest) tallied. Though we did not keep a running total of the claims admitted, I was vaguely conscious that the total exceeded the amount which Oboth-Offembi had estimated as total compensation when he had mooted the idea to the President. When in due course this sunk into the Ugandan team, the minister became nervous and angry. He peremptorily instructed his delegation that in the negotiations no more bank ledgers should be produced to verify the figures of the bank deposits. I knew this was the crunch. I informed my opposite number that consistent with agreed principles, we must continue to scrutinize the full list of claims. If the same principles are not applied for all claimants then, I said, with barely suppressed anger, I would have to break off the negotiations. To make credible my threat, I instructed the High Commissioner to book passages for myself and Ramachandran to Nairobi and from there by Air India to Bombay.

Having made the bookings, I sought an interview with President Idi Amin. The Ugandans knew that I was planning to go back to India, so an interview was promptly fixed. Before I was ushered into the presence of the President, his Minister, Obath-Offembi and senior members of the Ugandan team had gone and briefed the President. I had the formidable task of getting Idi Amin to overrule his own minister when the latter was sitting next to the President.

I recalled to the President what I had told him initially that, under his initiative, Uganda was making a path-breaking innovation in international compensation practice. I added he must consider me not just as the representative of the Indian Prime Minister but also his own future envoy to convey his generosity to all those poor claimants who went back to India three years ago. The compensation was small recompense for the hardship they had suffered and the assets which they left behind, but what they received would enable them to restart their lives. I put it to him in these words: how could I act to plausibly explain the compensation agreement, if the bank deposit to one 'Patel' was paid, but not to another 'Patel'? Consistent adherence to agreed principles alone could demonstrate the spirit of generosity implicit in the payment of compensation.

Idi Amin knew that I was booked to travel home later that Friday evening. Politely I informed him that I had to get instructions whether an arbitrary limit in the scrutiny of claims could be accepted, which would be found to be discriminatory by the recipients. I emphasized that I was not asking for any modifications of the principles which we had agreed on before commencing the negotiations. In the spirit of friendship, we had already accepted Ugandan ruling to abandon claims on many items, but a man's own cash savings should not be withheld. Somehow Amin saw my point and ordered that by 9 a.m. the next morning, all ledgers of the previous ten years from all branches of all banks, not only in the capital but also with banks in other towns, should be brought to the conference hall. Except for the Bank of Baroda, all other banks in Uganda were British—Barclays, Standard, Grindlays, etc. The managers later complained to the British High Commissioner that I was responsible for having spoilt their Friday evening engagements and their Saturday morning rounds of golf!

The next morning, truck after truck, loaded with heavy ledgers arrived and they were carried to the conference table to enable us to resume our scrutiny. After completing the examination of all claim forms, we went on to draw up a Memorandum of Understanding. We left the final total figure blank because nobody had kept a running addition as that required time and had to be jointly checked. But my south Indian colleague, Ramachandran, who had a mind like a calculator, assured me that our total was substantially augmented. He and someone from the Ugandan Finance Ministry converted the total in shillings into US dollars.

UNTHINKING VETO

I knew that Amin had embarked on this offer only as an image-restoring exercise. He was, therefore, interested in announcing the conclusion of the agreement and handing over a cheque of the agreed sum with a speech and the fanfare of maximum publicity. I was happy that in six weeks we had completed the exercise, which could have taken years. In the memorandum, we had registered our reservations for the right to have further negotiations on some items which required either physical verification, such as safe deposit vaults or more careful checking, such as social security entitlements and government bonds.

In my heart of hearts, I knew that expectations of further negotiations, on the retrieval of jewellery from safe deposits, were highly problematic, so I had readily agreed to fall in the line with Idi Amin's plans which were calculated to get him early international recognition at having paid compensation to a country that had not been hostile towards his regime.

I telephoned the Foreign Secretary in Delhi informing him of the satisfactory agreement reached and that a ceremony had been fixed for a formal handing over/receiving of the cheque the next day. I was aghast when the following morning, the Foreign Secretary telephoned and conveyed the instructions of the Foreign Minister that *the cheque should not repeat not be accepted without further legal clearance and examination of its implications*.

Meanwhile, preparations for the ceremony were already under way. Our High Commission staff were associated with the preliminaries. Photographers and a television crew had been notified and were assembling their equipment to cover the event due to take place in the early afternoon. The consequence of an Indian official insulting Idi Amin by refusal of a signed cheque for the agreed amount and that too under TV recording, put me in a cold sweat. Amin was no respecter of diplomatic immunity and such a public rebuff at his own planned and cherished finale could provoke him into an unimaginable rage. As it was too late to cancel the function, we duly reached the appointed office.

Amin made a statement for the benefit of Uganda TV and the press. In my response, after expressing appropriate sentiments of satisfaction, I added that I was instructed that the Government of India considered that I was not of sufficient standing to receive what was a great example of amicable negotiations. I promised that a higher level dignitary would come soon to receive the cheque from the hands of the President and express more adequately our gratitude. Amin was disappointed, but fortunately, he was mollified by the humouring of his vanity. I was greatly relieved that President Amin did not get openly furious at the last minute change in our consent. However, the Ugandan Foreign Minister told me when we were having refreshments, that if I was senior enough to be entrusted with the negotiations, I must surely be senior enough to receive the cheque!

I could not elaborate my fears on an international telephone connection to Delhi, as it might have been tapped and so had accepted the orders from my superior. Throughout the six weeks, I had received no instructions or even enquiry as proof of interest in the progress of the negotiations. I was angry at the last minute obstruction conveyed to me by the Foreign Secretary. In retrospect, I regretted my own decision of informing Delhi. I should have accepted the cheque for the agreed amount. (This was, perhaps, the most embarrassing moment in my previous or subsequent negotiating experiences. I had faced some tense moments during the protracted exchanges with China on the Sino-Indian boundary question and also had been baffled at delays in replies to instructions sought.)

I am persuaded that during such diplomatic negotiations, if in one's own mind there is confidence of the grasp of national interest including the possible political implications, one must be willing to risk peremptorily exercising plenipotentiary discretion on the spot and be prepared for chastisement from the higher authorities on return to headquarters. Careful and precise briefs, with clear limits of negotiating latitude should be given in advance, but delicate and difficult negotiations cannot be conducted with the exercise of last minutes veto, which repudiates the judgement of the man entrusted with the responsibility.

I duly returned to Delhi and explained the negotiating tactics which we had employed, resulting in a quantum jump of the compensation, perhaps, twenty times more than what was envisaged by the Ugandan authorities. The Foreign Minister, Y.B. Chavan, raised the point that the government and I personally did not have the power of attorney signed by each of the claimants and so they could go to the Indian courts, raising legal objections at the scaling down of their claims and create a storm in Parliament and the country. I mentioned to the Foreign Minister that Uganda had always made it plain that it would deal only with the Indian government but not with individual claimants. In any case, I was certain that no claimant was prepared to risk going to Kampala and make direct representations to Idi Amin's government. Anil Clerk, one of the most eminent Asian lawyers in Kampala, had unaccountably disappeared and no one else was likely to take on an Asian brief. Anyway, no one had shown any inclination to do so in three years. Moreover, many claims were obviously exaggerated and unverifiable, and it would be nationally embarrassing for the Indian government to say so in public or in the courts. I reiterated my fear that I was afraid that if we had not concluded the MOU and agreed to the compensation mutually arrived at, it was likely that Uganda would not have the capacity to honour the cheque in dollars.

However, in pursuit of the Foreign Minister's reservations, I went through the best method possible to confirm my judgement that the Asians would not challenge the Memorandum of Understanding. We arranged for groups of representatives from major areas of those expelled from Uganda, to come to Delhi for discussions in the ministry. It was a random but representative selection from four provinces. Altogether I must have met thirty or forty of them from different states in the large Committee Room of the ministry. The biggest group was from Gujarat, the second one from Goa, the third from Bombay and a few from the Punjab. After describing the process of negotiations, the principles mutually agreed, the total amount promised and the urgency of finalization, I asked them whether they considered the basis of the settlement acceptable to them. They knew Idi Amin's wayward ways even better than anyone in the ministry. Each group readily confirmed my impressions and stated that the result was better than what they could have ever dared to expect. None of them had any intention to go back to Amin's Uganda to seek legal or administrative recourse to obtain fuller measure of their paper claims nor to file suits against the ministry.

In order to live up to the argument which I had advanced to Amin, I urged, indeed beseeched the then Minister of State, Bipin Pal Das, to have the honour of receiving the compensation from Amin on behalf of the Indian citizens, to coincide, with our Republic Day in 1976. Das had even initially hesitated to undertake the assignment and was still concerned about his safety and dignity, but ultimately he agreed to go to Kampala. He duly received from the President Idi Amin, a cheque for the amount agreed in our MOU, $1,627,711.60 (one million, six hundred twenty-seven thousand, seven hundred and eleven dollars and sixty cents only), which was the equivalent of Ugandan shillings 13,445,414 (thirteen million four hundred and forty-five thousand four hundred fourteen shillings only). On his return, the Minister of State made a brief statement in the Indian Parliament and reported his friendly conversation with Idi Amin and, after expressing gratitude, expressed the hope of improved cooperation between India and Uganda. There was general acclaim in Parliament at the settlement.

I kept a photostat copy of the cheque under the glass of my table, but after the minister's statement, the follow up responsibility was left to the Africa division, which handled it with alacrity and sympathy. All the individuals were sent communications to the addresses in their claim forms, and announcements were also placed in the Indian papers to contact the ministry. Within a year or so, most of the claims had been disbursed to the individual claimants or their attorneys. While the gross amount was in dollars, the individual claims were converted from Ugandan shillings and were paid in rupees. In each case the amount had been agreed to the last paisa. If I remember correctly, one beneficiary got over 3 lakh (3,00,000) rupees. As far as I know, the ministry received no complaints of non-payment or of any corruption. There was no doubt that, compared to the assets left behind, the amounts received were a small fraction, but there were no serious protests.

Frankly, the expellees had abandoned even the slightest hopes of any compensation long ago. The richer Asians had opted for British nationality, but for Indian nationals, many of whom were poor craftsmen, masons, carpenters, bartenders, mechanics, etc., the amount, though small, was a gratifying bonus. Quite a few wrote to me personally and expressed gratitude for what they had received. In the intervening three years many had re-migrated abroad, specially those who already had families in the UK, Canada, and Australia. For some, notably the older ones, the compensation came as welcome relief and provided the capital for a fresh start.

There were a few Asians with allegiance to Pakistan and

Bangladesh but these countries, like the British, were not invited for similar negotiations. Incidentally, to justify the 'economic war' against Asians, it was discreetly revealed that the richer British Asians had left insignificant balances in their Kampala accounts, much less than was found in the accounts of the Indians. Apparently the richer ones were regularly and promptly repatriating their profits to the UK and Switzerland.

There were some interesting sequels to the negotiating escapade with Amin's Uganda. Oboth-Offembi had been the bane of my life for six weeks. But before I left Kampala, he sent word through our High Commissioner that he wanted me to arrange a scholarship for his son to study in a professional institution in India. I promised to do my best. Alas, for all Oboth-Offembi's contrived loyalty to Amin, in the following year, he along with the Catholic Archbishop of Kampala, became the victims of Amin's arbitrary brutality. Both died mysteriously in what was suspected to have been an arranged 'accident' on a lonely road.

Another sequel was that while the cheque given to India was duly cashed and the distribution of compensation started soon afterwards, a month or so later, a Ugandan Letter of Credit bounced for want of adequate exchange reserves. It was just as well we worked through half the night to complete the negotiations and the Minister of State went within two months and collected the cheque.

On the other side, a friend and colleague, then in the Finance Ministry, after expressing appreciation for the small windfall addition to our own low foreign exchange holdings, when my promotion was announced in February 1976, said it was Amin who had given us our next Foreign Secretary!

The most telling sequel was when Margaret Thatcher, then leader of the Opposition, came to Delhi in the summer of 1976. As Foreign Secretary, I was asked by Prime Minister Indira Gandhi, to play host to her and her party. Mrs Thatcher after criticizing the ineptitude of Heath first and later Callaghan in dealing so feebly with the 'monster' Amin, asked me to summarize the approach of our enviably fruitful negotiations. I did so briefly but she insisted that I call on her on my next visit to London. I duly did so when I was in the British metropolis, which happened to be only a few weeks later. She received me warmly in the House of Commons, gave me lunch and said she would speak to the Foreign Office and that I should go and brief on the negotiating strategy employed by us. I told her, I happened to know the able officers in the Foreign Office dealing with Africa. They were fully aware that Amin wanted his vanity to be humoured, such as by being invited by the Queen to stay at Buckingham Palace and have the Pipe Band of the Scots Guard play for him!

CONCLUSION

Idi Amin was finally displaced. Mussevini, a more sober and able Ugandan, assumed power. Over the years, under President Mussevini's leadership, Uganda has stabilized economically and moved again towards a more democratic dispensation. Some Asians have been invited back to take a hand in rebuilding Uganda but they have gone to help with management and technical know how and not with their own investments. I do not know if any of them regained any part of their own confiscated assets.

The Ugandan compensation was not substantial but even so it sunk home to the emigrant Indian communities that, contrary to the conventional wisdom, at least in some circumstances there were advantages in remaining loyal to the poor Indian homeland and not opting for the citizenship of advanced countries. It was evident that compensation which came to the Indians was a benefit which flowed from India's non-aligned position, Indira Gandhi's personal standing, and the diplomatic restraint exercised in not denouncing Uganda's right to nationalize assets even if they were built by earnings which came when they were serving as the adjuncts of imperialism.

What helped India was the show of respect for another developing country, the flexibility of arguments, and a more accurate perception of the points of soft vulnerability of Amin at that time. But however keen one may be on success, one also learnt that negotiations must always be projected around plausible principles of equity. In the face of blandishments such as that of Oboth-Offembi, one must remain firm and unflustered and not bend under pressure or be afraid to risk a break. Even when the odds are great, the negotiating strategy

Plate 1: Chairman Mao Tse-tung and Vice-President S. Radhakrishnan in front of Crysanthemum Hall inside Zong-nan-hai. The entire Chinese Politburo was present. Also Indian Ambassador R.K. Nehru and members of the Indian Embassy (the author is standing behind Chairman Mao).

Plate 2: Mrs Gandhi and the author at Sherathang prior to crossing Nathu La into Chumbi Valley—on the way to Bhutan with Prime Minister Nehru, September 1958.

Plate 3: Prime Minister Jawaharlal Nehru in Bhutanese formal dress (inscribed in Hindi 'Jagat ko').

Plate 4: Director Chang-wen-Chin and author during the discussions on Sino-India Boundary Question, 1960.

Plate 5: Chang-wen-Chin, the leader of the Chinese delegation and the author signing the report on Sino-Indian Boundary Question. Next to the leaders are deputy leader Yang-kung-su and S. Gopal, December 1960. The report was two inches thick with more than 1,000 typescript pages.

Plate 6: Jawaharlal Nehru and the entire Indian delegation in Prime Minister's office in South Block after the final session of talks on Sino-Indian Boundary Question, Rangoon, Christmas Day, 1960.

Plate 7: President Idi Amin of Uganda shaking hands with the author, November 1975.

Plate 8: Shri Kewal Singh ICS handing over the charge to the author as Foreign Secretary, April 1976.

Plate 9: B.M. Abbas of Bangladesh and the author signing the Accord on Farakka, 1 October 1977.

Plate 10: Foreign Minister Atal Behari Vajpayee being received by Foreign Minister Agha Shahi–on arrival–Islamabad, February 1978. The author is just behind Vajpayee.

Plate 11: Press Conference of Foreign Minister Atal Behari Vajpayee in Islamabad, February 1978. The author is on his right and K.S. Bajpai, the High Commissioner on his left.

Plate 12: Foreign Minister Atal Behari Vajpayee exchanging agreements on Salal Hydel Project with Foreign Minister Agha Shahi, New Delhi, June 1978.

Plate 13: Foreign Secretary of Nepal Udayan Bhatt and the author signing the seperate Treaties of Trade, Transit and Agreement on Controlling illegal trade, March 1978.

Plate 14: The author calling on H.M. King Birendra of Nepal after signing the separate Treaties on Trade and Transit between India and Nepal, Kathmandu, March 1978.

Plate 15: The two delegations from India and China, led by Deng Hsio-Ping and Foreign Minister Atal Behari Vajpayee, Peking, February 1979. The author is fourth from the left in the front row.

Plate 16: Reunion with negotiating adversaries. From left Udayan Bhatt of Nepal, Agha Shahi of Pakistan, the author, and B.N. Abbas of Bangla Desh, Kathmandu, 1992.

has to remain fine-tuned to optimal national dignity.

The Amin episode will remain a footnote in the troubled story of post-liberation Africa. It is, nevertheless, an interesting case study in diplomatic negotiations. It showed the capacity of defiance of a poor country against a powerful former imperial power. In an earlier century or even in an earlier decade, the sanction of power might well have prevailed. The pleas and threats of the British government and its coercive diplomacy did not yield compliance in the changed equations of the twentieth century. The conclusion emerged that punitive pressures only prove counterproductive. The US failure against Vietnam and in Iraq in 2003 must remain etched in post-war diplomacy. It also occurs to me, anticipating the future, that an operation like the Gulf War would have only given Amin a longer lease of power as happened with Saddam Hussein in Iraq.

No reimbursement was forthcoming for the 25 million pounds spent in the reception and rehabilitation of the British Asians from Uganda. It brings out that diplomacy is the craft of bringing intelligence to a dialogue between sovereign states.

The last fifty years have seen a great transformation in the patterns and destinations of migration, and as a consequence, many new and different minority problems requiring delicate resolution have confronted international diplomacy. There are, no doubt, millions who, though poor or displaced, are reconciled to their fate; but, equally there are many more who, aware of greener pastures elsewhere, and would like to vote with their feet. Some who have relations already established abroad, can legitimately unite with their families, but others will resort to desperate devices, risk great dangers, make terrible monetary sacrifices and in the end fail and face compulsory repatriation.

A democracy like India recognizes a citizen's right to a passport, which in effect gives him the freedom to seek a more conducive habitat wherever he can find it. But, while economic globalism facilitates the international movement of goods and resources, it is indifferent and even callous to the human frustration at being debarred by national barriers to gainful employment. The reality is that developed nations are advertising abroad for selective recruitment to meet the national shortage of specialists to sustain their own economic growth but, at the same time, enforcing stricter controls on immigration.

It is possible that persons of Indian origin may again suffer indignities and discrimination in rich countries. Nevertheless, by precept and example, India should not dilute its advocacy of the equality of races and nations and the right to settle to a life of dignity in multi-cultural, multi-racial societies. We have an exceptional civilizational tradition of toleration and assimilation and yet we also have a tradition of respecting other nationalisms and sovereignties. Our approach is no doubt flawed in consistency, but success in negotiations even with a man like Amin was only possible because the national discretion of another country was not questioned, and this left space for a dialogue of accommodation. Our own nationalism has no xenophobic content and should plausibly uphold the commitment to enlightened internationalism. India is morally most luminous when it chooses the diplomacy of reason and does not automatically turn to coercion as a way to protect its national interests.

CHAPTER 4

Diplomacy to Restore Severed Links and Mutual Confidence

The Normalization of India-Pakistan Relations – 1976

Until 1976 my professional involvement with Pakistan was peripheral and indirect. In the early years of my service (1947-9), I had opportunities to get close insights in the post-Partition holocaust from the outer office of the Secretary-General. I was a privileged junior member of the delegation in 1948 for discussions on the Kashmir question in the Security Council. Because the Pakistan division did not want to be the custodian for files on what was deemed an internal problem, and the Secretary-General was handling Kashmir related questions on its international ramifications (and also as he tended to be impatient with the drafting capabilities of the established hierarchy), I became the archivist of all papers related to Kashmir. For two years, until Vishnu Sahay was appointed Secretary for Kashmir Affairs but based in the Home Ministry, the cupboards in my office stored all the Kashmir related papers. I have described in the chapter on China how the Sino-Pakistan collusion led to an ultimatum given to me during the conflict of 1965. In 1971 my wife and I helped Dr Ghani, the Bengali High Commissioner for Pakistan, and his nervous chain-smoking Begum—both under the constant surveillance of the Punjabi First Secretary—to defect from Dar-es-Salaam. We did so by his coming to our embassy residence surreptitiously, late at night, and we conspiring to viciously denounce each other in public during the day so that Ghani's loyalty was not suspect, and his sons, who were academics in the Dacca University, were not brutalized and 'eliminated' by the West Pakistan military authorities.

Pakistan, of course, dominated India's diplomacy in all posts, but for us it was not the single-issue focus, as India was for Pakistan. Yet Indian missions everywhere watched Pakistan's diplomatic manoeuvres like hawks and sought to counter them. All this was 'routine' for most officials, but I was out of the loop in dealing directly with policy towards Pakistan. However, as Foreign Secretary it came as my first diplomatic challenge, and like other holders of the post, it remained a priority of official responsibilities throughout my tenure.

PARTITIONS IN HISTORY AND SPECIAL FEATURES OF THE DIVISION OF INDIA IN 1947

Lord Mansergh[1] (who put together 12 volumes of papers on the Transfer of Power in India and also wrote extensively on Home Rule and the establishment of the Republic of Eire), quotes Empress Maria Theresa of Austria, writing to her Chancellor Kuntz that she felt shame to show her face for having been responsible for the partition of Poland in 1772. Fredrick the Great reacted cynically and said she wept but remained only a little mindful of the untold suffering that followed because the partition was 'for reasons of state'. While the separation, the subsequent union, and then re-separation of Norway from Sweden, and of Belgium from Holland and the independence of Finland from Sweden have proved positive in their consequences, this cannot be said of partitions of Palestine or Cyprus.

Even more than Palestine and Cyprus, the two partitions that defied a majority community's definition of national unity (which brought into play the concept of minorities constituting separate political nations) were Ireland and India. These divisions were fostered by the policies of a third party—in both cases Great Britain. Objectively speaking, the Partition of India cannot be explained only by 'Divide and Rule'. As Urvashi Butalia observes, it brought out the conflict between the 'territorial logic' and the 'identity logic'. The bitterness that followed has been long lasting. It resurfaced after the demolition of the Baburi Masjid (1992), the riots in Mumbai (1992) and even more sharply after the Godhra torching of *karsevaks* and

[1] Nicholas Mansergh and Diana Mansergh (eds.), *Independence Years*, New Delhi: Oxford University Press, 1999.

the killing of the Muslims in Gujarat in 2002. The suffering and killings during in the Partition in 1947 cannot be compared to with any other political division in history. Penderel Moon, an ICS officer who stayed on in India for some years and then co-edited the Transfer of Power papers, has succinctly reflected, 'the Indian National Congress passionately desired to preserve the unity of India but acted consistently to make Partition certain'.

The magnitude of the tragedy of Partition was not anticipated by the British, the Congress, or the Muslim League. After the event, it has long been discussed whether Partition was in fact unavoidable even as late as 1947. Was it the lesser evil for the Muslims of the subcontinent? I (myself) have speculated that had the 100 days in the spring of 1947 not coincided with the beginning of the Cold War formalized in the Truman Doctrine (enunciated on 12 March 1947) and the appointment of Mountbatten and his negotiations with political leaders after arrival in India and the 3 June announcement of the transfer of power in the subcontinent on 15 August, the United States, in self-interest, might have prevented the bifurcation of the natural unity of the subcontinent.[2] Containing the perceived threat from the communist monolith straddling the Euro-Asian continent should have pointed to opposition of the division of a subcontinent already pledged to adopt a democratic constitution as early as December 1946. Be that as it may, what is certain is that for those who lived through the summer and autumn of 1947, the trauma remains. The independence of India was vitiated in the very moment of its fulfilment. We, of that generation, who came to maturity and official responsibility in the 1940s and straddled the transfer of power, are the seared witnesses of that time. Some were affected directly by the events that enveloped the Punjab and even Delhi, but the embers of rumour ignited communal tensions way beyond the two-way movement of people.

For many, the subsequent fifty years of events have reinforced the conviction that Indo-Pakistan reconciliation is a long way away; some feel it should not even be attempted, at least not until there is a radical transformation of Pakistan into a

[2] J.S. Mehta, 'The Two Cold Wars: Myopia and Misperceptions by the Great Powers and the Subcontinent', *India Quarterly*.

democracy. Others, including one-time 'hawks' like Atal Behari Vajpayee, came to recognize, that in enlightened national interest we cannot continue to live in the past. With measured vigilance we must not tire of exploring new forms of cooperation based on the unbreakable interdependence between India and Pakistan but only as two sovereign neighbours. Exceptions aside, the approach each individual brings to the problem dominates the thinking minds in the two countries and is based, at least partly, on one's experience, upbringing, and conditioning. I belong to the now thinning generation which lived through the experience of education before, and professional experience after Partition. We are, as it were, taking off from Salman Rushdie's title and could call ourselves 'Midnights Adults'. Consciously running the risk of stretching this paper into irrelevance, I shall introspect and describe at some length my own background as it may well have shaped my thinking and my somewhat unusual professional experience with Pakistan. I leave it to the reader to judge whether I am being an owl (in the figurative sense associated in the occident) as a wise old bird or, as the word normally signifies in India (a pejorative appellation) for a fool!

THE TRANSFER OF POWER AND MY EDUCATIONAL BACKGROUND

I was born not in British India, but in Udaipur where for generations my family were respected servants of the benign monarchy of Mewar. Amongst his titles, the Maharana was called *Hindu Surya* (the Sun of Hindus), and the ruling family boasted of never bowing to the Muslim conquerors. It is recalled that Rana Sanga led the combined Rajput armies against Babur and his grandson, the famous Maharana Pratap, was the only one who defied even Emperor Akbar. The interesting sidelight is that while Raja Man Singh, the ruler of Amber, led Akbar's forces at the battle of Haldighati, Pratap's own Commander-in-Chief was Hakim Khan Suri, a Pathan. Even after Partition, a good 10 per cent of the Maharana's subjects were Muslims. Communal relations in the state remained totally unaffected by the tensions prevailing in British India. All followers of the principal faiths seemed to have specially sacred shrines in or near Mewar. For the Shaivites the temple of Eklingji, for Vaishnavites and Krishna followers Nathadwara (second only to Tirupati); and for large numbers of Jains Delwara, Rishabhdeoji and Ranakpur; not too far is the *dargah* of Moinudin Chishti in Ajmer considered second only to Mecca and Karbala; lastly there is Galiakot, the most important mosque for the Bohras. Caste or religion never inhibited the celebration of all festivals. The word secularism was unknown but we lived in respect of the catholicity of all faiths. When aged 7, I was sent to Modern School in Delhi, my local guardian was not one of the many Hindu friends of my father, but Mohammed Hussein Bohra. The secondary school, which I attended in Udaipur from 10 onwards, had a defiant attachment to Gandhian nationalism. The school was the first in Rajasthan to prescribe a simple shirt and shorts as its uniform in order to obliterate visible symbols of caste, wealth, and religion. When in the 1930s, Hindu-Muslim riots vitiated social relations in northern India, religion-based tensions were totally alien to my experience.

However, when in the 1940s I went to the Allahabad University, I found strong loyalty to the Congress on the one hand confronting with protagonists of the Muslim League on the other, both having their play in the University Union whose membership was an obligation for the entire student body of 2500. I was Vice-President of the Union and H.N. Bahuguna was the Secretary when the Quit India Resolution was passed in August 1942. We were surprised that the protest march, in which one student was killed, was boycotted by most Muslim students. The Union, incidentally, was a kind of political nursery for Bahuguna and Narain Dutt Tiwari who became Chief Ministers and many others who after Independence went on to careers in public life. Some like myself went to the Civil Services or took short-term commissions in the armed forces. Amongst my personal friends at Allahabad were Nurul Hassan who became Central Minister, Ambassador and Governor; Zafar Zaheer, later Air Marshal in India and also Agha Shahi who became Foreign Secretary and then minister in Pakistan.

In 1946, while I was in the Navy with a wartime Volunteer Reserve Commission, I was posted in HMIS *Hamla* at Malad on the coast north of Bombay. While we were waiting to be demobbed, discussions in the mess were dominated by the politics of Independence, which was obviously round the corner. In February 1946 we found ourselves unexpectedly at the centre of the naval mutiny. It started with bad food in the ratings mess in HMIS *Talwar* (the Signals School) in Colaba but in the surcharged atmosphere it took a political complexion and quickly spread to all ships both at anchor and in the shore establishments. With 2000 ratings, our 'ship' was then one of the biggest in the Indian navy. The focus shifted to *Hamla* because Lt Ishaque Sobani, one of our colleagues, was the only officer in the entire navy to join the mutiny. The mutineers took charge of the armoury, the transport and the signal installations. The Commanding Officer (W.A. Windsor-Aubery) with thirty years in the first Punjab Regiment of the Indian Army, had been transferred to head a Combined Operations unit, and was totally stumped at such disaffection under his command. Sobani peremptorily demanded that he wanted to go to Bombay to represent the case of the ratings to the Flag Officer Bombay (FOB). The Commanding Officer (CO) deputed me and Lt Ranjit, to go with Sobani. He made believe that, as required by the Kings Regulations and Admiralty Instructions, he was keeping the 'mutinous officer' under custody. Both of us were junior to Sobani—I was only a Sub-Lieutenant—and so it was scarcely in compliance with the prescribed disciplinary rules. We were chosen only because we were friends of Sobani and acceptable to him. We drove Sobani in an amphibious jeep—his choice for maximum exposure to the rioting crowds—and reported to Captain Nott, the Admiral's Secretary in Vithal House. We were bluntly told that not only could Sobani not see the Admiral, but the officer was under arrest and our orders were to take him to HMIS *Firoze*, the Training Centre located on Malabar Hill. (It had been the club and office of the Western India Automobile Association and reverted to its original role after the war.) Sobani, we were told, would be put behind bars in the *Firoze*. Sobani, of course, was furious and had choice words about perfidious Albion. On coming out of the Navy office, he wanted to join the rioting crowd round the corner near Grindlays Bank or to go straight to the *Blitz* office to confirm the deception in print. (He was only assuaged by our making an unauthorized stop at the

Parisienne Dairy on the corner of Marine Drive for an expensive ice cream!). I recall this in detail because, unlike most of the Muslim officers, Sobani then was a firm secular-minded sympathizer of the Indian National Congress and a devoted admirer of Nehru. He disagreed strongly with other Muslim officers who echoed Jinnah's politics. The next time I met Sobani was in 1954 in Karachi, when during my home leave, I had gone to visit my father who was then High Commissioner for India. I had heard that like many Muslim intellectuals when Partition was accepted, Sobani too had lost faith in the Congress and decided to abandon his home in Bombay and become a citizen of Pakistan. Even though his politics had changed—and he knew I was in the Indian Foreign Service—he embraced me as if we were long lost brothers.

At Cambridge later in 1946 the old Majlis called the Tagore Society still had a membership of students from the entire subcontinent including Ceylon. In the refined atmosphere of a British University, there was then no spillover of the Congress-Muslim League tensions amongst the undergraduates but, while some went back home and followed their professional or academic inclinations, others who originated in that part which remained India defected to strange new surroundings in Pakistan. There were many at Cambridge who would attain distinction in the future including Shankar Dayal Sharma (a future President who was doing his Ph.D.), I.G. Patel (who was a young Fellow at Kings College), B.G. Verghese, Dharma Venkatraman (later Kumar) became nationally known economists in India. Rajgopalan joined AIR, Deshmukh, a younger brother of the Governor, went to the Reserve Bank, Akbar Imam, studying law, went back and eventually became a judge of the Patna High Court. There were others like Rahim who were 'progressives' at Cambridge and became passionate advocates of Pakistan's anti-Indian politics. But there was also Abdus Salaam in my college (St. Johns) who became a distinguished scientist and a Nobel Laureate, who went back to Pakistan but criticized both Pakistan and India for going nuclear and had the courage to urge reconciliation between the two countries.

I recall this entire intellectual spectrum to mirror the political and moral agony of the thinking elite in those momentous years before and after Partition. In no other country and even in India and Pakistan no other generation would go through such a love-hate experience, which cast a shadow on our lives and careers.

Old Colleagues, Relations and Friends Across the Divide

Out of a list of 62 notified in October 1946 as selected for the ICS against (war-time vacancies), thirteen were approved for the Indian Political Service (against the notified fifteen vacancies. The interim government deemed the Foreign Service the successor of the Political Service as the IAS was of the ICS. They were all called for training at Metcalfe House in March 1947. (In those months there still was a possibility that an independent undivided India will come into existence in which the central subjects will remain Foreign Affairs, Defence and Communications.) We were literally the last to be approved for the Political Service, between March and June 1947 and belong to a common 'Indian Foreign Service'. Out of the thirteen, there were four Muslim officers of whom three (Sultan Ahmed, Sajjad Hyder, and Iftikar Ali) opted for Pakistan. Sultan in his autobiography describes the agony of the decision and how he nearly decided to stay on in India. The fourth Muslim officer in our selection was M.A. Rahman (Ishi). He hailed from a distinguished Pathan family but opted to stay on in India. Having done his schooling at St. Pauls in London, he had gone on to get a first in classics at Cambridge and then came (out) to India and was commissioned by the elite Frontier Force Rifles (FFR), a regiment which went to Pakistan. Had he chosen to go to Pakistan he would have risen even quicker. Ishi's elder brother, 'Turk', also commissioned in the FFR rose to be a Lt General and for many years was Governor of Punjab (Pakistan) and Chairman of the Pakistan Public Service Commission. Sir Akbar Hydari, then one of the seniormost ICS Officers, who was about to take over as Governor of Assam and whose daughter was then engaged to Ishi, persuaded him to stay on in India. Ishi started working in the ministry as Under Secretary under Humphrey Trevelyan, then Joint Secretary (External, in effect Political) and who later had a distinguished career in the British Foreign Service. My first appointment without training was as Private Secretary to the Secretary-General. I had to keep very long hours. Cycling back during the curfew to a room in a private home was not without hazards of being questioned and harassed, if not worse. Ishi, whom I had never met before, put another bed in his single room in Western Court and gave me a more convenient roof. Sarwar, his batman from the FFR, served us both until he decided to go back to Pakistan. Ishi became a life-long friend. The other Muslim officer whom I got to know in the first year of my service and who chose to stay on in India even though he belonged to the Punjab Cadre of the ICS was Azim Hussein. It must be rare in the annals of diplomacy that at one stage two brothers, Azim and Naseem, represented political adversarial countries—India and Pakistan—but both were accredited at the same time to the government of Lebanon!

Such experiences are illustrative of the divisions and dilemmas amongst officers who, career-wise, straddled Partition; but this will never again be repeated for professional cadres anywhere. The result was divided loyalties and vigorous professional antagonism but most of us were not ashamed at nurturing old friendships and welcoming opportunities to meet old colleagues and classmates. This baffled diplomatic observers in many capitals around the world. When I was posted in Bern, Begum Liaqat Ali Khan, the widow of the first Prime Minister of Pakistan (who later, in her own right, served as Ambassador for Pakistan), telephoned and expressed a wish that she, along with her two sons, Akbar and Akhtar, and Kay Miles, her companion secretary, visit and stay with us. I was only a First Secretary and had a modest flat with three bedrooms, and one-and-half bathrooms just sufficient for ourselves, our own two small children and a German nurse. Rama's (my wife) father had known Nawabzada Liaqat Ali Sahib in UP before Independence, and I had got to know Begum Sahib's sister, Mira Sawhney, in Delhi. In 1952, there was no Pakistan mission in Switzerland and the British Embassy was looking after Pakistan interests. Sir Patrick Scrivener, the British Ambassador, had offered Begum Sahiba the hospitality and luxury of his residence, but was surprised—indeed even though it could cast a slur on his assigned representational responsibility of looking after Pakistan interests when Begum Sahiba insisted on staying in the flat, with no spare rooms, of a lowly officer of the Indian mission. Begum Liaqat at once started helping in the cooking and even bathing our children. Similarly without trace of ulterior purpose, Sajjad Hyder, who was selected with me, when he was posted as High Commissioner of Pakistan in New Delhi with a reputation as an uncompromising protagonist for his country, frequently took my sons out fishing to Okhla. I suppose I risked one more adverse mention in the Intelligence Bureau dossier on my reliability, but I did not forbid the boys from going. I don't know about the Irish and British diplomats, but I never saw a Federal German diplomat talking to somebody from the Democratic German Republic even on a social occasion when both Germanys had missions in Delhi. This sort of social and cultural magnetism and friendship between Indian and Pakistan representatives in the first post-Partition generation must be unique in the annals of diplomacy.

The Dividends of Personal Bonhomie

Personal equations were not without incidental professional advantages, and that I experienced also. When I took up appointment as Chargé d'Affaires in China in 1964. I was more or less ostracized by the Chinese Foreign office. Our relations had plummeted after the war in 1962. During my formal courtesy call, General Raza, the Pakistan Ambassador, expressed condescending sympathy and told me that in his first tenure in Peking, which was in mid-1950s, he had suffered the same kind of inconveniences and boycott as I was probably experiencing. In the 1950s, he recalled, the Indian Embassy was the favoured mission. India was allowed to buy the building of the Hong Kong and Shanghai Bank in the Old Legation quarter even though this part of Peking had a humiliating association for China, having been the defiant bastion during the Boxer Rebellion of 1897. All missions, starting with the extensive British mission, with many Chinese style bungalows, military barracks and a nine hole golf course, were subsequently dislodged from their historic compounds. Incidentally I came to the conclusion that the defence of the legation quarter was planned in my dining room in what must have once been the location of the bank counter. Even though India had purchased the building as a residence and a chancery from the People's Republic, we too were required to vacate the premises during the Cultural Revolution. General Raza, on his second coming, was instrumental in the Sino-Pakistan rapprochement. When I arrived in Peking he was the envy, indeed the legend, of the diplomatic corps. He could make the most unusual demands and the Chinese would bend backwards to satisfy them. For example, at his insistent request, the Chinese authorities located the same *ama* who used to look after their daughter ten years earlier but had then disappeared amongst the vast millions. Even in Communist China, General Raza had remained every inch a Sandhurst product. His residence was well-carpeted and tastefully furnished, but all cushions were covered with material made out of the turbans of the ceremonial uniform of the Rajputana Rifles in which he was commissioned in the late 1920s. To crown it all, he insisted on (and got away with) the rule that his domestic (Chinese) staff at home were to be dressed in monkey jackets with bow ties and behave as if they were mess orderlies!

Somehow General Raza took to me and Begum Raza became extremely friendly with Rama. For our part we showed deference to his age and seniority. On 4 September 1965 Rama and I were playing bridge at the Pakistan Embassy till the early hours of the morning with General and Begum Raza. There were no other guests. The Pakistan army had attacked the Chhamb Sector of Kashmir on 1 September, but neither they nor we had cancelled the engagement, fixed in advance.

The previous day, I had asked our Military Attaché, Col. Khera, to invite the other Military Attachés in Peking to his apartment and spread the maps of Punjab and Kashmir on his dining table and explain the prevailing military situation. By prior arrangement I had dropped in, and I asked the officers—the Russian and the Bulgarian were Generals—what they would do if they were in command of the Indian defending forces. All of them felt that militarily the operations could not be confined to the Jammu & Kashmir with long logistics but to put Pakistan under diversionary military pressure, India should make a counterattack across the International Boundary in West Punjab. Fortunately no one took our dining table strategies as anything more than hypothetical exercises. Pakistan still expected our counterattack would, as in 1948, be confined to the territory of Jammu & Kashmir. (When on 6 September, the Indian Army attacked in the Lahore and Sialkot sectors, the speculation among the military attaches was that only the Indian Embassy had been told in advance of the operational plans!) When we were playing bridge in the Pakistan Embassy we never spoke about the current fighting in Kashmir. Our bonhomie with the Pakistan Ambassador resulted in our two missions not descending to propaganda polemics locally. The Indian Embassy would have been at a decisive disadvantage as there was obvious partiality for Pakistan on the part of the Chinese government. (I have described the Chinese attitude in the study on Sino-Indian relations.)

As it happened, the inter-personal relations between the heads of missions of India and Pakistan gave me the clue for an important speculation. On 21 September at a Ghana Embassy dinner, my wife was making small talk with Ambassador Raza when suddenly he said to her he had to leave. Rama said in Hindustani, 'Nawab Sahib, why in such a hurry? Dessert and coffee have yet to be served'. He replied—again in Hindustani—*Bibi, tum samajhti nahi ho—Mujhe jana hai* (Bibi, you don't understand—I have to go). He was clearly intent on leaving and that too in a hurry without saying good-bye to diplomatic colleagues who were the other guests. I speculated that the urgency must have had something to do with the on-going India-Pakistan war. In the hypothetical scenario constructed in my mind, I thought he must have had an appointment with Chou En-lai. I have since read that Ayub and Bhutto paid a one-day secret visit to Peking on 20 September. Keeping in mind the prevailing circumstances and putting myself in the shoes of decision makers in Pakistan, I guessed that they would have been worried that China—which had a mind of its own and was not a surrogate of Pakistan—could go ahead but a diversionary incident on the India-China border, without full commitment, could complicate the cease-fire being urged in the Security Council with the support of both the United States and Soviet Union. In response to an appeal, collateral support for Pakistan had been pledged by China during the visit of Ayub and Bhutto in March 1965.

Operation Gibralter had not gone as was hoped by Bhutto. The people in the Valley had not joined the infiltrators. It was in this failure that operation Grand Slam—of direct Pakistan army attack—had been launched across the Jammu Sector. India, however, had not (as in 1947-8) confined operations to the 'disputed' Jammu & Kashmir but, following the military logic, Prime Minister Shastri had authorized a counterattack along the Punjab frontier. With tank battles stalemated, the appeal from Pakistan to China must have come around 12-14 September, which fructified in the ultimatum given to me on the nights of 16 and 19 September. Both had 3-day time limits and were calculated to create the apprehensions of a two-front conflict for India, which would ensure continued Indian restraint in launching an attack on East Pakistan but also immobilize possible reinforcements being moved to the Western front in the Punjab. Our army had frustrated Pakistani armour and the United States and Soviet Union had both got active in calling for a ceasefire. Pakistan did not want to alienate the United States and most of the world. If China were to go ahead and precipitate by direct involvement on the Sikkim front (or the NEFA), it would spike both US and Soviet diplomacy. Pakistan wanted a military victory but did not want to risk international condemnation by the Security Council. My broad understanding was always that China did not want to use its own military power to serve the interests of another country. Anyway, I concluded that General Raza's premature departure from the party must have been either to meet Chou En-lai, or to make sure that China did not go ahead and complicate options for future diplomacy for Pakistan. Not staying on at the dinner and telling Rama that he was in a hurry reinforced my speculative reasoning behind the long telegram in which, at variance with the consensus of anxieties in Delhi, I took the risk to argue in advance that on the expiry of the second ultimatum, China would climb down and do nothing. There were other analytical reasons for my prediction but telling Rama that he could not wait for dessert all but confirmed my speculation.

I recall a further incident where, in the hostile atmosphere of Peking, a friendship dramatically baffled the diplomatic corps. After the 1965 War was over I was called back for consultations and was away for almost two months. I was assigned to attend the proposed conference on the tenth anniversary of Bandung, to be held in Algiers, in which China was taking a deep interest—China hoped it could become the forum for tri-continental solidarity of the developing continents of Asia, Africa, and Latin America where the USSR would be excluded. (As it happened, because of awareness of Chinese diplomatic strategy, the Soviet Union started canvassing that it was also an Asian country and so we all dispersed from Algiers without the conference having even begun). I was then instructed to accompany Mrs Vijayalakshmi Pandit to some capitals in Europe to explain the recent Indo-Pakistan conflict and so only got back to Peking in December. When I did, the incestuous small diplomatic corps had already started the end of the year festivities. India-Pakistan relations had remained politically hostile. At the Moroccan Embassy during a dinner-dance General Raza went up to my wife and said to her 'Bibi, will you dance with me?' Rama replied 'Why not.' I saw this from another corner of the room and rushed to accompany Begum Raza on the floor. This was several weeks before Tashkent. I know of two envoys who went straight back to their chanceries that night and on the basis of seeing us dance, telegraphed to their governments, that Pakistan and India were defying China and had decided to normalize their relations! Needless to say, I myself was in no position to anticipate Kosygin's successful role in Tashkent.

THE BACKDROP TO INDIA-PAKISTAN NORMALIZATION, 1976

So much for the unique mix of personal equations and professional hostility that characterized India-Pakistan diplomacy in the decades after our respective independence. In my career, in which I had spent two-thirds at headquarters. I had 'dealt' from a 'desk' in the ministry with almost all parts of the world, but not Pakistan. In 1976 as Foreign Secretary, my first diplomatic foray was to be Islamabad. My own personal conditioning as well as intellectual reasoning had long nurtured in my mind that for our foreign policy nothing mattered as much as success in changing the chemistry and climate of relations with our neighbours and above all with Pakistan. Could I now make a beginning?

My predecessor as Foreign Secretary, Kewal Singh, was an ICS officer of the Punjab Cadre who was eight years older and as many years senior. He had served in the districts that became part of Pakistan. He was a Sikh and when I first saw him in 1948 he wore a turban and had a beard, which he shaved off in 1951 when he was in transit, by surface route from Berlin to Lisbon. He had familiarity with the language and special culture of what was now Pakistan and thus had an informed background on Indo-Pakistan problems. Moreover, he had been our High Commissioner in Pakistan at the time of the conflict of 1965. The one advice he gave me when handing over was to be firm with Pakistan and defer to the defence authorities on questions bearing on security. His own inclination on the prospective negotiations for normalization was to keep Pakistan on a short leash, allowing time for close observation that Pakistan adhered to the agreed letter and spirit of good relations. His advice was in keeping with the Simla Agreement which incorporated commitment to a step-by-step process of normalization. But Simla was nearly four years earlier before Kewal Singh took over. We could still rejoice, in the laurels and triumph of military victory and had reason to be diplomatically self-confident. In 1975, however, we had suspended our Constitution and proclaimed an 'Emergency'. Many correspondents of the international media had been expelled or withdrawn and the world had become critical of India. Even well-known friends of the country had been denied visas. Our international reputation as a democracy stood sullied and, for the first time, Pakistan could boast of being a working democracy, while India was imposing strict censorship and throttling human and political rights. In any case, I thought we should be ready with a more imaginative approach so that Pakistan could be brought on to a less hostile and more reciprocally friendly wavelength so that our image abroad improved.

Let me backtrack on the immediate context to the normalization process. In January 1971 pro-Pakistan Kashmiris had hijacked an Indian Airlines plane bound from Delhi to Jaipur, and diverted it to Lahore. In accordance with international law, India had demanded the repatriation of the passengers and the plane, and the handing over of the hijackers. Although the passengers were released and sent back by road, the hijackers, no doubt with local connivance, were allowed to set fire to the Fokker Friendship aircraft and destroy it. Not surprisingly, Pakistan refused to hand over the culprits. Indeed, Bhutto joined in a public march in Lahore applauding the hijackers. After the destruction of the aircraft and the refusal to hand over the hijackers, as a protest, India terminated the overflight rights of Pakistan Airlines across Indian airspace. Thereafter in February 1971 Pakistan filed a complaint with the International Civil Aviation Organization (ICAO) in Montreal, protesting at the violation of the Chicago Convention and we, in turn, filed a counter complaint about connivance in the destruction of our aircraft. In December 1970, in the all-Pakistan elections, there had been an overall victory for Sheikh Mujib and the Awami League. In March the independence of Bangladesh had been proclaimed. The denial of overflight rights meant that Pakistani -aircraft now had to refuel at Colombo when sending reinforcements and supplies to Dhaka.

The story of the 1971 conflict and the Simla meeting in July 1972 need not be recalled in detail here. As a follow-up of Simla, in 1973, 93,000 POWs had been repatriated and the Pakistan territory under Indian control had been vacated. Ten million refugees in India had returned to their homes in independent Bangladesh.

By 1976 much, of course, had changed. The 1971 American tilt against India had sought to be corrected by the visit of the US Secretary of State, Henry Kissinger, to Delhi in 1974. Pakistan for its part had effected considerable economic repair following President Bhutto's whirlwind tours. The Arab countries, flush with higher oil revenues, had helped Pakistan to rehabilitate its economy following the loss of the eastern half. Even so, the country had still not regained full international respectability. Some small steps for bilateral conveniences like postal connections, agreements for the protection and visits to religious shrines, direct shipping and telecommunication links, and agreement in principle for the grant of diplomatic and special-circumstances visas to enable visits to the other country had been agreed. Following an enabling trade protocol concluded in January 1975, state trading for specific goods like the supply of cotton bales had started. Similarly, agreements for the location and construction of boundary pillars had been reached.

Notwithstanding these small steps, Indo-Pakistan relations had not been 'normalized' even five years after the conflict in 1971. It was not just that Bhutto had gone back on his verbal pledge to turn the LOC into an international boundary, but the visible symbols of resident ambassadors and civil air links, had not been re-established. Mrs Gandhi had remained firm that until Pakistan withdrew the wholly unjustified complaint with the ICAO, India would refuse to restore these connections. Two informal meetings were held at the Foreign Secretary level in 1974 and 1975 when Pakistan showed impatience about wanting a resumption of overflights, but India remained unrelenting.

It was against this background that a letter was addressed on 27 March 1976 by Bhutto, the Pakistan Prime Minister to Mrs Gandhi, his Indian counterpart, regretting the stalemate in the envisaged pace of normalization, and, setting aside five years of hesitation, he indicated his willingness to withdraw Pakistan's complaint with the ICAO and expressed the hope that overflight rights and other pending questions could be resolved. Mrs Gandhi, in her reply of 11 April, welcomed the decision and indicated she would instruct her Foreign Secretary to contact his opposite number, to go forward to restore diplomatic relations and take other steps towards normalization. She went on to urge restraint in distorting India's position and policies. Mrs Gandhi's letter was acknowledged on 18 April and the decks were cleared for official talks.

I took over as Foreign Secretary from Kewal Singh on 1 April 1976, just four days after Bhutto informed us that he would withdraw the complaint with the ICAO. After the exchange of correspondence between the two heads of government, we obtained the approval of the Political Affairs Committee of the Cabinet for the restoration of all relations, which included not only diplomatic relations and civil air links but also road and rail connections, severed since the 1965 War. It was India's turn to go to the other capital. Since there were no commercial services between Pakistan and India, we had to fly to Islamabad by an aircraft of the Indian Air Force, which had detailed advice on the route to be taken, presumably so that we did not fly over sensitive military installations of Pakistan. I had taken a letter from our Prime Minister to Mr Bhutto, as the earnest of our now authorized purposeful approach because the preconditions had been satisfied.

NEGOTIATIONS IN ISLAMABAD

Our delegation for the normalization negotiations, which as Foreign Secretary I led, included Nirmal Mukherjee (the last ICS officer and later Cabinet Secretary) who was then Secretary, Ministry of Civil Aviation, and representatives of the Railway Board, the Ministries of Transport, Commerce, Home and my colleague I.P. Singh who was then Joint Secretary, in charge of the Pakistan Division. We also had with us representatives of our media. We arrived at the Rawalpindi/Islamabad Airport on the forenoon of 11 May 1976. Our delegation was met by Pakistani officials led by Agha Shahi, the Foreign Secretary. There was a large gathering of the representatives of the press, mostly Pakistani but some from the International media. It was my first official visit to Pakistan. I tried to improve my standing by recalling that in 1941-2 Agha Shahi and I were in the same hostel in Allahabad University but while I was an undergraduate he was several years my senior: indeed he got into the ICS from that academic stable. The assembled press representatives were in their characteristically aggressive questioning mood and were not content with bland friendliness. They wanted a statement from me reflecting India's approach to the forthcoming negotiations. I said I looked forward to fruitful discussions and then I added that I also wanted to see if I could go and salute Hamidullah Burki, who was the Commanding Officer of the LCM (Landing Craft Mechanized). I added I was his junior and can still recall that he was an exceptionally skilful navigator when we were both in a Combined Operations unit on the east coast of India. This public reference by an Indian Foreign Secretary recalling loyalty to a Pakistani commanding officer thirty years later, intrigued and deflected further questions. (I had heard that the former Lt. Burki was then a respected intellectual and an influential political commentator who was known to be very close to Bhutto.) As I expected, some journalists must have telephoned Burki on their return from the airport. Soon after we got to our hotel, Burki, whom I had not seen since 1946, rang me and after some non-moderate expletives in Hindustani, characteristic in wartime messes, said that I had embarrassed him by my flattering reference to him as a seaman and a friend. My purpose was to find an independent back channel direct access to the Pakistan Prime Minister in order to convey that I wanted to optimize the scope of my mission. Burki had been a strong supporter of the Muslim League in our pre-Pakistan mess discussions. When he telephoned to me, I used the opportunity to convey to him that I had come with full intentions to improve India-Pakistan relations and I hoped that from the Pakistan side old hesitations would not vitiate the process. (I had heard that Agha Shahi, was an extremely able but tough-minded negotiator, more so than his elder brother Agha Hilaly with whom my father had to deal in the 1950s.) I believe Burki conveyed the substance of my conversation directly to Bhutto and hopefully it might have mellowed the rigidity in the Pakistan negotiating brief.

In the initial plenary session Agha Shahi welcomed us and I replied with appropriate friendly sentiment. I said I had the authorization of the Prime Minister to work in the constructive spirit of the Simla Agreement. The composition of the delegation would itself be indicative that we were prepared to explore all strands of normalization. Thereafter we broke up into separate technical committees for civil aviation, transport, trade, etc., and I paid courtesy calls on Pakistan dignitaries.

Shahi and I readily agreed to re-open diplomatic relations. Nirmal Mukherjee and his opposite number agreed to restore civil aviation connections, extend overflight rights to national airlines, and establish direct air links between the two countries, specifically between Karachi and Bombay, and Delhi and Lahore. We pressed that we must try to facilitate human contacts for those who could not afford to travel by air—there must have been tens of thousands of divided families who for many years had just not been able to visit their relations in the other country. We offered to resume rail connections for passengers and goods. (Premier Hoyveda of Iran was in Delhi when I was in Islamabad.) I indicated that we would like to extend at least freight traffic through Pakistan to Iran but Pakistan probably wanted to keep this for separate bilateral leverage with Iran. Anyway, Pakistan was not prepared to agree with us to book goods to a third country: and insisted that such goods must be transhipped at the border. However, we agreed to the road connection being re-opened. Both for the rail and road links, the Wagah-Attari crossing were confirmed. While state trading and the supply of cotton bales had already started, we agreed to explore trade between private parties. We also agreed to mention that the two countries hoped to strengthen cultural ties. The experts in the delegation pointed out that functional and communication contacts required physical preparations: some rail tracks had to be re-laid and roads repaired, details regarding rolling stock and freight movements had to be discussed, for which supplementary technical agreements would be required. Similarly, roads were to be repaired to link to the frontier posts. I went on to suggest that the Ambassadors of India and Pakistan in a synchronized manner should present credentials to the respective Presidents at precisely the same time in New Delhi and Islamabad and this could be done in about two months but before that all preliminary agreements should be completed. I pressed my colleagues from the different ministries to enable me to make such a commitment. Even though none of them was quite ready for such a shortened and forced pace of normalization, I was convinced that that alone would make an impact on the public opinion in the two countries. Anyway all my colleagues reluctantly agreed to the deadline.

IMPEDIMENT: INTERVENTION AT THE PRIME MINISTERIAL LEVEL

The negotiations were protracted, at times lasting several hours and stretching over three days, but I do not recall any major difficulty except on one point. Agha Shahi insisted that in the Memorandum of Understanding, India should pledge that the question of compensation for the denial of overflight rights to Pakistan Airlines would in due course be considered. In his talks with Kewal Singh in the previous year, Agha Shahi had said that the diversion via Colombo was estimated to have cost

40 million dollars loss to Pakistan. I was adamant that when we were trying to open a new chapter in India-Pakistan relations, there should be no reference to old controversies. As against the cost of Pakistan aircraft having to make a detour, I reminded him that India also had a claim for the cost of the destroyed Indian aircraft by the hijackers, which must have had the connivance of the civil authorities in Lahore. Moreover, Indian Airlines had also suffered recurring losses by denying earning capacity by the *force majeure* reduction in its fleet. I argued that I considered it objectionable, and in any case undesirable, to vitiate the normalization process by mentioning these questions of monetary compensation. Agha Shahi's instructions obviously were to get India to agree to such a public pledge in order for Bhutto to be able to show to his domestic constituency that the complaint to the ICAO, which had remained unsatisfied for five years, was not wholly infructuous and that Pakistan's grievance was still alive.

I was hosting a lunch at a Rawalpindi hotel for the Pakistan delegation when one of the bearers came to me and said that the Prime Minister wanted to speak to me on the telephone. I could not think why Mrs Gandhi should want to give me further instructions since I had not sent any reports to Delhi. (We had no diplomatic mission and so no cipher links for confidential communications was possible.) As I got up from the table to go to the telephone I was told it was Mr Bhutto who was calling from Gilgit where he had gone on tour. As reported in the *Dawn* paper of that morning, Bhutto had made a not too friendly speech towards India, which included a reference to Kashmir and India's high defence expenditure. In the telephone conversation with me he was very suave and somewhat flattering to me personally. He recalled that his father Sir Shah Nawaz Bhutto as Chief Minister of Junagadh had occasion to meet my father at ministerial meetings under the auspices of the Chamber of Princes. As a counterpoint, I mentioned that my daughter, when she was at Smith College, had met his daughter Benazir, who was then at Radcliffe because both were under the *loco parentis* of the Galbraiths and their sons, Peter and Jamie Galbraith (who were then undergraduates at Harvard) were common friends. Moreover, my son Vikram had seen Benazir quite frequently when both were at Oxford in the mid-1970s. Indeed I let slip that Vikram had even campaigned for her in the Oxford Union elections!

Recalling these old connections was really the preliminary to Bhutto pressing me to agree to the mention of compensation for the monetary loss for the diversion of PIA flights. I tried to explain the inadvisability of doing so but he then said that he wanted me to transmit his personal request to Prime Minister Indira Gandhi to modify the instructions he assumed I carried. (I had no such specific negotiating restraints.) He said he would order the appropriate Pakistan authorities to give me a quick telephone connection to the Prime Minister in New Delhi so that I could obtain approval to include mention of compensation in our Memorandum of Understanding. This, he said, would remove the impediment to full normalization. I could not refuse, and returned to the lunch a little at a loss what to do.

In the after-lunch speech I made polite mention of the progress we were making and my hopes not of a stalemate but of a diplomatic breakthrough with a win-win satisfaction for both sides. Taking the clue of irrelevant flattery as an aid to diplomacy, I recalled my old admiration for Agha Shahi's distinguished uncle, Sir Mirza Ismail, the Prime Minister of Jaipur. After his achievement in building up the technological infrastructure of Bangalore and Mysore, we in Rajasthan were awestruck at the transformation of Jaipur, where in a short period he had also laid the foundation of improving the old planned city and given an economic gallop to the state. In a more frivolous way I said I was pretty confident of the results of our negotiations because the previous day, while the expert groups were meeting, I played golf with borrowed clubs, and on the sixth hole—allegedly, the most difficult on the Rawalpindi Golf Course—I had got a birdie two with a 20 ft putt. Agha Shahi's reply to my toast was also friendly and complimentary and hoped that the one remaining impediment could be sorted out, and added that he hoped next time I played golf here I would do better and get a three instead a two on the same hole! Not being a golfer he did not realize that three was only a bogey and worse than a birdie. Shahi was surprised at the giggles around the table.

As soon as the afternoon session started, Agha Shahi

reminded me to seek approval of the mention of compensation in the Memorandum of Understanding. Even though I was reluctant to do so, since it was the Prime Minister Bhutto's express wish I could not very well refuse to transmit his request. I was put through to Delhi and I spoke to P.N. Dhar, the Principal Secretary to the Prime Minister. I explained to him what Bhutto wanted but almost deliberately made myself even less coherent than I usually am. I did not appear to be enthusiastic for the requested authorization. Dhar's reply in Hindustani was somewhat as follows: *Jagat, mere to samajh me nahin ata hai, tum vapas aakar samajha do aur phir nae instructions denge* (Jagat, I do not quite understand the request, you had better come back and explain the problem and then we will give you fresh instructions.) When this conversation was taking place from my sitting room in the Rawalpindi hotel, the Pakistani delegation had discreetly left the Indian team alone. They all came back a little later after the conversation was over. I told Agha Shahi that I did not have to repeat to him what my instructions were; he would have gathered—hinting that they must all have been eves-dropping—that I had been told to get back to Delhi without concluding the MOU. Agha Shahi must have already conveyed the sense of my instructions to his Prime Minister. Substantial progress had by then already been made in preparing the draft MOU by I.P. Singh and his opposite number, Mr Mehdi, the Director General dealing with India in consultation with the specialists, leaving only this question of compensation open. The Pakistan side, I believe, had been favourably struck at our forthcoming attitude, enlarging the scope of understanding and did not want to be on the defensive in insisting on a residue reservation, as a reminder of an ugly controversy. Anyway, Agha Shahi dropped the insistence on mentioning the right to raise the question of compensation in the body of the MOU and we progressed to finalize the joint statement. As a sop I said—what really went without saying—that once diplomatic relations were re-established, both countries would have the option of using the established means of raising any problems according to their discretion. In fact, the question of compensation, as claimed by them or by us, was never raised.

TIME BOUND AGREEMENT: PROBLEMS OF IMPLEMENTATION

In the end we agreed to the comprehensive normalization of relations and the restoration of all suspended connections—diplomatic, air, road and rail links and private trading. I had said that within roughly two months, the process should be completed but within a few days after my return to Delhi I would indicate the date and time of the synchronized presentation of credentials of the two ambassadors. (This required the approval of the President, which I could not presume in advance.) Before signing the MOU, Agha Shahi mentioned that we should re-affirm that the Kashmir problem would be discussed on the basis of the UN Resolutions, once relations have been normalized. I told him that our mandate was to complete the process envisaged in the Simla Agreement, which had not been superseded, and there was no need to bring in questions that enlarged or repeated the Simla provisions. The reference to Kashmir could not have lasted more than one minute. I rightly guessed that Agha Shahi was raising it before the conclusion only in order to be able to answer the Pakistan media that Kashmir had not been forgotten.

It was nearly seven in the evening when both of us came down to hold a joint press conference and release the copies of the four-page long Memorandum of Understanding. It was more comprehensive than any other single document signed between India and Pakistan since Independence. The Indian Air Force plane had been waiting on the tarmac for almost seven hours to take us back to Delhi by the prescribed diversionary route. The press correspondents were understandably weary and impatient at having to cool their heels for six hours. Bill Borders, the *New York Times* correspondent in Delhi, had travelled up to Islamabad to cover this meeting. He was so fed up of waiting that he had composed his report, more or less, saying that the Indians and the Pakistanis have tried again but remain gridlocked in hardy old rigidities and have failed to reach agreement on the normalization process. When we announced the comprehensive nature of our agreement I saw Bill Borders rushing out to cancel the story he had already filed. (I wish I could get a copy of his original report as a souvenir.) We were of course asked whether Kashmir had been raised, Agha Shahi in all honesty answered in the affirmative and with equal honesty I could say that India stood by the Simla Agreement and there was no discussion on the subject.

Implementing the understanding was a formidable task for our slow moving bureaucracy. Normally in the Foreign Service we allow four to six months for a transfer but here was a committed deadline of only two months. Establishing even a new minor diplomatic mission required months of preparations, in finding different kinds of personnel, giving them leave to visit families, assembling manuals and ciphers and much else besides. Islamabad was a major and sensitive mission with complex problems and getting ready to re-open the mission after five years called for an emergency approach requiring cooperation of many ministries and agencies. Above all I had to think of and to look for an ambassador of exceptional qualities. The deputy and others also had to be carefully chosen, but we looked for them at headquarters and then left the deputy-designate to coordinate the complex but time-bound preliminaries. I persuaded Kiran Doshi to 'volunteer' for the challenge. But the choice of headship was critical. Soon after this meeting I was due to go to London for Foreign office level consultations. I requested K. Shanker Bajpai, who was barely half-way through his tenure as Ambassador to the Netherlands, to meet me in the Air India lounge at Frankfurt airport while I was in transit. I urged him to wind up quickly at The Hague, come to Delhi, and be briefed to take on this challenging assignment. Meanwhile on our side broken rail tracks were re-laid and some culverts on the approach road were repaired. All the other concerned ministries warmed up to a sense of emergency implicit in the deadline. The separate technical agreements for rail and air links were signed by the respective ministries on 28 June, and on 5 July 1976, both before the deadline. Anyway, K. Shanker Bajpai for India and Fida Hussein for Pakistan duly presented their credentials to the two Presidents on 21 July 1976 at precisely the same hour.

While we were negotiating on restoring these functional links, it had occurred to me that we could really gild the lily and have even greater public impact if we had agreed and announced the opening of Consulates General in Karachi and

Bombay. India had extensive properties in the port city, which were vacated when the capital moved to Islamabad. I had visited my father while he occupied the beautiful residence in Clifton and I believe made a good garden on what used to be a rather sandy compound. The vast number of Mohajirs—who had migrated from India—were impatient to visit relations across the border, and would have been enthused with the convenience of a local visa office. I mentioned this to Agha Shahi and he did not demur but thought it was premature to finalize it during these negotiations. Pakistan, of course, hoped that they could get the old house of the Quaid-e-Azam in Bombay for their Consulate/Deputy High Commission.

But I jump ahead. On my return to Delhi, P.N. Dhar the Principal Secretary and G. Parthasarathy, Chairman of the Policy Planning Committee and a close adviser of the Prime Minister, after politely felicitating me said that in signing the Memorandum in Islamabad I had exceeded my brief. I was reminded that the expectation was that I would negotiate on the gamut of problems but Bhutto would come to Delhi to sign the Agreement with our Prime Minister. This was not part of the written decision of the Cabinet but had been verbally mentioned to me.

In Islamabad after I felt that comprehensive and politically significant understanding was within our reach, I had discussed the pros and cons of signing a memorandum with my colleagues specially Nirmal Mukherjee, who was many years my senior. Pakistan, I knew, was impatient for overflight rights. Keeping a half-hostile atmosphere for several more weeks, possibly months, in my view, would not have been in India's national interest or our international standing. I had not departed from the authorization in any detail, and the programme and strategy of settling the outstanding issues was left to my discretion. I felt there was decisive advantage in making the process comprehensive and time-bound and give it the stamp of finality. This approach had taken the Pakistan team by surprise, but a positive one, which would confound the extremists in both countries and the Bourbons abroad who despair of Indo-Pak friendship. Anyway, I was convinced that there was no hope of Bhutto humiliating himself in this manner especially as he was probably planning to go for a general election in about a year's time. It was, to my mind, unrealistic to expect the Pakistan

Prime Minister coming to kowtow before Indira Gandhi, whom the *Economist* on its cover page had portrayed as 'Durga, the Goddess who brooked no lesser Gods'. The Prime Minister herself was gracious and congratulated me, never expressing any disapproval at having finalized the memorandum in Islamabad. As it happened and as I had expected, there was worldwide acclaim to the comprehensive scope of the agreement. Tass, the Soviet new agency was the first to welcome the Agreement.

A digression on Soviet attitudes to the subcontinent may not be irrelevant. Except the few days of overlap with the Cuban missile crisis in 1962, and after the Kissinger visit to Peking in July 1971 and the final stages of the Bangladesh crisis, the USSR was moving to improve relations with Pakistan without weakening its relations with India. This careful approach had been evident in Kosygin's role at Tashkent (January 1966). Since my posting in Peking, I had come to believe that we had been conveniently wishful in laying store by the Soviet Union's hostility to Pakistan on the grounds that it was an ally of the West. After the Sino-Soviet rift, the ideological and security rationale of Soviet foreign policy was being corrected by non-ideological pragmatism with efforts, wherever possible, to match the Chinese influence. Indeed in one of my last despatches from Peking in 1966, I had mooted the possibility of Soviet Union providing arms to Pakistan not in order to dilute the connection with India or significantly bolstering Pakistan's military capability, but in order to be seen as not unfriendly towards Pakistan and balancing the growing Chinese ascendancy in that country. I felt that if we anticipated the possibility and were mentally prepared, it would have created less of a shock. Ambassador T.N. Kaul in Moscow when he came back to Delhi to take over as Secretary, thought that Soviet arms to Pakistan was 'unthinkable' on strategic and ideological grounds. Yet, in 1968 Soviet arms were given to Pakistan, which created unnecessary surprise and distress in India because we (and the Communist Party of India) had dismissed the possibility of military aid to our adversary which was a Western ally. Not for the first time, it occurred to me, the ideologically oriented friends of the USSR had discounted its non-ideological realism, often removed from its propaganda.

The West, of course, welcomed the 1976 normalization of

Indo-Pakistan relations but there was a tinge of surprise at its scope. The Third World, specially Muslim countries, were relieved that they did not have to take the line of 'equal friendship'. The worldwide approbation naturally and deservedly went to the Prime Minister Indira Gandhi; anyway the suggestion that I had exceeded my brief was never reiterated, even in private.

A few days after the normalization agreement, Bhutto was flying over India on his way to North Korea. This was the first time after five years that a Pakistani aircraft was in our air space. Bhutto sent a message to Indira Gandhi, which she reciprocated, but Bhutto while abroad could not resist voicing criticism of India. He made unfriendly remarks in Peking and our Chargé d'Affaires, Lakhan Mehrotra, following my own innovation of registering diplomatic protest when unwarranted slurs were made against Indian policies, walked out of the function. But we continued the policy of deliberate restraint to underline the positive benefits of the good neighbourliness with Pakistan.

The agreement, in fact, did set the tone of friendship in India-Pakistan relations for the next three years. It yielded greater dividends than would have been the case if agreement on specific items had been made piecemeal ('in coffee spoon doses') and stretched over months or years. The comprehensive agreement also lowered the decibels of both official and even non-official propaganda against India. The bonus was, in fact, in concrete benefits that have not been adequately noticed.

THE POSITIVE DIVIDENDS FROM THE NORMALIZATION OF RELATIONS

In August 1976 another IAC flight, also going from Delhi to Jaipur, was hijacked and the two hijackers indicated to the pilot they wanted to go to the Gulf, Libya, or Pakistan. They were pro-Pakistan Kashmiris, demanding the release of Maqbul Bhat who had been convicted of murder in Kashmir. Mrs Gandhi called me and in accordance with a pre-arranged crisis drill, all the emergency management group, led by B.D. Pande, the Cabinet Secretary, assembled swiftly at Safdarjang Airport. On my recommendation, the pilot was advised to land in Lahore.

(In any case, a Fokker would have had to refuel to fly to the distant airports.) On return to my office, I promptly telephoned Agha Shahi and he sent down the Additional Foreign Secretary, Shah Nawaz and I asked Shanker Bajpai, who was in Delhi, to proceed to Lahore. Naresh Dayal, who was first Secretary in Islamabad, rushed down from Lahore reaching even before Shankar Bajpai. My guess was that with the transformed climate of good relations, the Pakistani government could not expressly be behind the pro-Pakistan elements in this escapade. Anyway I was persuaded that we would have had much better leverage in Lahore and with the Pakistan government than on distant airfields and possibly more hesitant governments even if fuel and permission were available.

For a whole day my office became the operational centre, with the Cabinet Secretary and Nirmal Mukherjee, the Civil Aviation Secretary, and some others sitting with me sharing in the decision-making. Scores of phone calls came from Shah Nawaz and the Pakistan authorities in Lahore. We were asked what terms to offer to the hijackers—how near should the Pakistani officers move to talk with the hijackers? We gave considered reactions, but allowed the Pakistanis wide margin of discretion. The Pakistani officers proved patient, tactful, and resourceful. It was obvious that Pakistan did not want the embarrassment of the loss of Indian lives and aircraft on their soil. It was entirely due to the Pakistani officials that, by the small hours of the next morning, I was informed that all the passengers had been released. The women and children were allowed out first, and later other passengers were permitted to disembark from the aircraft. I believe all this happened by the Pakistani officials first winning the confidence of the hijackers and then immobilizing them by mildly drugging the food sent to satisfy their gnawing hunger. Both the passengers and our plane were flown home the following day.

In these telephone conversations, I had taken the risk of hinting to Shah Nawaz that as long as the hijackers were seen to be taken into custody, we would not ask where they were being 'imprisoned', how soon they would be tried, or what punishment would be meted to them. Y.B. Chavan, then Foreign Minister, who came to the office a couple of hours after the plane had already landed in Lahore, called me on the internal telephone and said that obviously Pakistan was behind this crime and we should have told the pilot to refuel and go elsewhere than be allowed to land in Pakistan. In a situation like hijacking, one has to make an instant decision without higher consultations; in fact, my hunch proved correct. It was one of the first examples of success in handling plane hijack without loss of life or, as happened in 1971, the destruction of the aircraft or as in Kandahar in December 1999, without suffering the humiliation of giving in to the highjackers' demand for the release of those convicted and in our custody. This, I believe, was only because some element of mutual trust had been established by the comprehensive normalization and by adhering to a time-bound programme. Pakistan, one assumed, was placed on its mettle and had to live up to its professed goodwill towards India and demonstrate it even against the sentiments of the disaffected Kashmiris. In January 1977 the hijackers were released, and we protested for the record, but in a low key. I felt there was little point in showing impotent anger and vitiating the improved climate of relations. We had got our passengers and aircraft back but to expect that the Pakistan government would take serious criminal action against Pakistani loyalists, or return them for trial in India, was wholly unrealistic.

Other bonus advantages were even more important. The Salal Dam negotiations had been going on for eight years and, in exasperation, the Prime Minister had approved the recommendation to consign the question to international arbitration under Article IX of the Indus Treaty of 1960. I submitted and the Prime Minister decided reverse her decision. I wrote to Agha Shahi to try another round of bilateral talks. After several reminders and only after two or three months, Pakistan agreed to do so. We held discussions in Delhi in October 1976 and then a second round soon afterwards in Islamabad. (The following chapter covers the Salal negotiations.[3]) Instead of having another internationalized problem on our hands, it ended in an agreement by which we got 690 megawatts of power for our north India grid.

[3]See chapter on 'Fresh Water Diplomacy for Resource Optimization' in this volume.

In November 1976 Farakka issue came up before the UN General Assembly. It is not widely known that Pakistan helped India by quietly advising Bangladesh to withdraw the item by accepting the promise of bilateral discussions, which we had offered. This not unfriendly attitude was because of the climate created by the comprehensive normalization.

I would like to mention two more developments, which have so far never been publicized. In the run up to elections in Pakistan in March 1977 which was soon after our general elections, we received copies of a 'White Paper' which was being issued under Bhutto's initiative and direction to show how, since the early 1960s, he had personally been strongly committed to Pakistan's policy on Kashmir. (Bhutto and PPP were well placed to win the elections but he wanted a dramatically improved majority.) I.P. Singh, the Joint Secretary, and I quickly read through the copies of this Pakistan White Paper which we received by bag from our Mission in Islamabad. Having done so, I decided to call the Pakistan High Commissioner and urged him to request his government not to vitiate the improved climate of India-Pakistan relations by such a publication. I mentioned that in our own general election campaign, just concluded, foreign policy issues had been scrupulously eschewed by the principal parties including the prominent leaders. This not un-friendly climate should not be spoilt for temporary political advantage. Our quick scrutiny had showed that in the pamphlet, there were no new facts or arguments. If they distributed the publication, then, as had been the practice over decades, we would have no alternative but to put out a rejoinder. We gathered later that a second White Paper on 'India-Pakistan relations' was under preparation, which too aimed to show Bhutto's consistent militancy for Pakistan on national security issues. As a result of our discreet diplomatic intervention, the Kashmir White Paper was arrested from further distribution and the India-Pakistan White Paper was not even published. These successes were deliberately not publicized in order not to cause provocative embarrassment to Pakistan and reduce needless polemical duels with no gains to foreign policy.

I am persuaded that in our times, when the media and public opinion are of great importance, the atmosphere should not be vitiated during sensitive negotiations. Discreet restraint in small incidents can yield far greater dividends to the national image than knee-jerk reaction of ritual adversarial public denunciations. How to mix diplomacy with another country and consolidation of support from the domestic audience requires great sagacity. All too often, immature diplomacy succumbs to the easy temptation of one-upmanship, but the overlooks the longer-term damage to good relations. I have little doubt that neither the satisfactory denouement of the hijacking incident nor 690 megawatts of power from Salal project in Kashmir, nor acquiescence (if not discreet support for India) on the withdrawal of the Farakka question from the UN, would have been possible if the climate of relations had not been positively transformed by a comprehensive time-bound normalization or had we sought to advertise them as success for India and defeat for Pakistan. One could recognize that in all of them, Pakistan had little to gain, except Indian goodwill. The greater concrete benefits were for India.

As a further proof I recall a small little personal incident. The Arab countries, unlike public opinion in the West, had not looked with favour at the dismemberment of Pakistan in 1971. The normalization agreement had created an impression that the India-Pakistan acrimony was at last being buried. This started in Mrs Gandhi's time, but to the Arabs, it continued, surprisingly, after the Janata government came to power in April 1977. As a result the Muslim countries became more spontaneously friendly towards India. Because I was known to have been involved in the negotiations for both governments, in 1978 the Saudi Foreign Minister extended a personal invitation to me to come to Riyadh for a friendly visit. There were no specific items to be discussed. To my knowledge the Saudis had never taken such an initiative towards a mere official in the past. I sought the approval of the Foreign Minister and the Prime Minster. The Prime Minister, Morarji Desai, was always reluctant for officers to travel without a concrete purpose and turned down my request. However, some months later he approved of my stopping off in Riyadh for a day, en route to a meeting of the Non-Aligned Foreign Ministers in Belgrade. I was treated like royalty in Riyadh, and was able to explain that the new government, like the previous one, was sensitive to ensure full protection and freedom of faith to the Indian Muslims.

During the discussions I discovered that the Saudi government had decided not to attend the Non-Aligned meeting for which I was bound, on the ground that they were now averse to meetings in 'Communist' countries. I reminded the senior officers that Saudi Arabia was an original member of the Non-Aligned Group and was present at the first Belgrade conference in 1961 and urged that they should not now keep detached. When we were in the conference hall in Belgrade, the Saudi Arabian Ambassador in Geneva came to where the Indian delegation was seated and asked for 'Mr Mehta', saying his instructions were to join the meeting and to get the brief from Mr Mehta! As it happened it was at this conference that Pakistan's request for joining the non-aligned fraternity came up and, on behalf of India and in accordance with prior approval of government, I indicated that we had no objection to the request. All the other delegations were visibly relieved and came to applaud our positive attitude. For three years from 1976 to 1979, in various international forays, the diplomatic recrimination between India and Pakistan were noticeable by their absence and subsisting problems were mentioned only in a low key for the record. India's international standing was certainly enhanced when it was perceived that we were rising above the familiar old bilateral political friction.

BI-PARTISANSHIP ON INDO-PAKISTAN RELATIONS—VAJPAYEE'S VISIT IN 1978

This interlude (1976-9) of trusting relations between India and Pakistan heralded a period of bipartisanship in foreign policy at a time when dramatic changes had occurred in the complexion of governments of both countries. The 1976 normalization achieved agreement on major items still outstanding on the agenda at Simla. In 1973, the prisoners of war and territory controlled by India had been returned, but the verbal (secret?) understanding in the one-to-one conversation between Mrs Gandhi and Bhutto—of step-by-step moving to turn the LOC into an international frontier—was not fulfilled. Even so there was no promotion of disaffection in the Valley of Kashmir from the Pakistan bases. This restraint had meant that, in practice, the LOC had come to be respected and so there was a *de facto* reconciliation to the *status quo*. In the 1976 memorandum gains were mutual, if anything more to India's advantage. After the apparently transparent fair elections in Jammu & Kashmir in 1977, I made bold to confidentially suggest to Morarji Desai and A.B. Vajpayee, his Foreign Minister, that the Kashmir problem was on the way to solution, but I pleaded not to claim it in public as it would then be denied aggressively. Ritual references made by Pakistan dignitaries should be ignored. At the General Assembly of the UN in 1976, unnecessary attention was focused when Foreign Minister Chavan, since he was himself in New York at the time, felt it was politically imperative to instruct our Permanent Representative to 'reply' when Agha Shahi made reference to old UN resolutions on Kashmir. (Agha Shahi formulation was no different from such statements in previous years.) In exercising the 'right of reply', we also repeated what we had asserted time and again in the previous decades. I would have advised ignoring Agha Shahi's redundant affirmation but I had not gone with the Foreign Minister when the general debate started, as I knew that the Farakka item was on the agenda and that was directly more important for us and would be coming up for the first time. The slinging match that followed attracted wide and at times sarcastic media attention. Next year in 1977 Vajpayee ignored the low key mention of Kashmir and it went totally unnoticed in the world media.

From Nehru's times, notwithstanding nuanced differences projected by the Swatantra Party on the right and by the Communist Party on the left, there was a broad consensus on the foreign policy of Non-Alignment. The general elections in 1977 were entirely on domestic issues, notably the recent outrages to the spirit of democracy as embodied in the Constitution and the brutalities perpetrated during Emergency. In the elections, Mrs Gandhi was dramatically defeated, and for the first time a non-Congress coalition came to power in Delhi. Yet, bipartisanship in foreign policy was actually reinforced. It is true after the Janata government led by Morarji Desai assumed office in March 1977, he spoke of 'genuine Non-Alignment' and this raised eyebrows in India whether it implied a rightward deviation from the old thrust of policy. Gromyko was invited by the Janata government and he rushed to Delhi, fulfilling a long overdue visit, and went home duly reassured. Prime Minister Desai was invited to Moscow in October 1977 not by his opposite number (Kosygin) but by President Brezhnev. Pakistan was curious and even anxious at the policy implications, because the Janata coalition included Jan Sanghis, with Vajpayee as Foreign Minister. Using the excuse that the Salal Agreement, though initialed in October 1976 had yet to be formally signed, a delegation led by Agha Shahi (who in the meanwhile, had been elevated to become Foreign Minister) came to Delhi. He too went back assured that there would be no significant deviation in foreign policy. Agha Shahi went back reassured though the Salal agreement was signed two years later.

Even so the deep suspicions in the people and many officials in Pakistan remained entrenched. After paying visits to the other neighbouring countries, A.B. Vajpayee announced his intention to go to Pakistan as a gesture to improve relations. This was to be the ultimate proof of wanting good neighbourliness in the subcontinent. It required great political courage for him to undertake the mission. For months before Vajpayee's actual journey in February 1978, the Pakistan media, especially the Lahore papers, wrote critically of the old Jan Sanghi, who had opposed the creation and existence of Pakistan, and led a demonstration against the Simla Agreement in 1972, was being allowed to come to the country. I was myself nervous that possible hostile manifestations might mar the visit which, of course, I had recommended. The Foreign Minister must also have been apprehensive, but he did not cancel his visit. While in Islamabad, he showed great sagacity and diplomatic restraint. He did not react in anger at the mention of Kashmir in the banquet speech but simply said India's position was well known. The positive metamorphosis came not so much because of his conversations with General Zia-ul-Haq but from the open press conference of Vajpayee—the first ever held on Pakistani soil. I recall a packed hall of media representatives of Pakistan and quite a few foreigners. Vajpayee started by taking the wind out of the sails of curiosity and criticism by reading a statement honestly confessing to his political past and his earlier deep hostility towards the very existence of Pakistan and then went on to affirm a new faith in friendship and sincere wishes for the well-being of Pakistan and its people. He pledged categorical respect for its present frontiers and answered all questions, many in fluent Urdu.

It is difficult to think of a comparable transformation in the climate of adversarial national opinion by a brief high level visit in the annals of diplomacy. The Rippentrop-Molotov talks in August 1939 also signalled a dramatic change in Soviet-Nazi Germany relations which took the West by surprise but, it led to the German attack on Poland and the beginning of Second World War. Anyway public opinion did not matter in either country. The nearest comparable summit leading to positive change and improved relations between adversaries was when President Sadaat went to Jerusalem in November 1977. However, Sadaat did not have a decade-long record of personal activism and protest against Israel as did Atal Behari Vajpayee against Pakistan. Vajpayee's visit was acclaimed but he never got the sustained international applause as did Sadaat, though in this case, it was even bolder. (Carter and the US were more interested in the Middle-East and in bringing about the Camp David accord which followed the Sadaat visit some months later.) The 1978 visit of Vajpayee catalysed and confirmed improved official relations between India and Pakistan; it assuaged the deep suspicions of the Pakistani people and a new confidence percolated down the line and lasted as long as the Janata government remained in power.

I recall that even Vajpayee was surprised. After a tour to Nagpur, he told me that his own party colleagues had expressed satisfaction and felicitated him. I would like to add that though the Vajpayee visit as Foreign Minister was then the highest point in India-Pakistan relations in years, it was traceable to the normalization authorized and negotiated when Mrs Gandhi was in power and Vajpayee's visit gave it a welcome bipartisan character. The lesson to be distilled is that the willingness to confess and compromise for the sake of the larger future goals of socio-economic progress is a mark of statesmanship. Vajpayee had understood that even while holding firmly to vital national interests, the approach requires nothing less and nothing more than sensitivity to sovereign 'otherness' and demonstrated recognition of the long-term permanent interdependence.

Incidentally as a collateral and concrete earnest of this new approach of friendliness affirmed by Vajpayee during his visit to Pakistan in 1978, the opening of the Consulates General in Karachi and Bombay were announced. I had been thinking about the choice of the first incumbent of this important post since the normalization in May 1976. Somewhat unusually, Mani Shanker Aiyer's reports from Baghdad had percolated up the hierarchy to the Foreign Secretary's desk. I had received some complaints about Mani Shanker Aiyer from the ambassador in Baghdad but I was most impressed at the style and content of his analysis. I had only met him briefly in the 1960s when he was a Junior Secretary in Brussels. Anyway he came to my mind when we were looking for an officer for Karachi who could combine exceptional intelligence, and sober political sensitivity. The post required somebody in a higher rank for it would have very large consular and commercial responsibilities. Mani Shanker Aiyer was still a First Secretary and not quite senior enough for the grade of Counsellor. I felt a somewhat accelerated promotion would be justified, and he was duly nominated. His subsequent official, and then political career with Rajiv Gandhi and the Indian National Congress, and as minister in the Manmohan Singh government are public knowledge but for the rest of my tenure as Foreign Secretary I was extremely happy to have him in Karachi. He brought to the assignment an imaginative zest and a diplomatic skill which was closer to my own approach than that of many other colleagues. He was immensely popular and highly respected in Karachi. His subsequent distinctions are his own but his assignment in Karachi gave him an early high professional profile in the service. I could not help regretting that, some years after I retired he decided to give up the Foreign Service but may be this has been a gain for our politics. His 'Pakistan papers' are testimony to his unusually enlightened perspectives.

Within weeks of opening of the post, Karachi became one of the most active consulates in the world, certainly in India's consular network. It was flooded with hundreds of thousands of visa applications, which only reflected the pent up desire to visit kinsmen and friends in India (and no doubt in the other direction). It also revealed the potential of commerce, the latent cultural nostalgia on both sides and highlighted the multi-layered interdependence between the two countries.

The period 1976-9, with a *de facto* bipartisan endorsement of Indo-Pak friendship, straddling the Congress government of Mrs Gandhi and the Janata government of Desai (and correspondingly Z.A. Bhutto and General Zia-ul-Haq in Islamabad) and has come to be looked upon by thoughtful observers in both countries as what is possible through diplomacy in our troubled bilateral relations. But it all came to an abrupt end after the Soviet intervention in Afghanistan in December 1979. By January both countries went back to the old Cold War stand, seeking psychological and security linkages with the rival super powers rather than remaining faithful to their national interest in independence, internal stability, socio-economic development, and regional non-alignment in their immediate neighbourhood.

REVERTING TO 'BEGGARING THY NEIGHBOUR': TWO DECADES OF DETERIORATION

During the period 1976-9 both super powers had applauded the striking improvement in the climate of the subcontinental relations. Even though the global Cold War was by no means over, contrary to some expectations, neither the USA, nor the USSR were in any way alarmed that a sublimation of tensions would amount to a loss of their own competitive advantage.

The events which led to the Soviet invasion in Afghanistan would overstretch the scope of this study. They have been covered extensively in a separate study.[4] What is relevant here is the unplanned coincidences which led to knee-jerk misjudgements and precipitated the sharp deterioration in India-Pakistan relations.[5] The invasion came only a few weeks after the storming of the American Embassy and the taking of hostages in Iran which needlessly unnerved and alarmed the Carter administration that the Soviet Union was being tempted to exploit the situation by southward strategic thrust to a warm water port and the control of the oil artery of the Gulf. The intervention also happened to come in the week when the

[4]M.S. Aiyer, *Pakistan Papers*, 1994, UBSPD.

[5]*The March of Folly in Afghanistan 1978-2001*, New Delhi: Manohar, 2002.

General Election campaign in India was coming to its culmination. During the campaign in 1979, Indira Gandhi, in electioneering distortions, charged that during the Janata period relations with USSR had deteriorated and she promised to restore them to the old friendliness and understanding. In the election manifesto of the Congress party, specific commitments were made (again needlessly) such as recognizing the pro-Vietnamese and pro-Soviet Heng Samrin government in Kampuchea. This caused a long-term setback to the ripening relations with the ASEAN nations.

The Soviet invasion was an impetuous folly, totally ignoring the lessons of history, but it was compounded by the erroneous reactions of the United States and with India striking a pro-Soviet posture. These began a disastrous slide in India-Pakistan relations that continued for more than two decades. I have speculated that if Indira Gandhi had had more time to reflect on the implications of the Soviet invasion or had invited honest MEA advice culled from the Kabul reports and its own analysis, her decision might well have been different. Similarly, had Morarji Desai remained in office for his full term of five years—he was voted out in July 1979 when Choudhry Charan Singh assumed office which lasted only six months—the official Indian attitude to the Soviet intervention would not have been so fatally flawed. In January 1980 when there was near universal condemnation of the Soviet armed attack on a non-belligerent friendly neighbour by all including our neighbours, India departed from the principles of the non-aligned and abstained and thus from her pre-Independence empathy with the Pathans, indeed with Afghan nationalism. I was no longer Foreign Secretary but discreetly I did everything possible to warn against the potential consequences of going against the fundamentals of our foreign policy. I felt that we were giving a gratuitous opening to Pakistan and risking a reversal in the prevailing improving climate of relations. Predictably, taking advantage of India's abstaining vote and US alarm, Pakistan seized the opportunity to plead that the US should resume substantial military aid to Pakistan (and not just what President Zia-ul-Haq called the Carter offer of $400 million as 'peanuts'). After President Reagan assumed office in 1981, the US began the massive remilitarization of Pakistan as a 'frontline' country facing the so-called 'Evil Empire' and Pakistan made believe that this kind of aid would continue. The US's worry about threats to the Gulf oil artery proved unfounded, but the spectacle of the Soviet Union being bogged down in its own 'Vietnam' was malevolently relished. The US did everything possible to bolster Mujahideen guerrilla capabilities and thereby aggravate Russia's military problems in Afghanistan. The CIA brought Islamic fundamentalists to be trained in Pakistan and then got them inducted as 'Jehadis' to fight the 'godless Communists' along-side the Afghan Mujahideen. However, after Gorbachev came to power, he was quick to recognize the mistake of the Soviet intervention and in 1986 indicated his intentions to unilaterally withdraw the Russian forces from the country. Gorbachev confided his intention to the Indian Chargé d'Affaires, but Delhi virtually instructed that the Soviet leader should be dissuaded from leaving Afghanistan.[6] We thought the Soviet intervention was a guarantee that the country would stay secular against the rise of religious fundamentalism. Once the Soviet forces did withdraw in 1989 as a result of protracted negotiations with UN's mediator Cordovez, the US lost interest in Afghanistan and summarily terminated its involvement. Afghanistan went off the Western radar screen but as a by-product of the US financed militarization and the CIA operations, Pakistan became awash with sophisticated arms illegally held and abetted by narcotics smuggling which only went to aggravate the instability of the country. The region—Afghanistan, India and Pakistan—was thus left a terrible legacy of super power misjudgements.

Even after the super power's withdrawal, instead of re-establishing credibility with mainstream Pushtoo sentiments, India persisted in backing Najibullah who, in Afghan opinion, was suspect, as an anti-national Soviet 'stooge' and a renegade to Afghan nationalism. Soviet arms supplies continued even after the departure of the Soviet forces and this enabled Najibullah to remain in administrative control for three years. Yet bitter ethnic, tribal, and leadership rivalries continued to plague the country. Initially through a Shura assembly in

[6]Conversation with C.V. Ranganathan, Deputy Chief of Mission, Indian Embassy, Moscow.

Peshawar, Pakistan tried but failed to unite the factions under the leadership of the of ISI-backed Hikmeteyar. It was the Rabbani group that won power in Kabul, and they denounced and dislodged Najibullah, who was obliged to take refuge in the UN compound. It was in this situation of internecine conflict that Pakistan started recruiting 'Talibs' from the refugee camps and its own madrasas. With training guidance and Pakistan supplied arms, launched them for the 'conquest' of Afghanistan. The Taliban overran Kandahar in 1992 and captured Kabul in 1996. Najibullah was then dragged out of the UN precinct and, evoking no Afghan sympathy, was strung up on a lamp post. Medieval orthodoxy, allegedly in accordance with the Sharia, was imposed in the areas brought under Taliban control. India's hopes of restoration of influence in Afghanistan could not be revived with the ouster of Najibullah. Pakistan, enthralled with the delusion of a Pakistan-Afghan Sunni Confederation, fantasized that the Khyber was moving to the Oxus, which would give Pakistan strategic depth in the event of a future conflict with India.

Since 1980 our relations with Pakistan lost the semblance of the mutual trust of the 1976-9 period, not even with American direct intervention in 2001 (after 11 September). Indian analysts have tended to slur over the misjudgements of the 1980s. In national self-righteousness, in the UN, with the Afghan factions, and in Kashmir, we have tended to minimize the fact that we have unsuspectedly contributed to the Jehadi anger and insurgency against India. Ill-advised acts of commission and omission catalysed conditions for cross-border terrorism. After Sheikh Abdullah passed away, the government in Delhi played unprincipled politics which only accentuated the disaffection in the Valley. The Governor, B.K. Nehru, was not prepared to be party to the political shenanigans of the unprincipled Farooq-Congress coalition that systematically rigged the elections in 1987. This further alienated the Kashmiri people. The build-up of disenchantment burst into violent insurgency in 1989. Many observers, publicly or privately, acknowledge that the insurgency started indigenously, and it was Kashmiri youth who first went out to fetch arms from Pakistan and only later did the ISI rush in, recognizing it as an great opportunity for its old purpose.

During the decade of the 1980s, there was a moment of hope on Indo-Pak relations when Rajiv Gandhi as Prime Minister met his opposite number Benazir Bhutto. Yet this did not change attitudes on Afghanistan. There was even stronger euphoria when in February 1999 Vajpayee made the bus journey to Lahore and physically and symbolically embraced Nawaz Sharif and concluded a series of confidence-building agreements. However, all too soon the promise was destroyed by intrusions in Kargil. General Musharraf is supposed to have been the planner and architect of the Kargil operations. What is often overlooked that some of the Jehadis who took part in the Kargil intrusions included Arabs who were originally brought to the region to fight the Soviet infidels. They were influenced by the Afghan disappointment at India's betrayal of their struggle against the foreign invader. Against great odds, the Indian army made a magnificent defence in Kargil: it was diplomatically helped by Vajpayee resisting domestic pressures for 'hot pursuit' into Pakistan controlled Kashmir beyond the LOC. Kargil, however, was ultimately resolved by the intervention of President Clinton who demanded that the intruding Pakistan forces, Afghans, and foreign Jehadis should all pull back to the Pakistan side of the LOC. These 'freedom fighters' complied obediently. Hopes were again dramatically revived in July 2002 when, overlooking his initial revulsion at the overthrow of democracy and the takeover by the military, Prime Minister Vajpayee extended an invitation to General Musharraf to come to India. The media and even cognoscenti on both sides had great expectations from the Agra Summit but while the meetings were not officially deemed a failure, the fact was that no joint statement could be finalized. It again looked like the old gridlock had been resurrected. Pakistan wanted to discuss the 'dispute' in Kashmir first and all but refused to acknowledge the illegality of rampant cross-border terrorism across the LOC.

11 SEPTEMBER AND INDIA-PAKISTAN RELATIONS

Dialectical reversals both, international and regional, followed the attack on the World Trade Center and the Pentagon. Pakistan was confronted with an urgent demand from the USA to join the crusade against terror. This meant direct military operations against Osama bin Laden, al-Qaida and the Pakistan created Taliban. For a country born under the theory of nationhood based on religion, the US demand to fight Islamic faithfuls posed a painful dilemma. General Musharraf, however, made a quick somersault and agreed to provide facilities for the fight against 'terror'. Pakistan was rewarded with the lifting of sanctions, economic rescue, and the promise of diverse kinds of support by the United States. But even when Pakistan once again turned into a partner of the West against terrorism, it continued to connive at cross-border infiltration against India, justifying it as support for 'freedom fighters' in Kashmir. But this dichotomy was embarrassingly exposed when on 13 December 2001 pro-Pakistan terrorists attacked the Indian Parliament. Unless he distanced himself from this blatant act of terrorism against the citadel of Indian democracy, General Musharraf risked being considered either a mercenary or a hypocrite in his condemnation of international terror. Musharraf seemed to realize that the suspicion of selectively condoning terrorism by allowing unhindered latitude to Islamic extremists could be a menace to the economic progress of Pakistan itself. In a national broadcast on 12 January 2002, he went much further than any previous decision maker in Pakistan to dissociate himself publicly from the Islamic fundamentalists.

Musharraf's intentions seemed genuine but it was still questionable whether he had the will and the capacity to disown the involvement of militants in Kashmir and all over India. Could he order the winding down, if not closure, of all the moles and linkages in India and in neighbouring countries like Nepal and Bangladesh? The attack on Parliament caused anger in India and crystallized into the demand for a military riposte such as an attack on the terrorist camps in Pakistan-occupied-Kashmir (POK) and abrogation of the Indus Treaty. As an immediate response, the level of diplomatic relations was scaled down and the Indian army was moved to forward battle positions. The demand was raised for the extradition of twenty 'criminals' known to have been given refuge in Pakistan. Notwithstanding these strong reactions, the framework of policy perspectives in India and Pakistan had yet to emerge.

It was not only a low point in India-Pakistan relations but also in the internal cohesion and self-confidence of both countries. On 27 February 2002, in the Sabarmati Express, the bogeys of *karsevaks* returning from Ayodhya after pledging to build the Ram Janmabhumi Temple were torched at Godhra station and over 50 persons died in the inferno. This in turn led to massacres and damages to the homes and economic assets of hundreds possibly thousands of Muslims in Ahmedabad and other cities of Gujarat. Strong suspicions were articulated that the BJP led state government under Modi had not only connived, but with the help of party activists from VHP and Bajrang Dal, encouraged the worst incident of communalism since 1992, possibly after 1947. The Godhra/Gujarat conflagration came soon after the elections in UP where the verdict was a 'disappointment' to all parties but pointedly so for the BJP government, which had been in power. This reversal was compounded by the dramatic defeat in the local elections in Delhi and some other states. These were all political setbacks for the NDA government and brought out serious tensions amongst the partners in the coalition. The country was even gripped by an anxiety on the essentials of the national ethos, the prospects of secularism, and whether fundamental rights of equality for minorities were not in jeopardy. Democracy remains well-established in India but there is a barely concealed cynicism and distrust of the rulers in the mind of the man-in-the-street. What made it more serious was that there was a nationwide financial crunch, which was aggravated by populist politics, administrative profligacy, general inefficiency, and rampant corruption. While the public debt continues to soar, the delivery of entitlements declines. A disenchanted people will not accept the imperative of financial discipline from a government that loses moral credibility; the revival of investment, domestic and foreign, cannot optimize if stability becomes a question mark.

The situation in Pakistan, if anything, was more serious. There was no established safety valve to give vent to people's political, economic, and social aspirations, or their discontent. Democracy was overthrown for the third time in 1999. As on previous occasions, the takeover by the military was justified with the promise of cleaner government, greater economic dynamism and the pledge of early restoration of democracy. However, infact disabilities were placed on political parties and their leaders. While remaining Chief of the Army, Musharraf launched a non-opposed referendum, and on the basis of the result, claimed to have obtained overwhelming legitimacy for a five-year tenure as President. *The Economist* dubbed the device a 'bogus' political exercise: it was blatantly the violation of the established constitution. Musharraf promised to hold parliamentary elections to share power with a Prime Minister but the supreme authority would be vested in the National Security Council in which the President and the Army Commanders would have overriding control. The experiences of Ayub and Zia-ul-Haq were being repeated to legitimize a military dictatorship. Musharraf survived because of the economic munificence of the West but Pakistan still had a long way to go to improve its low human development indicators.

The Indian and Pakistan armies remained in forward positions; the cost and security justification for this eye-ball-to-eye-ball confrontation was never vindicated. Periodic terrorist incidents continued. The question was, could they master their separate problems, including curbing domestic religious extremism and uphold law and order without a sea-change in their bilateral relations? Was there not a parallel imperative of easing the burden of non-productive expense? Could they continue to deflect people's anger and cynicism by pointing to the old enemy and rejoicing in malevolent satisfaction?

Ultimately it is for India-Pakistan themselves to find ways to again start as if they were back in 1947. Obviously history cannot be unwritten or even forgotten, but the point to underline is that our leadership and intellectuals have to recognize that these years look like wasted decades of under-achievement, flowing from a succession of misperceptions. The permanence of geography, the imperatives of some rich, some scarce or dwindling natural resources have to be juxtapositioned against a mounting population explosion and the challenge of pervasive poverty. Looking back, we must quietly recognize that Partition was perhaps not the lesser evil for either country or even the Muslims of South Asia. The British, but also those in India and Pakistan who accepted it, were partners in a fallacy and not just victims of 'divide and rule'. The breakaway of Bangladesh was proof of the inherent flaw in the original concept of religion-based nationhood. But there should be no further political unscrambling in South Asia and any suggestion of reunification or confederation must not be contemplated: indeed it should be summarily rejected. Pakistan and the Jehadi militants should recognize that, whatever it costs, India cannot be displaced from Kashmir without running the risk of measured or expansive retaliation. For either country to depend on the nuclear option is only relying on a hypothetical response, which carries both a moral as well as grave military hazards for the user. India's own problem of national confidence can take no consolation from the dilemmas or difficulties of Pakistan. India itself faces a challenge to prove on the ground and in practice that democracy works for the people's rights and welfare. Let us face it: the lesson of 9/11 was that established international frontiers give no immunity against terror and that fanaticism in one country only feeds extremism in the other.

CONCLUSION

The main focus of this paper was to recount the role diplomacy played in the 1970s. It is being written in the spring of 2003. One cannot deny that at Simla, when India held all the trumps, the agenda was left incomplete, but too much must not be made of the omission. Even if there was no 9/11, there could still have been misgovernance inside Kashmir as in the 1980s and cross-border terrorism from Pakistan as in the 1990s. As this paper has tried to show, credit must be given to Indira Gandhi for firmly rejecting full normalization for four years until the unjustified complaint filed with the ICAO was withdrawn and then not hesitating to authorize the most comprehensive framework ever which facilitated trusting and cooperative relations with Pakistan. The highjacking and destruction of the aircraft in 1971 was symbolic of the old malevolence and the normalization approved in 1976 was proof of what is feasible, with purposeful diplomacy. The many positive gains of 1976 included saving two other problems from internationalization, retrieving undamaged another highjacked plane and all its passengers, and obtaining power for India from a Pakistan assigned river and Pakistan acting as bridge-builder with Bangladesh on the Farakka item in the UN. The sea-change culminated in the unparalleled success of Vajpayee in Islamabad in 1978. These are overlooked by many commentators who despair of diplomacy but they remain proof of what can be achieved by enlightened perspectives towards conflict resolution. Two valid questions which encapsulates all others and fifty years of ugly history must be asked. For India the question is: Is it in India's interest—in its own march towards the promised 'tryst with destiny'—to have next door Pakistan as a failed or 'hostile state'? And Pakistan must ask—'Could it cope, if India were not secular and democratic which gives votes to the 15 crore Muslims?' Pakistan must not presume on India's capacity and national determination to contain the blowback and protect the Muslim minority. Pakistan cannot be indifferent to their becoming second class citizens in India from which only a handful more can flee, but massive number of co-religionists would suffer degraded lives. The answers do not alter with nuclear weapons or periodic conflicts or even with random terrorism.

For decades the leaderships of both countries surrendered their independent discretion too readily and got hypnotized by superpower strategies and rival intellectual concepts. Both countries became psychologically dependent on external help and beneficence. No doubt, powerful distant friends bring some advantages, but as we have seen in Afghanistan this kind of support lasts only as long as it fits in with the donor's own perceptions and fears. The advent of terror has exposed the limitations of military power and correspondingly underlined the importance of multi-layered indigenous strength. In the globalized interdependence, beggaring your immediate neighbour invites risks, even more than before, of your own house being torched. The defence capability has to be calibrated so that it does not jeopardize real national socio-economic strength and stability. Smothering the roots of international terror may be far more difficult than containing communism. Both India and Pakistan must heed the alarming rise in people's cynicism which can ignite the tinder of desperation. The refugee camps in Gujarat are ghettoes of pathetic suffering but, as in Palestine, they could become the breeding ground of future terrorists. The only real answer is planned modernization, accepting plurality, toleration with urbanization, equitable and transparently just economic progress but always with people's participation. This mix alone could take the nations away from violent extremism, be it religious or ideological.

President Musharraf has made a brave decision that Pakistan must choose modernization in which extremists wedded to the Sharia laws are kept at bay. However, one cannot be confident (nor one hopes is he complacent) about achieving success. But it is a bold conceptual beginning and India must give it a benign benefit of doubt. In the rise of Hindu fundamentalism, India faces the test of fidelity to its own enlightened constitutional directives. Prime Minister Vajpayee confessed that the communal killings (and by implication the sluggishness in the exercise of responsibility by the Gujarat government in not promptly smothering the reactions to Godhra) and the attack by the VHP and Bajrang Dal in Orissa were shameful blots on India's prestige and principles. Alas, presumably after being reminded of the calculus of party politics, in Goa, he tried to defend the Gujarat government and drew attention to militancy amongst some sections of the Islamists. But he seemed to be going against his own liberalism of the last quarter century. Subsequently he became aware that not only was the NDA cohesion under internal stress, but the fundamental strength of India with a tolerant secular tradition was under scrutiny. Paradoxically the top leaders in both countries, be they civil or military, now have a vested interest in the restraint of the other. By now both recognize or should do, that only the centre can hold and govern these huge countries; only maturity and sagacity can manage a modern civil society. These last years have called for agonizing introspection in both countries. If another conflict ignites, it will put an end to any hopes of either country emerging to real development; rationalization of Indo-Pak relations in the end hinges on enlightened bilateralism. Fundamentally the peace process requires weighing and proclaiming the long-term penalties of retarded human development for the people of the two countries. To regain and secure the civilizational pride, India will have to aim at an integrated package of secularism at home and functional cooperation simultaneously with all its neighbours. We could not eradicate communalism if we were poised along battle stations on the frontiers. India has to revert to be an example of an open tolerant humanist society which is perceived by the world as a rational blend of nationalism and principled internationalism. We should not be ashamed to acknowledge that our mindsets were mummified by the passions aroused by Partition, and accentuated by our accepting the superimposed fallacies of the Cold War. Leaders on both sides must now overcome prejudices against the 'otherness' of the kind which a generation earlier took place between France and Germany. We must, however, be clear that conflict resolution through diplomacy must resist the temptation of public relations for home consumption. Diplomacy is, no doubt, concerned with the immediate specific issues but at the back of the mind there must always be an integrated vision, even if it is a distant one. Most (not all) politicians, intellectuals and even professionals on both sides of the frontier, in their arguments have selective amnesia; we cannot afford innocence to the concept of economic opportunity costs and continue to justify rigidity with no compromises. As this paper has tried to illustrate, hardy stalemates have been and can be overcome. Eminent citizens like Amartya Sen, the late Mahbub-ul-Haq and Abdus Salaam have strongly urged that national priorities in both India and Pakistan must be reoriented to reconciliation and peace.

BIBLIOGRAPHY

Aiyer, Mani Shankar, *Pakistan Papers*, New Delhi: UBS Publishers, 1994.

Akhund, Iqbal, *Memories of a Bystander—A Life in Dilomacy*, Oxford: Oxford University Press, 1997.

Chari, P.R. and Parvaiz Iqbal Cheema, *The Simla Agreement: Its Wasted Promise*, New Delhi: Manohar, 2001.

Dasgupta, C., *War & Diplomacy in Kashmir 1947-48*, New Delhi: Sage, 2002.

Dixit, J.N., *India-Pakistan War and Peace*, New Delhi: Books Today, 2002.

G. Wirsing Robert, *Kashmir in the Shadow of War*, New York: M.E. Sharpe, Armonk, 1993.

———, *India, Pakistan and the Kashmir Dispute*, New Delhi: Rupa & Co., 1994.

Gupta, Sisir, *Kashmir: A study in India-Pakistan Relations*, Bombay: Asia Publishing House, 1966.

Jaffrelot, Christophe, *Pakistan: Nationalism Without a Nation*? New Delhi: Manohar, 2002.

J. McMohan, Robert, *Cold War on the Periphery—the US India & Pakistan*, NY: Columbia University Press, 1994.

John, Wilson, *Karachi: A Terror Capital in the Making*, New Delhi: Rupa & Co., 2003.

Jones, Owen Bennet, *Pakistan: Eye of the Storm*, New York: Viking, 2003.

Korbel, Josef, *Danger in Kashmir*, princeton, New Jersey: 1966.

Kux, Dennis, *The US and Pakistan 1947-2000*, Oxford: Oxford University Press, 2001.

Lamb, Alastair, *Crisis in Kashmir 1947-66*, London: I. Routledge & Kegan Paul, 1966.

———, *Kashmir: A Disputed Legacy 1846-1990*, Hertfordshire: Roxford Books, 1991.

Malik, Hafeez, *Pakistan Founders' Aspirations and Today's Realities*, New Delhi: Oxford University Press, 2002.

R. Sawhny, Karan, *Kashmir: How far can Vajapyee and Mushrraf go*? New Delhi: Peace Publication, 2003.

Sareen, Rajendra, *Pakistan—The India Factor*, New Delhi: Allied Publishers, 1984.

Sharma, B.L., *The Kashmir Story*, Bombay: Asia Publishing House, 1967.

Singh, Jasjit, *Kargil 1999: Pakistan's Fourth War on Kashmir*, New Delhi: Knowledge World, 1999.

Stanley, Wolpert, *Zulfi Bhutto of Pakistan*, New Delhi: Oxford University Press, 1993.

Strategic Foresight Group, *Cost of Conflict*, New Delhi: International Centre for Peace Initiatives, 2004.

The Kargil Review Committee, *From Surprise to Reckoning*, New Delhi: Sage, 1999.

Victoria, Schofield, *Kashmir in the crossfire*, London: L.B. Tauris Publishers, 1966.

Widmalm, Sten, *Kashmir in Comparative Perspective*, London: Routledge Curzon, 2003.

Zakaria, Rafiq, *The Price of Partition*, Mumbai: Bhartiya Vidya Bhawan, 1998.

CHAPTER 5

Fresh Water Diplomacy for Resource Optimization

The Salal Hydel Project – 1976

BREAKING THE DEADLOCK WITH PAKISTAN

When reflecting on their post-Independence political problems India and her South Asian neighbours have never fully grasped that the interests of the subcontinent taken together could be maximized only by exploring the collective potential and respecting the logic of geography. The present political frontiers may have their religious, ethnic, linguistic, and cultural logic, but they do not correspond to the flow of the rivers or the rational use of water which is be the key to optimum development. The massive Himalaya remain a barrier to the monsoon clouds, and the rains are seasonal, the rivers from melting glaciers flow southwards. These rivers are the lifeblood of India, Pakistan, Nepal, and Bhutan and broadly speaking determine the parameters of 'Indian' civilization. The Indus Treaty, hailed a success, was the imposed reconciliation with the lesser evil but remains one of the major political blunders of the century. The Salal Agreement was reached after eight years of deadlock, but was a small corrective towards the optimization of benefits—green revolution and power to 175,000 tube wells in India but the important point to note is that it caused not one cusec of loss to Pakistan! This was an example of scarce resources spreading benefits through rational diplomacy in cooperation atleast after a political impetuosity.

THE CANAL SYSTEM OF THE PUNJAB IN THE COLONIAL PERIOD

The canals taking off from the major rivers of the Punjab were started by British engineers in the second half of the nineteenth century in order to settle the soldiers of the defeated army of Maharaja Ranjit Singh and to create a grain surplus that could help consolidate the British empire. The implications of the decision to transfer power not to one but two successor dominions was that the boundary would cut across the rivers and the canal system on the Indus tributaries that had so far been an integrated one. Apparently little discussion took place, either in the Central or the Punjab Partition Council, on the consequences of Partition on the functioning of the canal system, which straddled the new frontier. One cannot help speculate that the two affected parties—India and Pakistan—unconsciously (or thoughtlessly) presumed that the working irrigation network would not be adversely affected. The Standstill Agreement of the Punjab Partition Council dated 27 July 1947 and the Continuation Agreement of 20 December 1947 after the meeting of the Chief Engineers of the two Punjabs, and the fact that the arbitration provisions of all Partition related questions would expire on 31 March 1948, all passed off without apprehension. The working of some of the canal system, it was assumed, would continue without noting that the headworks lay in the sub-Himalayan range, in India, but provide irrigation to areas lying mostly in West Punjab in Pakistan. These colonies had turned scrubland into a thriving agricultural surplus and were the richest assets of the future Pakistan. When the canal system was built—long before the vivisection of the country had been contemplated—they followed the natural gravity slopes from the north-east to the south-west, involving minimum expense on storage and pumping.

Long before Partition, it had become plain to the engineers that the 'easy' part of the irrigation potential of the Punjab rivers had been exhausted and further development would require major structural innovations. Even before Partition, some other anomalies had become evident. A population of 25 million, resident in what became the Pakistan part of Punjab were dependent on the Indus irrigation system, but some 21 million living in the eastern part of old Punjab, which also had vast cultivable land, could prosper only with irrigation facilities that had yet to be developed. To put it differently, out of 39 million acres of cultivable area in the new Pakistan, 21 million were irrigation areas. Out of the 26 million acres cultivable land in India, only 5 million had such access. Had Punjab not been divided, there would have been proportionately greater new investment in the east than in the west. As mentioned earlier, the Punjab provincial engineers were already contemplating the Bhakra Nangal multipurpose project, including generating power at Nangal, from a major storage dam at Bhakra on the Sutlej. Such future developments were predicated on the logic of a united India.

PRECIPITATING THE CANAL WATERS DISPUTE

This expectation of the undisturbed continuity of the canal infrastructure was jolted when the stipulated arbitration deadline expired on 31 March 1948. Meanwhile, after the transfer of power in August 1947, the climate of relations between the two dominions deteriorated. Jinnah may well have contemplated that peace would subsist by relying on a balance of hostages in the two new nations—Hindus and Sikhs in West Pakistan and Muslims in East Punjab and the rest of India. What followed, as we all know, was a holocaust: roughly half a million were killed, between 17 and 18 million migrated from one side to the other, and the West and East Punjab were virtually purged of their respective minorities. In October 1947 there were tribal intrusions in Kashmir; the Standstill Agreement was superseded by the accession of the state of Jammu and Kashmir to India on 27 October 1947, eventually leading to a conflict between the Indian and Pakistan armies, which ended with a ceasefire brokered by a UN Commission on 1 January 1949. When the Standstill and Arbitration Agreement expired, there was no response to the demand for seignorage to cover the administrative costs of operating the headworks, so on 1 April 1948 the East Punjab government stopped the flow of water from the Madhopur headworks into the Upper Doab Canal into West Punjab. The standing *kharif* crop stood endangered. Pakistan came to a grim realization its own viability could be in permanent jeopardy as in all rivers,

India was the upper riparian. Within eight months, the fundamental weakness of Partition was painfully exposed: while a homeland for the Muslim majority had been carved out of a land with historically enmeshed religions and cultures, the geographical interdependence with India could not be undone.

The central government under Prime Minister Nehru, with more enlightened instincts, quickly overturned the East Punjab's impetuous decision. The Chief Engineers of East and West Punjab met in Simla on 18 April and the flow into the canal was resumed but the matter was left for ratification by the two central governments. An inter-dominion meeting was held in early May where Pakistan was represented by Ghulam Mohammed, its Finance Minister with Nehru himself acting as the spokesman for India. On 4 May an understanding was reached that the canal system would continue to operate as before. However, the question of sovereignty over waters, seigniorage, the rights and patterns of future development, all remained undecided. Sir Cyril Radcliffe, presiding over the Boundary Commission, had hinted that the joint control of the canal system would be logical. Specifically he had in mind that the canal taking off at the Ferozepur headworks should be jointly administered, but his terms of reference were limited to the delineation of the boundaries of the new dominions. During the period 1948 to 1952, both countries made intermittent diplomatic manoeuvres to support and strengthen their respective rights and claims. Pakistan bracketed the question of the Indus Canal System to the Kashmir dispute under discussion in the UN Security Council. It even suggested reference to the International Court of Justice for adjudication. Broadly speaking, Pakistan expressed its downstream anxieties and India wanted to continue with its pre-independence plans to develop its vast unirrigated areas and hydel potential. Correspondence was exchanged on the subject of canal waters between the two Prime Ministers, but there was no real progress.

It was at this stage that came the constructive suggestion of David Lilienthal, the retired president of the Tennessee Valley Authority and the American Atomic Commission. He met Nehru during the latter's visit to the USA in 1949, and at his invitation, visited India and Pakistan. In an article in the *Colliers Weekly* in August 1951 entitled 'Another Korea in the Making', he argued that the availability of waters for productive use in the Indus basin could be substantially augmented. He even speculated that the additional economic gains could be so great that it would deflect and sublimate the prevailing tensions between the two newly independent countries. He asserted that such developments could save India (and Pakistan) from being 'lost' like China or relapse into a conflict as happened in Korea. Lilienthal had a greatly respected position in the United States. He met Dean Acheson, then Secretary of State, and was encouraged by President Truman himself. There was even a hint that he fancied holding responsibility as head of the contemplated independent Indus River Basin Authority.

INDUS TREATY NEGOTIATIONS 1952-1960

Lilienthal put his ideas to Eugene R. Black, the President of the World Bank, who readily showed interest in optimizing benefits from the Indus system. However, before the World Bank got involved with its expertise and financial support, Eugene Black wrote to the two Prime Ministers about what he believed should be accepted as broad principles by the two governments. The two countries would be expected not to interfere with the existing pattern of distribution of the canal system; moreover, both should pledge to cooperate towards a comprehensive solution 'on a functional and not a political basis'. On behalf of the Bank, he offered the services of an experienced engineer as an impartial adviser. The overall purpose he envisaged was the most effective utilization of the total water resources of the Indus River system for the development of the region. It was only following the consent of both governments that the tripartite discussions got started in March 1952.

Gulati in his monumental work (1973) on the Indus Waters treaty describes the tortuous story of eight years of negotiations in perspective and in detail. The relations between the countries were vitiated by massacres and migrations. Through the years, the Lilienthal and Black approach of optimization slowly withered and narrow national advantage became assertive. Initially and periodically the negotiations were supervised by Eugene Black himself, but more regularly they were shepherded by W.A.B. Illiff, the Vice-President, with the assistance of General Raymond A. Wheeler, an engineer and Davidson Sommers, a lawyer.

To begin with India and Pakistan were invited to submit their own 'optimal plans' and not surprisingly these were found to be irreconcilable. In consequence in February 1954 the Bank put forward its own plan, which was then discussed over the years in Washington, London, and Rome, before the final approach crystallized. The over-simplified compromise basis was to allocate the three western rivers (Indus, Jhelum, and Chenab) for the exclusive future utilization by Pakistan and, after a period of transition of ten years extendable by three years, the three eastern rivers (Ravi, Sutlej, and Beas) for use and development by India. All the rivers, whether they originated in India or (as with the Indus and Sutlej north of the Himalayan range in Tibet), flowed through India before entering Pakistan. The canals from the different rivers, which cut across the new frontier, were to be substituted so that Pakistan could feel sanguine that it was not at the malevolent mercy of India. What made Pakistan finally withdraw its claim to a share in the eastern rivers was the pledge by the Bank and six other countries (Australia, Canada, New Zealand, Germany, the United Kingdom and United States) of US $1.2 billion to finance the development of storages and replacement canals. There was a small allocation of $56 million for a dam on the Beas in India. The most important elements of the programme were the Tarbela Dam on the Indus, and the Mangla on the Jhelum. These would make Pakistan independent of repetition of an impetuous decision of withholding normal flow by upstream India. India was to pay 62 million sterling for the cost of substitution of waters from the eastern rivers. The Treaty also constituted a permanent Indus Commission with senior engineers from both sides. Through regular contact and data exchange, they were responsible for the smooth implementation of the treaty provisions. These include provisions for the reference of disputes to a neutral expert and if that should fail, then to a court of arbitration whose terms were spelt out in the Treaty. Indus Treaty signed by Jawaharlal Nehru and Ayub Khan in Karachi on 19 September 1960.

The Indus Treaty was less than fair to India. Nehru had

hoped it would bring peace, but he had reservations about such optimal gains from the beginning. There seems to have been an in-built hesitation to provide for the water allocation to develop eastern Punjab. According to the calculation of one Indian expert on the basis of drainage and cultivable area, India should have been allocated 42.8 per cent but received only 20-5 per cent of the total 'available' waters earmarked for utilization in the east. The considerable potential for hydel generation on sites on the Jhelum and Chenab lying in Indian controlled Kashmir was made subject to Pakistan's consent. The Chenab has 20 BCM of mean annual flow and could spare waters for link canals to augment waters in the Ravi for final enlargement of the cultivable area in Rajasthan. The final solution was certainly very different from the engineering vision of David Lilienthal for optimum development of the Indus system. The treaty thus fell short of the Helsinki rules, which lay down that the total of the basin must be shared equitably on the basis of the drainage area, balancing prescriptive rights against future needs, and to meet the potential needs of the inhabitant population. Pakistan as an ally of the US in CENTO and SEATO got greater indulgence and so was able to obtain pledges of a very substantial financial subvention. Notwithstanding all these factors, it was a major achievement for fresh water riparian diplomacy. A contentious question was out of the way and for 43 years, the Treaty has worked smoothly and has enabled the two countries to greatly and freely expand the water uses.

However, it bears mention that taking a long-distance enlightened view, India and Pakistan both lost an opportunity to demonstrate to the world that they could rise above the myopic paranoia of mutual suspicions and, for the sake of the poor millions in the countries, extend the advantages of an integrated river basin development. The odds were no doubt against such a perspective, but good neighbourliness entailed in not dividing an inherited integrated irrigation system and the wastage of enormous additional funding by an artificial separation and substitution, when supplementing them would have been in keeping with hydrographic logic and natural conditions.

Having expressed this criticism, let me quickly add that in

the decades that have elapsed since the Indus Treaty was signed, there have been two wars and long periods of suspicion and tension, but the Treaty provisions have been respected and the canal flows have not been tampered with. Teclaff *River Basins in History and Law* lists all the riparian treaties signed since the seventeenth century. The Indus Treaty is the only one concluded between two known adversaries. Teclaff's listing includes treaties concluded between USSR, Poland, and Hungary when they all belonged to the Warsaw Pact and were under Soviet military domination but none provided for the sharing of waters. There are no treaties for functional cooperation between the extremities of the Soviet Union/Russia on the one side and Alaska of the US on the other, although these virtually touch each other. There is thus no parallel to the Indus accord.

II

WITHDRAWAL FROM THE DECISION TO GO FOR ARBITRATION

The Indus Treaty, signed in 1960 and with validity in perpetuity, was a 'given'—an established fact when I became Foreign Secretary in April 1976. I gathered that soon after it was concluded, the Indian Central Water and Power Commission located a site at Salal for a major hydel power plant. As required under the Treaty, in 1968 India submitted the plans and construction designs to the Indus Commissioner for Pakistan's concurrence. Salal was critical for the economic progress of Jammu & Kashmir and for the needs of agriculture in the Punjab. It was an outstanding problem in the relationship with Pakistan, and I had to familiarize myself with the background.

As a run-of-the river project, Salal was to have dead storage for only three to four days. This restriction was to ensure that the river did not carry an inbuilt threat to irrigation in downstream Pakistan. But there lay the rub. Anything emanating from India, it was feared in Pakistan, must have a hidden purpose for use in military contingencies. The Pakistan establishment was convinced that peremptory releases, even from a non-storage dam, could be used to obstruct or cut-off

Pakistani tanks and forces, when they embarked on capturing Kashmir. The other hypothetical scenario was even more worrisome to Pakistan. Once the storage was viciously emptied and, until the dam was replenished (which could take up to a week), the 'dry' riverbed would permit Indian armed forces to cross over in an offensive pincer on Sialkot. Uninformed or tutored public opinion was inflamed with suspicions that such diabolical purpose was really behind the Salal project. Pakistan, therefore, had persistently stalled on its consent for eight years. To cover its real anxieties, the negotiating arguments advanced were that even a limited storage behind a comparatively low dam carried the potential of extensive flood damage to fertile fields in the adjoining Pakistan districts. The Indian side was not unaware of the hidden rationale of operational contingencies but we emphasized our rights under the Treaty and the economic benefits to India and skirted the security anxieties of Pakistan. It is possible the Central Water and Power Commission felt that these anxieties were irrelevant and the Ministry of External Affairs chose not to focus on them.

The Salal project, its designs and its positive benefits were discussed in seventeen meetings of the India-Pakistan Indus Commissioners and was raised half a dozen times by my predecessor Foreign Secretaries. However, since the necessary concurrence was not forthcoming, in exasperation the Ministry of External Affairs, on the advice of the Ministry of Irrigation and Power decided that we resort to the arbitration procedure provided in Article (IX) of the Treaty for the settlement of differences and disputes. It is a long and elaborate Article, which provides for the selection of a neutral expert on minor problems but it goes on to lay down provisions that, in the event of it being categorized as a dispute, a court of arbitration could be constituted with two nominees from each country and three outside 'umpires' of whom one of them was to be chosen as the Chairman. The arbitration court, after weighing the evidence, would adjudicate in writing. The process was bound to be long, during which the climate of public opinion would remain surcharged and turn into propaganda; national attitudes would harden and obstruct the rationalization of relations between the two countries.

Soon after I became Foreign Secretary, I was instructed to

negotiate the normalization of relations with Pakistan (see Chapter 3). Following the hijack of the Indian Airlines plane by Kashmiri separatists in January 1971, after the passengers were released the aircraft was destroyed and the government fostered or connived at a public rejoicing. In consequence, the civil aviation connections between the two countries were broken; overflights in Indian airspace were forbidden and Pakistan then filed a complaint with the International Civil Aviation Organization in Montreal. Diplomatic relations between the two countries were broken in 1971 in the wake of the Bangladesh conflict and not restored at the Simla meeting of the two Prime Minister in 1972. The rail and road connections had been severed after the conflict of 1965. In the intensive three-day long negotiations in Islamabad in May 1976, we were able to conclude a compre-hensive Memorandum of Understanding to restore all links including diplomatic relations within eight weeks to the day. Having met this deadline, the general climate of relations improved significantly.

At this stage, I discovered the looming spectre of the decision, already taken, that we had decided to go for arbitration over Salal. It did not require much perspicacity to foresee that even though the process of adjudication would take a long time but in the meanwhile, the atmosphere would become so vitiated that it could complicate the resolution of other issues. Anyway the construction of the hydel project would remain deferred and the delay could extend into years, perhaps indefinitely. I feared the hazard of another 'Kashmir', that is, a bilateral problem being internationalized. I put my apprehensions to Prime Minister Indira Gandhi. She readily reversed her approval and authorized me to make another attempt at diplomatic negotiations. I promptly wrote to my opposite number (Agha Shahi) for a further round of bilateral talks over Salal. The nodal responsibilities were taken over by the Ministry of External Affairs.

Pakistan, of course, had no interest in Salal. No reply came for weeks. Meanwhile in the wake of the normalization, we had restored other severed links and found that greater co-operation had been forthcoming. Pakistan had proved ingenious and effective in handling another IAC plane, hijacked in August 1976. People-to-people contacts had been welcomed on both sides and there was a significant improvement in the climate of relations and so I could politely taunt the Pakistan Foreign Secretary with reminders on Salal. It was only after several such reminders and a lapse of nearly three months that Agha Shahi finally conveyed agreement to the re-opening of talks. One gathered unofficially that the delay was because Bhutto was planning to go for a general election—the first after the loss of East Pakistan—and he did not want his image as an old anti-Indian hawk to be diluted. From his point of view, he would have been quite content if Salal had remained deadlocked!

Though I was by no means confident of overcoming the old resistance, we embarked on the negotiations with serious purposefulness. Two rounds of negotiations were held in October 1976, the first in Delhi and soon thereafter in Islamabad. As a generalist with no grasp of engineering concepts and even terminology, I had to make great efforts to understand the design and broad rationale of the project. After considerable internal diplomacy, our government authorized some concessional parameters such as reducing the height of the proposed dam and, in order to assuage the hypothetical apprehensions of deliberate downstream flooding, the permanent closure of the diversion canal after the hydel plant had been commissioned. During the negotiations, the real *arriére pensé*—the military contingencies—were never openly articulated but it became evident that they were strongly entrenched.

SALAL AS A MICROCOSM OF INDO-PAKISTAN RELATIONS

Salal is a microcosm of the whole range of India-Pakistan problems and, in essence, similar to US-Soviet relations during decades of the Cold War. The economic benefits of cooperation and interdependence got obscured by entrenched national security suspicions. Although Salal had been discussed a score of times, we from India had never seriously attempted to expose them as technically fallacious and even contingency-wise unsound. I had no illusion that simple pledges of goodwill even following the comprehensive normalization would not have a telling impact. Before embarking on the second round of negotiations, I urged one or two of our irrigation and power engineers led by R. Rangachari and Leela Poonappa, then a young Under Secretary in the Ministry of External Affairs, who were part of our negotiating team, to examine a worst-case contingency as if they were Pakistanis. I requested these competent and dedicated officers to draw up a balance sheet of possible loss and damage if, in fact, we were to abuse the storage at Salal in the way probably suspected by the Pakistan diplomatic professional and technical experts. After nightlong calculations, they came forward with a range of facts that had never previously been marshalled. For example, on the basis of the known storage capacity of the dam and geological data for the Punjab kind of reverine terrain, they worked out the rate of ground water absorption in the riverbed and the banks of the Chenab.

Our officers concluded that the impact of a peremptory release of the stored waters from a dam site 30 miles inside the frontier would substantially be contained within Indian controlled Jammu & Kashmir itself. The storage capacity being limited, the residuary flow would have greatly reduced the hypothetical flood damage in the adjoining areas of Pakistan. They also worked out that from such a one-shot release and subsequent temporary slowing of the river flow, the reduction in the availability of water for the canals would, at best, delay the downstream irrigation cycle by one to one-half days. This would be insufficient to do permanent harm to a standing wheat crop in which the normal watering cycle is once in three weeks. On the other hand, for India, the emptying of the storage would mean immediate stoppage of the power plant for at least four days, possibly a week—the time required to have the pondage level restored so that the turbines could operate again. These and other calculations in detail were put to the Pakistan experts, but they continued with their refusal to an agreement. The Pakistani Cabinet had clearly confirmed that unless we made further major adjustments they would continue to disagree.

I therefore sought an appointment with Prime Minister Bhutto. I reaffirmed that subject to Pakistan's consent, the Treaty gave India the right to non-consumptive utilization on the western rivers. As politely as possible, I pointed out to him that 'there was a limit to the extent that India would cut its economic nose to cause minor irritation to Pakistan'. I also added that according to our calculations, the feared peremptory release of the waters and shutting down of the power plant for three days would lead to a direct loss of Rs. 8-10 crore in revenue, from the non-supply of electricity. As a consequence, 1,75,000 tube wells would have to stop for want of power. This would have a multiplier adverse effect on agricultural productivity. 'No Prime Minister—be it in India or Pakistan—could take the risk of provoking the wrath of the Punjabi farmer.' I went on to argue that if he were the Prime Minister of India, even if malevolently inclined, he could not significantly harm Pakistan. Riaz Khokhar, later the Foreign Secretary, who served in Delhi as High Commissioner, was the note-taker and confirmed to me that I had urged these and such arguments to Bhutto.

Our case was strong. While the economic logic of India was irrefutable, the military fears of Pakistan could not stand objective scrutiny. Agha Shahi, on Bhutto's instructions, asked me to defer my return to Delhi and I readily agreed. We learnt that a Cabinet meeting was called by Bhutto and senior military and civilian professionals, including some summoned from Lahore, were asked to scrutinize our calculations. The Pakistan government had to decide whether to re-affirm the old veto or to accept the logic of the 'new' arguments.

WIN-WIN COMPROMISES

In reversing its attitude, however, there remained the political problem for Bhutto: not appearing to go soft or 'surrender' to India on the eve of the elections envisaged in a few months time. Opposition to Salal had for years become a populist cry, particularly as it was in Kashmir. I had asked for a second meeting with the following day with Bhutto. Much to our gratification, I was told our calculations were not disputed and that the Pakistan government would in principle drop its reservations and go along and concur with the marginally modified design, but that no agreement could be signed immediately. I had an intuitive sense of Bhutto's dilemma. I made clear that we were anxious to go ahead with electricity generation, not in scoring debating points against Pakistan. I hinted that the newly marshalled facts had not so far been publicized by us. We reached an interesting compromise. He approved that the Foreign Secretaries could go ahead and initial a Memorandum of Understanding, but the formal signing must be deferred. As a diplomatic gesture, I volunteered not to publicize the terms. (In that respect, I knew I could take advantage of the prevailing restrictions authorized under the Emergency.) However, as I was leaving, I unilaterally but confidentially informed the Pakistan Prime Minister that we would continue preliminary work on the basis of the MOU as an earnest of the formal signing of the agreement. I added my saying so could be subsequently denied by Pakistan authorities. Being a civil servant, I would risk possible condemnation and punishment. I had won some credibility by volunteering to keep the details of the agreement confidential and so saving the Pakistan government the embarrassment of making a climb down.

This, however, was not the end of the story. General elections were duly held in the spring of 1977 back-to-back in India and Pakistan. Mrs Gandhi was defeated but Bhutto was re-elected. Yet, despite irregularities, Bhutto did not get the plurality he had hoped. He was soon arrested and displaced by General Zia-ul-Haq. With the Janata coalition coming to power in Delhi, for the first time a non-Congress government—there was curiosity and uncertainty on a possible re-orientation in our Foreign Policy, specially with A.B. Vajpayee, an old Jan Sanghi, as Foreign Minster. A Pakistan delegation led by Agha Shahi, by then elevated to the status of Foreign Minister, came to Delhi to make first contacts with the new government and to ascertain whether they would stand by the letter and spirit of normalization of relations negotiated under Mrs Gandhi. The Salal Agreement was not on the agenda in the hurried visit but obviously it was part of the carryover of unresolved problems between the two countries. Morarji Desai and his Foreign Minister publicly and privately gave assurance of continuity of non-aligned policies. It would seem that Agha Shahi and his colleagues went away reassured after the frank and friendly conversations. The Janata government, in word and deed, had underlined the priority to be given to good relations with all the contiguous neighbours.

In February 1978, A.B. Vajpayee, even in the face of a hostile press, visited Pakistan and in a remarkable diplomatic performance, turned round Pakistan public opinion by a mix of non-denial of his anti-Pakistan past and the sincere promise of friendliness towards the government and people of the country in the future. It was following this successful visit that in April 1978 Agha Shahi led a delegation to New Delhi to formally confirm the initialled but not signed agreement on Salal. During the formal conversations, Agha Shahi once again tried to urge Atal Behari Vajpayee to review the dam specifications. As a gesture of goodwill the latter was urged to further lower the height of the proposed dam. The old arguments were refined. While welcoming the reiteration of friendliness, he urged that as a matter of abundant caution against possible malevolence and abuse of the Salal Dam, Pakistan would have to unilaterally build expensive defence works costing, he estimated, about Rs. 25 crore. He, therefore, urged that the height of the dam be lowered by another 5 ft (We had already agreed to lower the height prior to the negotiations in 1976.) I could not help feeling that Agha Shahi, who is an able and polished diplomat, was banking on Vajpayee's non-familiarity with the background of previous discussions and the technical implications in the loss of power generation. I was sitting next to the Foreign Minister and passed a slip urging a small coffee break. As a civil servant, I had straddled the two governments. I got hold of the new Pakistan Foreign Secretary (Shah Nawaz) during the coffee break. I told him that in international relations this was a rare case where bipartisanship was easy but political one-upmanship would be courting disaster. If the height of the dam were to be varied by even an inch (not to mention lowering it by 5 ft as suggested by Pakistan Foreign Minister), it would raise a political storm in India. On the other hand, neither Indira Gandhi nor Zulfikar Bhutto—both having approved the initial agreement when in power—could have any grounds for objection if the terms remained unaltered. This was conveyed to Agha Shahi and his last minute attempt to improve the agreed specifications of the initialed understanding to Pakistan's advantage was abandoned. The old terms were confirmed and the Salal Agreement was signed by the two Foreign Ministers in April 1978 in the Committee Room of the External Affairs

Ministry. The photograph taken on the occasion clearly shows the Indian national motto 'Satyamev Jayate' (Truth triumphs) behind the figures of A.B. Vajpayee and Agha Shahi when they were exchanging the signed copies. Incidentally as far as I know, Pakistan has not constructed any special defensive barriers or floodwater abutments as a precaution against India misusing the Salal Dam. Since 1987 when Salal was finally commissioned and started feeding the north India grid, it may well be lighting some bulbs in Delhi and irrigating farmlands in Punjab, Haryana, and Rajasthan from a river whose waters, under the agreed treaty, belong exclusively to Pakistan.

After nearly 20 years Salal has got silted and the power generation has greatly reduced as compared to what was originally estimated. Whether there are technical solutions to restore the power potential is for the engineers to decide, but Salal has not been abused and the climate of relations was much improved for functional cooperation between the two countries.

LESSONS FROM THE NEGOTIATIONS

There are many lessons, which can be gleaned from the Salal story:

(a) Salal was a small—perhaps not so small—example of conflict resolution. While the logic of an integrated basin had already been compromised when the Indus Treaty was concluded in 1960, the Salal negotiations and agreement retrieved to some extent the optimal beneficial gains, for India, from a tributary assigned to Pakistan without inflicting any disability or handicap on Pakistan. India has demonstrated faith in the enlightened principle of interdependence and optimization that lies in treating the river basin as an integral whole. Rising above the restrictive limitations of terrestrial sovereignty is the essence of International Law and specifically the Helsinki principles on rivers.

(b) When objectivity gets vitiated by the red herring of security, negotiations get needlessly locked into mutually reinforced national self-righteousness and consequently the economic opportunity costs are virtually banished from consideration.

The delay in concluding the agreement was because our diplomacy failed to foresee and assuage the unwarranted suspicions that had taken root in the Pakistan diplomatic and technical establishments. In consequence India must have lost hundreds of thousands crores of rupees in revenue and productivity.

(c) A healthy tension-free climate of relations is essential for the constructive modification of rigid old postures. These can be lubricated by measured unilateralism in small concessions. Initially reducing the height by 5 ft, and agreeing to close the temporary diversion, facilitated in easing a long-standing impasse. The small concessions authorized by Mrs Gandhi's government led to the giving up of an old veto on the part of Pakistan. The success, indeed the beginning of the Salal negotiations, was facilitated by the time-bound comprehensive normalization of relations in May 1976.

(d) To rescue a problem from needless internationalization and inoculate it against populism, it is expedient to consign negotiations to a process of bilateral exchanges. We negotiated in secrecy and resisted the temptations of public relations upmanship. Such discussions thus make for more purposeful and swift progress do not get unnecessarily protracted.

(e) There is advantage in volunteering not to air jubilation or advertise a climb down. Successful diplomacy must resist the temptation to rejoice in rubbing the others' nose in the mud: with neighbours where many problems exist or may erupt, diplomacy must seek to appear as a 'win-win' situation.

The task of diplomacy through effective leadership of the Ministry of External Affairs is to steer between the professionalism of the military mind (which is paid to contemplate worst-case capabilities) and the technical exoticism of the civilian experts which are inclined to exaggerate the unilateral economic benefit and damages. In this case most civil, mechanical and electrical engineers had held out for nothing less than optimum benefits of power generation. Diplomatic negotiations must not be approached with a warlike aim like unconditional surrender, nor can complex problems be looked upon as a marketplace for a zero-sum-game.

(f) Successful snegotiations depend on a sensitive understanding of the political constraints of the adversary. Mrs Gandhi did not crow over the triumph in Salal. (Incidentally she did not even mention progress in Indo-Pak problems during her election campaign of 1977.) It thus became possible to restrain Pakistan from playing up Kashmir during the Pakistan elections in 1977. In exercising restraint, as mentioned, we were incidentally helped because the final stages of negotiations were held in Islamabad and India was under an emergency when press freedom was circumscribed.

(g) Because Salal remained off the headlines, the Janata government readily accepted what it had inherited and did not get tempted to repudiate the initialled agreement. Bipartisanship in foreign policy, wherever feasible, facilitates diplomatic solutions.

(h) Not infrequently the pressures of domestic politics are apt to imprison the typical political leaders into uncompromising postures. The decision-maker shirks from asking timely unloaded questions of his advisers as it may expose his own ignorance. Even without genuine prior consultations, the professional has a duty to offer objective advice. The diplomatic professional must argue for the long-term opportunity costs and the economic benefits in avoiding further delay. There have been, no doubt, dire consequences for honest advice but not infrequently these are exaggerated.) In any case this obligation is implicit in guaranteed lifelong tenure for senior civil servants in the parliamentary system. Indira Gandhi had approved the resort to arbitration but she also readily reversed her decision when the logic of another 'Kashmir' was put to her.

SPECULATIVE RAMBLING THOUGHTS AND DEEPER IMPLICATIONS

The Indus dispute may not have been precipitated but for East Punjab's unilateral stoppage of water on 1 April 1948. Too many of our experts slur over our guilt in precipitating the Indus River Dispute. Conceivably but for this peremptory action, there might have been improved chances for the survival of the integrated canal system, the realization of the imaginative vision originally projected by David Lilienthal and supported by Eugene Black. If one billion dollars at 1960 prices—the equivalent may be 6-8 billion in 2003—could be internationally marshalled and used productively, for *supplementary* benefit for both India and Pakistan, at least hypothetically, poverty levels could have been significantly reduced and the per capita income increased substantially.

Janata government *could not have started* these negotiations, at least not until after the Vajpayee's visit to Islamabad in February 1978. Even if it had, the negotiations might not have been completed by June 1979 when Morarji Desai government went out of office. Thereafter we had no government enjoying the confidence of Parliament for six months.

By January 1980, our relations with Pakistan started slithering downhill. The Soviet intervention in Afghanistan in December 1979 more or less coincided with Indira Gandhi's return to power and, based on ill-conceived advice, she got out of step with the non-aligned consensus in not condemning the invasion of Afghanistan. The USA was even more out-rageously wrong: Carter/Brezenski raised an entirely false strategic alarm. When President Reagan came to power, carrying the notion of fighting the 'Evil Empire', he re-militarized Pakistan, supported the Mujahideen, assembled the Islamic extremists as reliable anti-Communists and laid the seeds of terror. January 1980 may prove to be as much of a turning point as Pearl Harbor. In hindsight it was just as well that Mrs Gandhi authorized the reopening of the Salal question in 1976. Had we gone ahead with arbitration, it could have gone on for several years and, after the Soviet intervention in Afghanistan, the adjudicatory judgement might well have been influenced by the US tilt for Pakistan as was apparent during the Indus Treaty itself in 1960. Who knows, as with Karnali in Nepal ready for consideration since 1964, Salal may still have been on the drawing board!

Many scholars, American, Indian, and Pakistani, have selective amnesia for the period from 1972 (Simla Agreement) to 1989 (the beginning of insurgency) or 1998 (the nuclear tests). The arms race revived in 1980 with the American false alarm. Pakistan had fully respected the LOC up to 1979 because the bilateral climate was friendly. The cross-border infiltration, combined with the Indian misjudgement in the Kashmir Valley in the 1980s, is conveniently overlooked. These antecedents triggering the insurgency forfeited the prospect of functional cooperation between the two countries. Neither Chari[1] (Indian) nor Cheema (Pakistani) nor Wirsing[2] (US) mention the successful bilateralism of 1976. Wirsing dwells on the Indus Treaty (1960) but though his book is written in 2002, it has no mention of Salal and the uninterrupted power flowing since 1987 and through all the crises of the 1990s. Wirsing gives the Indus Treaty 1960 as an example of third party facilitation but omits mention of Salal Agreement in 1976, which was wholly bilateral. In financial terms the total benefits must be several thousand crores of rupees. What is worse is the pontified presumption that India and Pakistan diplomacy cannot solve any problems bilaterally.

Salal was a gain for power-starved India, with no corresponding loss to Pakistan. We can learn from the American experience of the Harmon doctrine. He argued for upper riparian sovereignty over the Rio Grande but ever since, notwithstanding America's size and strength, the doctrine has proved an albatross in subsequent relations with Mexico. The Harmon doctrine proved pointedly embarrassing, when decades later the US came to urge Canada to undertake flood control and power generation on the Columbia for benefit to lower riparian Montana and other adjacent American states. India desperately needs renewable power from Nepal but just as US coercive diplomacy failed, India likewise has so far forfeited the chances of hydel power surplus from Nepal by insensitivity towards a small country. Nepal is now plagued with Maoism because its water wealth was not harnessed. Using the advantage of mountain heights and tumbling waters, it could have prospered like Bhutan. The conclusion is obvious: whether it is narrow self-interest or adherence to international morality

[1]P.R. Chari, Parvez Iqbal Cheema, *Simla Agreement 1972: Its Wasted Promise*, Manohar, 2001.

[2]Robert G. Wirsing, *Kashmir in the Shadow of War*, Armonk, M.E. Sharpe, pp. 233-4.

and principles, in the long run, the aim should be to see benefit in resource optimization by integrated river basin development. It certainly suits countries like India and USA.

In a perspective view, this logic is reinforced by ecological considerations. An econometrician can work out the multiplier benefits from a renewable source of energy, year after year, but it is not implausible to speculate that it might have saved millions of hectares in depleting forests and slowed the unrequited export of billions of tonnes of silt, which clog the riverbeds and cause rampant floods in India.

Notwithstanding the success in Salal, there is no denying that optimal benefit from the waters of the Indus is by no means exhausted. Aside from potential gains from additional storages and hydel projects in Pakistan itself—there are known locations on the Indus—there is unsatisfied demand for power in Kashmir; indeed all over north India. Baglihar, another run-on-the-river project on the Chenab has much similiarity to Salal. Navigation on the Jhelum has unrealized advantage but that is contingent on the consent of Pakistan. Irrigation in west Rajasthan and Gujarat could be more cost effective if waters of the main Indus could be consumptively used instead of emptying unutilized in the Arabian sea. As mentioned, beyond Salal there is the untapped potential of power and link canal diversion from the Chenab to Ravi. But such dreams as Lilienthal's can only be realized if there is a political will. If, as some suggest, the Indus Treaty may be abrogated to punish Pakistan for a temporary provocation, we will not only earn international opprobrium but be left to rage in impotent fury. It is in the interest of both countries to always keep in mind their riparian interdependence. Salal shows that beggaring the neighbour and paranoiac negativism can only be overcome by patient, steady sensitive negotiations. While Partition cannot be undone, the future of both India and Pakistan, specifically their peoples is in never despairing about cooperation, which emanates from the logic of geographical interdependence.

The overriding lesson of Salal is a reminder that there is an array of possible riparian projects of benefit to India and her neighbours, which (setting aside the constraints of resources) are hostages to false fears and myopic politics. The economic opportunity costs are astronomical. Further delay is fatal for all countries. The aggravation of poverty fuels Maoist insurgency. The seasonal monsoon may not be as merciful as in the temperate lands where it rains all through the year saving on artificial irrigation, but we are more fortunate than the vast deserts. We must harness and husband our seasonal good fortune. In effect this is what the governments of India and Pakistan did in a small way on Salal and so left a positive example for bilateral diplomacy.

BIBLIOGRAPHY

Gilmartin, David, Colonialism and Irrigation 'Technology in the Indus Basin', *Journal of Asian Studies*, no. 53, 1994.

Gulati, N.P., *Indus Waters Treaty*, New Delhi: Allied Publishers, 1973.

Hafez-ur-Rahman, 'Indo-Pakistan Waters Dispute', *Pakistan Horizon*, vol. XII(4), 1959.

Mehta, Jagat S., 'Challenge of Water', paper for Woodrow Wilson Centre Diplomacy, Washington DC, 1982.

———, 'Opinion: Indus Water Treaty: A Case Study in the Resolution of an International River Basin Conflict', National Resources Forum United, vol. 12, 1988.

Rangachari, R., 'Indo-Pakistan Cooperation', *Water Resources Development*, Surya Foundation, 2002.

Warikoo, K., 'Perspectives of the Indus', *Hindustan Times*, 1998.

Workshop, Luxembourg, 'The Management of International River Basin Conflicts (Austria)', Headquarters of International Institute of Applied Systems Analysis, 1986 (Follow up at George Washington University, 1987).

CHAPTER 6

Diplomacy for Equitable Allocation on International Riparian Flows

The Sharing of the Ganga Waters at Farakka – 1976-1977

When I was deputed to lead the Indian delegation to the UN Conference on Water held in Mar-Del-Plata in March 1977, the background publication put out by the UN listed 214 river basins shared by two or more states.[1] Since then, the Soviet Union and other countries have splintered, and there have been other definitional refinements. The Ganga-Brahmaputra-Meghna (Barak) are now generally accepted as three separate basins. The latest tally of international river basins mentioned in the UN publication is alleged to be close to 300. It is formally recognized that fresh water is the ultimate natural resource for life and development; the hydrological cycle is fixed and cannot be augmented; 7/8th of the water on the planet is in the oceans and cannot be consumed or economically used without an expensive process of desalination. Deep in the mythology of all religions remains the embedded belief that water is abundant, pure and a cleanser of mind and body. Thoughtful minds have predicted for some time that future conflicts will be around water and its control. I cannot help reiterating that nothing is as symbolic of the problems of balancing considerations which flow from national sovereignty and the growing international interdependence, as rivers shared between two or more states.

[1]UN DOC E/C7/71, 11 March 1977.

RIPARIAN INTERDEPENDENCE OF SOUTH ASIA OVERLOOKED

No part in the world is as fortunate in having a rough geographical definition, that is coterminous with the limits of its civilization, as in the sub-Himalayan watershed of South Asia. Yet—there lies the problem—nowhere was this natural advantage for optimal future development so thoughtlessly overlooked as in the political fragmentation of India. Subsequent developments have confirmed that Partition was one of the greatest blunders of the twentieth century. If the British had had a shred of enlightened inevitability when quitting, they should not have squandered goodwill by partitioning the subcontinent. The tragedy was compounded when India, which had pioneered the quest for self-government on grounds that mastery over national destinies will dramatically enhance the welfare of independent peoples, did not see that Partition, cutting across the major river basins, would jeopardize these aspirations. Surprisingly in the rush to gain political power, the leadership of the Indian National Congress and the Muslim League were both myopic on the riparian consequences of the division. Drawing frontiers across the Indus, the Ganga and the Brahmaputra system has had terrible, perhaps politically irreversible, consequences for India, West Pakistan, and what became Bangladesh. The optimum future now looks like a distant mirage because of nationalist short-term perspectives. The Ganga-Brahmaputra basin covering India, Bangladesh, Nepal and Bhutan by 2020 may have a population of two billion and, not surprisingly, these interconnected basins have one of the densest concentrations of poverty in the world. As a monsoon region, South Asia receives a heavy rainfall that is unevenly spread through only four months of the year. Development is dependent on human and technical inputs in irrigation in order to draw beneficial advantages from the rich soil of the Ganga basin. The area of 1.8 million sq. km lying in India, Nepal, Bhutan and Bangladesh is only half the size of the Mississippi basin but has four times the annual rainfall. A further striking feature is the short distance—at places only 90 km—from the coast of the Bay of Bengal to the outer Himalaya and thereafter in an equally short distance from near sea level along the riparian plains ascending to the highest and longest mountain range in the world. It is because the slopes of Himalaya are so steep that they carry the potential of 250,000 MV of hydel power, perhaps the greatest anywhere in the world. If fresh water is the resource for determining the future economic health of the region, the importance of this basin can scarcely be over-estimated.

A recognition of the increasing demand for and limited availability of water was a challenge to development and political leadership in all countries. It was overlooked that water wealth, in flowing rivers, must be equitably shared and not selfishly appropriated. As against this, every constituent nation has marshalled convenient precedents and legal arguments against the overriding reality that optimization for every country is only in marshalling the totality of the waters. Fresh water diplomacy has been at the heart of the problems of South Asia and failure is writ large in the consequential poverty of India, Bangladesh and Nepal.

FARAKKA IN THE POST-INDEPENDENCE PERIOD

The main channel of the Ganga (referred to in Bangladesh as the Ganga and later as the Padma) shifted eastwards 200 years ago into the present delta and is now part of the Bangladesh. That was about the time that Calcutta became the most important port of the English East India Company serving half of India. Even a hundred years ago, Sir Henry Cotton, the Chief Engineer of the Company (and many subsequent British appointed engineers or committees) recognized that to save the port from creeping siltation (brought down from the Himalayan slopes and brought up with the tides from the Bay of Bengal) would require a strong downstream flushing action by a massive canal diverting the main flow of the Ganga at Farakka. Although this was considered a possible solution, such a man-engineered improvement carried the hazard of causing distress in the eastern part of Bengal, now Bangladesh, notably the Khulna district and the deltaic Sunderbans. Even then it was recognized that it might not be a permanent solution. Generally speaking, river ports get clogged up even when there is no such double-sided threat of siltation and tidal sandbars. (This has been the fate of London, Delaware, and many others.)

The improvement could slow, if not halt, the creeping deterioration and enable ships of deeper draught to come up to discharge or pick up cargoes along riverine docks but in the long run, it seems to have been professionally recognized, that it would be a losing battle. Massive dredging helped but in the flat deltaic surroundings, there was not sufficient elevated ground to dump the silt where it would not again get captured and enveloped at the time of high floods or periodic massive tides. Moreover, the non-consumptive use of such a massive flow of waters implied enormous opportunity costs upstream in agricultural and developmental uses which, once committed for flushing action, could not be politically reversed. 40,000 cusecs could yield millions of tonnes of food if utilized for irrigation purpose. The historic importance of Calcutta, then capital of British India, could not be lightly set aside but it was the prospect of slow emaciation and eventual death of the port for international commerce, which was the logic of establishing a subsidiary port at Haldia south of the confluence of the Damodar River. The Farakka Project must have remained a technically debatable proposition, and so in the last 100 years of the British rule over India, the scheme for a diversionary canal from Farakka was not pursued.

However, following Partition and the constitution of the province of East Pakistan (and the precipitation of the Indus dispute since 1948), the idea of Farakka canal was revived. As envisaged, the engineers contemplated the diversion out of the main river flow of the Ganga. The problem was not in the monsoon or post-monsoon months but during the 'lean season' beginning in January, when the flow starts steadily declining. According to the statistical average, the flow at Farakka is only 55,000 cusecs in the latter half of April and the beginning of May. When the scheme was approved by the Government of India, the importance of Calcutta port was of course fully recognized, but the opportunity costs in alternative consumptive uses were never fully examined. The tragedy of Farakka, in my opinion, is linked to the blunder of looking upon Partition as unavoidable or the lesser evil. In the prevailing passions and distrust in some minds on both sides, there was a shortsightedness: in India it was 'good riddance of anti-nationalists' and in Pakistan, a welcome 'liberation from Hindu majoritarianism'. In fact, it was a blunder from the point of view of the peoples of both India and Pakistan.

This provides the background to the Farakka problem. The scholarly and polemical literature relevant to Farakka runs into hundreds of books and monographs. One cannot help suspect that there was a presumption of irreconcilable hostility between Pakistan and India and even after decades, there could be no optimization of benefits for both countries. It was in the prevailing mood of mutual suspicion and narrow nationalist concerns that the idea of a diversionary canal from Farakka was resurrected.

THE SHADOW OF THE INDUS WATER DISPUTE

It may be worthwhile to digress briefly on the evolution of the law on international waterways. The Harmon doctrine of absolute sovereignty was advanced in 1894 (when Harmon was the US Attorney General) against Mexico's complaint of radical reduction in flow but it cast a shadow on the political relations and has progressively been modified. The US faced a contrary position when wanting flood control and surplus hydel power on the Columbia, where Canada is the upper riparian state. Exercising the rights of the upper riparian state in relationship to the lower riparian helplessness has proved short-sighted.

It has often been forgotten that India is both the upper riparian on rivers such as the Chenal, Jhelum, Ravi, Beas and the Ganga, but the middle or lower riparian on the Indus and Brahmaputra (in Tibet called Tsangpo) and many of the Nepalese tributaries of the Ganga. The Helsinki principles were enunciated by the International Law Association in 1992. Yet as early as 1942, B.N. Rao (later Constitutional Adviser to our Assembly), as a judge of the Calcutta High court, presided over the Indus Commission and adjudicated on the inter-provincial dispute between Punjab and Sind on the then proposed Bhakra dam. He enunciated the principle of 'equitable apportionment' that must seek to balance existing uses and construction on hand and the future potential of all the riparian partners. This vision transcends narrow nationalism and embodies enlightened internationalism and is the essence of the Helsinki principles accepted after many deliberations of the International Law

Institute and the International Law Association. It was subsequently embodied in the United Nations Framework Convention to ensure the utilization, development, conservation, management and protection of international water courses with the object of promoting optimal sustainable utilization for the present and for future generation.

There is no evidence, at least on any paper that I have seen, how and why the idea of a major diversion from the main flow of the Ganga at Farakka was revived by independent India. It seems to have been pulled out of the dusty shelves and resurrected when India and Pakistan got embroiled in strife. The crisis for the canal system in the Punjab with headworks in the 'Indian sub-Himalayas' feeding the colonies in West Pakistan (as has been described elsewhere), started on 1 April 1948. What followed were twelve years of negotiations which, with World Bank mediation, ended in a lesser evil treaty signed by the heads of governments in September 1960. The Indus Waters Treaty, it may be recalled, originated with the idea of supplementing the existing canal system from the tributaries of the Indus but after eight years of negotiation (1952-60) and the supplement of a billion dollars subvention of the World Bank, it ended with the proposal to make Pakistan water independent by having its own reservoirs at Tarbela and Mangla.[2] The Indus treaty is based on the simple solution of three rivers to each country: it has worked satisfactorily for over forty years, but it has meant India only got 21 per cent of the total waters of the Indus system when it had a higher population in the basin.

With a riparian crisis on the Indus precipitated in 1948, it may well have occurred to some Indian minds that before demands for continuation of 'normal' flow for downstream East Pakistan was advanced, India might go ahead with the old solution to save Calcutta port. The idea of such a canal with a carrying capacity of 40,000 cusecs flowing into Bhagirathi was advanced in 1951—three years after an inter-dominion representation at the highest level had got engaged with Indus waterways now 'internationalized' and threatening to become a subject of discord. Pakistan protested from the very beginning

[2] See 'Fresh Water Diplomacy for Resource Optimization' in this volume

about the 'Farakka' plans. India continued with the technical preparations for the dam. The Farakka project was formally approved in 1960 and construction began in 1961. The economic importance of Calcutta port serving virtually a third or even half of India was obviously vital and must have been pressed by B.C. Roy, one of the most influential Chief Ministers at the time. In the prevailing mood of exasperation and hostility towards Pakistan, the possible downstream damage was, if anything, a perverse encouragement to Indian civil engineers. India's case was based on the fact that nearly nine-tenths of the river flowed through Indian territory, which made it virtually an Indian waterway. East Pakistan expressed concern at the damage to agriculture and industry but this was deemed as irrelevant or dismissed as exaggerations. Diplomatic protests did lead to periodic meetings of experts between 1960-8 covering the Ganga, Kobadak, the Ganga Barrage, the Tista Barrage Project in East Pakistan and the Tista Multipurpose Project in India. India and Pakistan both advanced arguments quoting conveniently chosen precedents as upper or lower riparian respectively, but it was essentially a dialogue of the deaf. Pakistan's plea that consent of the lower riparian should be taken in advance was ignored by India and the construction at Farakka continued.

EAST PAKISTAN BECOMES BANGLADESH

To cope with 10 million refugees spilling over into the country, in 1975 India was initially hard put how to respond to the demand arising out the all Pakistan elections giving the Awami League led by Sheikh Mujibur Rehman an overall national majority. Bangladesh decided to wrench its freedom and became independent in 1971 with last minute collateral intervention by India. The climate of India-Bangladesh became transformed from hostility to cooperation and understanding after Bangladesh proclaimed its independence. I cannot help wondering if India had not been divided in 1947 or if 1971 had happened in 1951 or thereabouts, whether Farakka would have been conceived and launched in a more or less unilateralist manner. As it happened, following 1971 there was a burst of mutual goodwill in India and Bangladesh which showed purposeful determination to set aside a quarter century of alienation. In this spirit in March 1972, Mrs Gandhi for India and Sheikh Mujib for Bangladesh signed a Treaty of Friendship, Cooperation, and Peace with no specified duration and simultaneously a joint River Commission was established. Meanwhile, by 1974 Farakka was on the way to completion. The diversion canal to Bhagirathi/Hooghly was completed during the early months of 1975. In April 1975, when Farakka Barrage was ready for commissioning, negotiations took place first in Delhi and then in Dhaka. I am told—and this is nowhere on the record—that notwithstanding a dramatic change of atmosphere, even at this stage, President Mujib was reluctant to agree to *any* diversion of the flow into the Hooghly canal. However, in the friendly atmosphere, Bangladesh eventually assented to a test flow with specified releases for a 10 day period from 21 April to 31 May, gradually increasing from 11,000 cusecs to 16,000 cusecs. After 31 May, by which time the monsoon rains would start, the withdrawals continued. There was relief not complaint when the full envisaged capacity of 40,000 cusecs was diverted into the feeder canal as Bangladesh was glad to have the flood intensity being correspondingly moderated. India suggested that there could be a similar augmentation of water by a gravity link canal from Brahmaputra starting in Jogipara in Assam up to Ganga upstream of Farakka. The canal would run for a third of its length across north Bangladesh. Bangladesh even then insisted that augmentation at Farakka should be from the Ganga basin itself and not from Brahmaputra; storages could be built at identifiable locations in Nepal. But a canal of 80,000-1,00,000 cusecs would be like a massive river virtually bifurcating the country.

The tentative discussions conducted in April 1975 were in a constructive and friendly spirit but they turned acrimonious and politically hostile after the assassination of Sheikh Mujib on 15 August 1975. All through the winter of 1975 and the lean season of 1976, the feeder canal was worked to its full capacity. Bangladesh argued that the April 1975 understanding was only reluctantly agreed and that too as a test run for a limited duration when Justice Abu Sadat Mohammad Sayem was President, but later when Major General Zia-ur-Rehman became the Chief Marshal Law Administrator, Mrs Gandhi was obviously distressed at the military takeover. With Sheikh Mujib, she had developed a political rapport and personal friendship, but with his killing all that was gone.

Not surprisingly following Mujib's assasination the climate of relations with India deteriorated sharply. Both officialdom and the people in Bangladesh were angry at the callous unconcern at the ill-effects in the reduction of river flows in the Ganga/Padma. As one gathers from G.M. Abbas's book, *Ganges Water Dispute*, throughout the winter of 1975-6, there were several internal meetings, and many diplomatic approaches were made to foreign governments. An intensive campaign was also launched at home and abroad to publicize the Bangladesh's case. Maulana Abdul Hamid Bhasani addressed a letter to Prime Minister Mrs Gandhi, urging normal flows for Bangladesh to continue. The reply from Mrs Gandhi was not considered satisfactory and Maulana Bhasani threatened to lead 'a million' men from Bangladesh to demolish the barrage.

In the winter of 1976, Abbas went to the USA, UK and was prominent at the preparatory conference on water proposed by the UN. In Dhaka, these efforts aimed at emphasizing the adversarial consequences of the drop in the river flows when the feeder canal was receiving the greater share of the Ganga. The Soviet and Czechoslovak ambassadors in Dhaka spontaneously showed concern and seemed to share the apprehensions of the harmful effects by the intrusion of saline waters into the delta, as fresh water flows of the Padma were dramatically reduced. The extent of damage may have been exaggerated, but there could be little doubt that diversion into Hooghly was affecting the economy of downstream Bangladesh.

INVOLVEMENT IN FARAKKA AS FOREIGN SECRETARY

I became Foreign Secretary on 1 April 1976. Following the withdrawal of Pakistan's complaint with the ICAO on 27 March my first important assignment was the normalization of relations with Pakistan. The MOU of May 1976 in Islamabad was comprehensive and time bound. It went some way in assuaging anti-Indian pubic opinion in Pakistan and was quietly welcomed by India's neighbours and more enthusiastically by international opinion. My first involvement in the ongoing Farakka negotiations was in June 1976 when I accompanied G. Parthasarthy, then Chairman of the Policy Planning Committee in the Ministry of External Affairs, to Dhaka leading a 'goodwill' delegation. As Foreign Secretary, I was second in rank but not in any position to alter or mould the brief which carried the approval of the government of the day. The Indian side had already emphasized the importance of Calcutta port and how it was necessary to ensure effective flushing action to enable the accumulating sandbars to shift in order that ships of deeper draught could sail into Diamond Harbor. Bangladesh asserted that during the depth of the lean period, if, out of the normal flow of 55,000 cusecs, 40,000 cusecs were diverted, it caused such severe human distress, that it could be visible from the air. Not surprisingly, the Dhaka meeting was infructuous.

On 26 August 1976 Bangladesh decided to inscribe the Farakka question on the agenda of the forthcoming United Nations General Assembly. The item was entitled, 'The question of unilateral diversion of the international river Ganges in contravention of all international laws, regulations and traditional usages and in violation of solemn pledges on the use of such water'. An explanatory memorandum was attached. On 8 September the title was changed to 'Situation arising out of the unilateral withdrawal of the Ganges waters at Farakka'. When we learnt of the inscription, India invited Bangladesh to send a delegation to Delhi for further discussions. These took place between 7 and 10 September. Babu Jagjivan Ram, the Minister of Agriculture was appointed leader, with G. Parthasarthy as his deputy, and myself as the third ranking member of the Indian team. The Bangladesh delegation to Delhi was led by Rear-Admiral Khan, the Deputy Chief Martial Law Administrator. The delegation called on Prime Minister Mrs Gandhi, during which I was present. One was hoping that the call could lead to the withdrawal of the item from the agenda of the General Assembly. In my experience, it was the coldest and shortest meeting between two leaders of government that I have ever attended. Abbas reports the conversation verbatim which looks plausible enough. The conversion did not last more than a few minutes.

FARAKKA IN THE UN

We in India obviously did not like the idea of Bangladesh complaint being discussed in the General Assembly of the UN. It was evident that there was overwhelming sympathy for the Bangladesh case. Our mission to the UN did its best to contain the embarrassment, opposing the inscription on the ground that this was a bilateral problem and internationalizing it would only complicate a constructive resolution. While the Soviet bloc expressed reservations, the item was accepted without a vote and placed on the agenda. The idea of discussion in the Plenary was fortunately rejected, but our efforts to have it consigned to the second or the seventh committee failed. It was finally allotted to the special Political Committee of the Assembly, which takes up questions of secondary public interest. Bangladesh's attempt to obtain priority of discussions also failed. It was the general expectation that Parthasarthy, who had been continuously associated with Farakka talks and had been Ambassador to the UN for many years, would himself lead our delegation, at least when the Farakka item was being discussed. But Parthasarthy, was probably apprehensive of a negative resolution, and declined to take on the responsibility, so I was assigned to field our case. After the imposition in 1975 of the Emergency the boast of India's functioning democracy had suffered a setback. As it happened, Shirley Amar Singhe of Sri Lanka, previously High Commissioner to India, was the Chairman of the Non-Aligned Group but there was little consensus support for India even amongst the non-aligned. While the developed countries, were reluctant to publicly join in criticism of India, the undercurrent of sympathy for Bangladesh could easily be discerned. Handling Farakka before the assembled world community, had odds staked against India. The only positive factor was the comprehensive normalization with Pakistan concluded in May 1976. When I embarked on the task to lead the Indian delegation on the Farakka, I had no illusions of success. I recalled not just Kashmir but the passage of the Pakistan's proposals on a Nuclear Free Zone in South Asia. I knew I had been given a difficult and delicate responsibility.

It was gratifying that our delegation had succeeded in having the discussion of this item postponed till November thus somewhat diluting the focus of international attention. There was an attempt to obtain international mediation by a high dignitary, but we had resisted the suggestion. When the item came up, Bangladesh presented a draft resolution, following a complaining statement and I made a statement underlining the spirit of constructive cooperation between two neighbours. The discussion was adjourned for a week. It required very assiduous efforts with senior members of the Non-Aligned Groups—with Sri Lanka, then Chairman, Egypt, Yugoslavia and many other delegations—to prevent the item coming to a vote. Abbas, who carried great personal standing amongst 'water and riparian experts' round the world, was able to gather support from Islamic, Latin American, and African countries as well as the developed countries. I decided that the only way one could ensure minimum embarrassment to us would be to win a measure of confidence from the members of the Bangladesh delegation itself. I remember approaching Rear-Admiral Khan, the leader of Bangladesh delegation and a suspected hardliner against India. I told him that I was an ex-Sub-Lieutenant naval officer but during my entire career had never got within 500 yards of an Admiral and therefore I felt privileged to be shaking hands with him. He laughed and somewhat mellowed. I met B.M. Abbas frequently. He had told me previously that he was a civil engineer who started service in pre-partition Bengal and had since been associated with Farakka in East Pakistan, to eventually become head of the Water and Power Commission for the whole of Pakistan, before Bangladesh became independent. He disclosed that over the years, he had attended about 150 international meetings, seminars, and conferences on riparian problems, where he had invariably focused of Farakka. (We used to refer to him as Farakka personified and *The Economist* called him a 'one-man international lobby' on Farakka). I told him that in comparison, I was an innocent generalist but I did believe that good neighbourliness depends on bilateral diplomacy and not hauling a country over the coals. I said to him, no doubt they might get a resolution to their liking, but surely what they wanted was additional water in the Padma. A resolution would only harden public opinion in India. I myself privately felt that in the face of obvious distress in Bangladesh, we should show greater flexibility. I promised him that if the item was not put to vote, I would guarantee a further meeting in Dhaka within a week of the end of discussion on the subject in New York. With personal rapport established, Abbas seemed to accept the sincerity of my plea. I took the risk that government would uphold my commitment. Somehow I felt I could explain to the Prime Minister that it was in the national interest not to be internationally embarrassed.

Abbas's account[3] of Bangladesh at the UN is understandably one-sided but, more surprising is the World Bank publication by Salman and Uprety entitled *Conflict and Cooperation in South Asia's International Rivers*.[4] They were not aware of, and give no credit to the friendly manner in which the members of the Indian delegation spread out to prevent the resolution coming to a vote. (Print academic publications often do not get the flavour of behind-the-scenes informal diplomacy.) A few countries were certainly encouraging Bangladesh but it was crucial that we neutralize Pakistan's propensity for mischief. Fortunately having comprehensively normalized relations with Pakistan a few months earlier, I seemed to command some respect personally and so I approached the Pakistan Ambassador to forestall support for Bangladesh. While expressing sympathy for Bangladesh, Pakistan did not discourage the idea put forward by me of withdrawing the item when diplomacy from our side was being reasonable and plausible. A consensus statement was worked out in informal negotiations with the help of prominent non-aligned countries. It was read out by the Chairman of the special Political Committee, adopted by consensus on 24 November, and subsequently approved by the Plenary on 26 November. It was a gratifying outcome. I must acknowledge the standing of Rikhi Jaipal, our Ambassador to the UN, for his influential support.

[3]B.M. Abbas, *The Ganges Water Dispute*, Dhaka: The University Press Ltd., 1982.

[4]A. Salman and Kishor Upreti, *Conflict and Cooperation in South Asia's International Rivers: A Legal Perspective*, World Bank Report, no. 25580, January 2003.

The fact however remains that in the entire history of the UN, this is the only case where an item, once on agenda of the General Assembly has been withdrawn without a vote having been cast. This was possible only because the sponsor nation agreed not to press for a vote. The consensus statement conceded the importance of the item but did not go as far as to condemn India for its recalcitrant stance. I would like to believe that the success was attributable to the credibility and consistent approach of refurbishing diplomatic sensitivity towards all our neighbours in an even-handed way.

I considered it important that the item should not become a regular feature of the General Assembly agenda, like the South Asia Nuclear Free Zone question. Abbas makes out that the consensus had the same validity as a General Assembly resolution, but this is not tenable and anyway has not been proven. What was and remains important is that we adhered to the pledge of urgent negotiations towards expeditious settlement.

1977: CHANGE OF GOVERNMENT—PURPOSEFUL BILATERALISM

In accordance with the promise made in New York, the Indian delegation led by the then Minister of Agriculture, Jagjivan Ram, held talks in Dhaka between 6 and 9 December 1976 and again between 14 and 16 January 1977. The third round started in New Delhi on 21 January 1977. Sensing the element of validity in the Bangladesh's complaint, though short of their hope for a condemnatory resolution but generally more sympathetic consensus in its favour, both delegations reviewed the commitment that a minimum and continuous flow of 40,000 cusecs was not absolutely essential for the Farakka project for safeguarding Calcutta port. Prime Minister Indira Gandhi accepted in principle that during the lean months, a larger proportion of flow should be released for Bangladesh. Out of 55,000 cusecs (the benchmark at 75 per cent availability from the observed data on the lowest flow in May) India's share could be limited to roughly 24,000 cusecs. Our engineering experts, notably the then Chairman of Water and Power Commissioner, C.C. Patel, had continued to argue for nearly twice that amount and was reluctant to accept anything less. Rear-Admiral Khan leading the Bangladesh team called on Jagjivan Ram and indicated that this was below the minimum they could accept. (Their concessional limit was 35,000 for Bangladesh with only 20,000 being diverted to the Hooghly River.) While we were bandying around these allocations, there was a last-minute cancellation of a meeting because we waited the return of Mrs Gandhi from an internal tour. We could not proceed beyond this gridlock without her authorization.

While we were haggling with these allocations it had been announced that the Emergency would come to an end and fresh general elections would follow within two months. This meant that Morarji Desai and all other leaders who were in custody would be free to campaign in the elections. The conventional wisdom in officialdom was that Mrs Gandhi would come back to power even if it was with a diminished majority but no one openly predicted the surprising results that there would be a strong swing in favour of a hurriedly cobbled Janata Party. As it happened, Z.A. Bhutto had already scheduled elections in March 1977 and so the two election campaigns were more or less under way in both countries. My own concern was that while electioneering enveloped the countries, the atmosphere should not deteriorate and vitiate relations with either Pakistan or Bangladesh. This was not easy, but we in the Foreign Office made an earnest effort. The actual steps are described elsewhere.[5] On the whole foreign policy did not figure as an election issue.

The long prepared first UN Conference on Water was scheduled to be held in Mar-Del-Plata in the second and third week of March. Our election results were due on 21-2 March, halfway through the conference. At the Water Conference, after the General Assembly consensus, Farakka was on everybody's mind and we had to field it so that it did not find critical mention, to be picked up by the Opposition as ammunition to criticise the government or invite an explosive 'change', tempting at election time, that national interests were not being effectively safeguarded. The Bangladesh delegation was again led by Rear-Admiral Khan, the number two in the country in martial law regime. In the absence of an available minister or

[5]See 'Normalization with Pakistan' in this volume.

dignitaries like Parthasarthy willing to run the risk of embarrassment, again I had to lead the Indian team, alas at a much lower level than that of Bangladesh. B.M. Abbas was of course there and commanded great international respect for his experience on international riparian questions. He was elected Chairman of the committee that covered regional riparian cooperation. One of the items for the plenary was 'Recommendations for Action'. Which urged that in the case of transboundary rivers, no new major works should be started if there was an existing or a possible dispute. Countries took up their respective positions on whether they were upper or lower riparians. Fortunately, even the diluted draft on this proposal was defeated in the plenary. We certainly were nervous. Any of these items could bring up Farakka and polarize opinion, and perhaps compel a right of reply from India. Knowing that Bangladesh wanted to marshal support, it was my endeavour to ensure that Farakka or any other dispute with Bangladesh did not find specific mention in the speeches. Though there were general recommendations urging cooperation for optimizing non-navigational uses of international waterways, Farakka itself was not mentioned a single time. (It certainly was discussed informally in the corridors around the conference.)

I had reached an informal prior understanding with Abbas that Farakka would not be brought up. In the statements, I set the tone by pledging Indian commitment to constructively harness national and international rivers. It surprised not so friendly delegations that Bangladesh did not specifically refer to Farakka. In dignified praise for each other, we managed to enhance diplomatic respect for both countries. Rear-Admiral Khan himself left after his general statement in the initial plenary.

On 21 March 1977 half way through the conference, I myself left by making a series of long hops to New York, London and then Geneva. I had hoped to be in Delhi on 22 March when the results of our general elections were due, but our aircraft was deflected at Cairo due to an obstructed runway and we had to land in Athens. The crew had to be given 24 hours rest and so I spent a day glued to the radio of Ambassador Krishnan who being concurrently elected to Greece was on a visit. Appropriately I visited the Acropolis, the symbol of the ancient democracy of Athens. It became clear that the Indian electorate had not voted for Mrs Gandhi; the Congress party had suffered a severe defeat and that there would be a change of government in New Delhi. On reaching Delhi, I called on Mrs Gandhi in her Akbar Road office and she felicitated me at keeping Farakka out of the conference. Within days of the swearing in of Morarji Desai as Prime Minister, it was decided to resume the interrupted dialogue with Bangladesh. Jagjivan Ram had switched allegiance to the new Janata coalition, and was appropriately designated the leader and I was now to be his deputy.

Through previous experience of negotiations, I was convinced that the political atmospherics outside the specific issue under discussion had to be harmonious and free of friction if the chances of success were to be maximized. In international politics there is always a psychological 'linkage' with other current anxieties of the negotiating parties. Though never officially informed, I had learnt that after Sheikh Mujib's death, the Mukti Bahini freedom fighters had been withdrawn from Bangladesh and were deployed along the Garo Hills from where they were making nightly raids to destabilize the post-Mujib regime in Bangladesh. I took the initiative to inform the Prime Minister that if the proposed negotiations on Farakka were to be meaningful, this kind of coercive interference and hostility was counterproductive. The Prime Minister appreciated the point and apparently directly confronted the head of RAW and asked him if Tiger Siddique and his colleagues were in fact indulging in such nefarious forays into Bangladesh. The Ministry of External Affairs had been kept in the dark, but the fact could not be kept from the head of the government. In any case, some of the raiders were captured and shown on the Bangladesh television services. The Prime Minister ordered that within the next few days, Tiger Siddique and the remnants of Mukti Bahini should be withdrawn completely from the border of Bangladesh and redeployed far away in the Darjeeling area. This removal was soon noticed in Dhaka and, of course, interpreted as proof of the sincerity of the new government in Delhi. While it was never mentioned across the table, it certainly eased the will to compromise in the subsequent negotiations.

Jagjivan Ram was a persuasive and able negotiator. Better than any engineer he understood that India had perhaps made a mistake in committing a substantial amount of water to be consigned to the Bay of Bengal to an ultimately doomed river port, when the corresponding use in irrigation and industry could have been beneficial in augmenting upstream productivity. It was a great folly but by 1976 it was politically irreversible. Ram indicated his willingness to scale down India's demand for the diversionary canal to 21,000 cusecs so that 34,000 cusecs would be available for Bangladesh in the last ten days of April. This, however, was not good enough for Rear-Admiral Khan and the Bangla Desh negotiators. Eventually Jagjivan Ram accompanied only by myself called on General Zia-ur Rehman where Admiral Khan and Tabarak Hussain, the Bangladesh Foreign Secretary, were present. As a final concession, it was agreed to split the differences, adding 500 cusecs to Bangladesh's share. In other words, between 21 and 30 April, based on 75 per cent availability from the data observed in the past, India would withdraw 20,500 cusecs and 34,500 cusecs would be released to flow into Bangladesh. Admiral Khan, I suspect, was not in favour of this compromise; tensions was evident in the conversations with the press before we took off for the return flight. It was left to me to announce the agreed basis for sharing the waters reaching Farakka and that it was a breakthrough on a crucial point. Only somebody who had the political standing of Jagjivan Ram could have signified his consent to a reduction below 21,000 cusecs. It was nevertheless 5,500 cusecs more than what was conceded by Sheikh Mujib himself in April 1975 in conversations with Indira Gandhi and that too on an ad hoc trial basis for one season only.

However, the full agreement covering many other ticklish issues remained to be negotiated, and for these I was designated the leader of the Indian team. Abbas, by now elevated to Cabinet level, was to lead the Bangladesh side. There were three more negotiating sessions between May and September. Before proceeding to Dhaka on the second visit, I called on Jyoti Basu, the newly elected Chief Minister of West Bengal, and urged that in the larger interest, we must scale down the amount of water to be spared during the lean months for the Calcutta harbour. He did not demur. The agreement was initialed by myself and Abbas on 30 September but the formal document was signed by Sardar Surjit Singh Barnala, the Minister of Agriculture, and Rear-Admiral Khan, the Deputy Cheif Marshal Law Administrator of Bangladesh, on 5 November 1977.

In his book Abbas gives details of the ups and downs of the negotiations in the three sessions in New Delhi and Dhaka and again in New Delhi. They were by no means smooth sailing. I kept no notes and have not sought permission to refer to the relevant records. Abbas gives a fairly lengthy description of the process from his viewpoint. The Indian delegation had to overcome a number of problems, some merely semantic, but others like the duration of the treaty of a more substantive nature. The atmosphere had obviously improved. The basis of mutual confidence established between Abbas and myself certainly helped and from my side enabled me to overrule some of my more hawkish colleagues. Among the tricky issues, was to assuage anxieties of India arbitrarily reducing the flow upstream. We reached compromise on many issues but conceded on a specific calendar of ten days periods based on previous flow statistics. The hub was on two points—long-term augmentation, and the guarantee of a minimum share regardless of fall in the river flow. Both sides agreed to jointly take note of the actual flow at Farakka, and at Harding Bridge in Bangladesh. We assuaged Bangladesh anxiety by agreeing to guarantee 80 per cent of the declared minimum flow even if the total went below the statistical average. Both countries, however, remained committed to their own long-term augmentation plans.

I had kept Prime Minister Morarji Desai, Foreign Minister A.B. Vajpayee, Defence Minister Jagjivan Ram and the Cabinet Secretary, Nirmal Mukherjee informed. Abbas in his book refers to the internal discussions in the Bangladesh government prior to each bilateral discussion. What he did not know is that there were last minute hitches from our side, specifically from Charan Singh, then the Deputy Prime Minister holding the Finance portfolio. The Cabinet had cleared the full draft agreement but just before the last meeting, Charan Singh demanded that the commitments already made for the duration of the agreement, should now be stretched further and there should be no commitment to review after the specified period. It was embarrassing for me to get Abbas to agree to this last minute modification. We had agreed that the duration would be five years with the option to extend it further. The agreement contains the schedule of withdrawals from 1 January to 31 May each year. I had informed Abbas that I was due to leave for New York to join the Foreign Minister Vajpayee. Abbas hummed and hawed but finally said he would try to get the approval of General Zia-ur-Rehman, the *de facto* Prime Minister. After a whole day's attempt at establishing telephonic contact with his President, who was on tour, some time around 8 p.m. he received the final clearance to the proposed modification. Meanwhile, we had to get the administrative machinery geared so that the formal document could be ready for our signature. After knowing that we would be concluding the agreement, late that night after all the teams were in a relaxed mood, and I took the two delegations for a lavish Mughlai dinner in a Jor Bagh restaurant. There was much relief and mutual satisfaction and great bon homie prevailed.

As stated, the basic difference was on how the flow at Farakka should or could be augmented. The long held view of Indian engineers was that it should be from the Brahmaputra at a point in Assam (Goalpara) by a canal which initially would carry between 80,000 to 1,00,000 cusecs to be emptied above Farakka. Bangladesh's view was averse to treating the Ganga-Brahmaputra as a single basin. They insisted that the additional waters at Farakka should come from storages in the Ganga basin itself, built in the foothills of Nepal. This question of augmentation in some way was the long-term nub of the problem. In a spirit of compromise, letters were exchanged that both sides could make any proposal they chose, but specifically that it would not exclude reservoirs in the upper reaches of the Ganga in Nepal. Both sides committed themselves to studying the problem during the period of the agreement.

The final initialing of the agreement was forty minutes after midnight on 30 September 1977. I boarded the Air India flight at 2 a.m. The interim agreement was widely welcomed in Bangla Desh because India had come halfway in favour of the initial demand. With floodlights and the press in tow, there was a sense of satisfaction all round. Abbas acknowledged that the agreement came after a quarter century of deadlock. International interest and offers to finance any agreed long-term project came during the visits to New Delhi of President Carter and of Prime Minister Callaghan and Robert Macnamara of the World Bank to Dhaka. The offers were registered in both capitals but there were unbridgeable differences on the most appropriate solution.

During 1978, the Joint Rivers Commission, first established in 1972, was revived but Farakka was an unspoken impediment to the survey of the totality of the potential of cooperation of all rivers which flowed from India into Bangladesh. Although the climate was improving, there developed a stalemate, specifically with Bangladesh insisting that there should be a joint approach to the government of Nepal to explore the possibilities of storage sites on the tributaries of the Ganga. There were several meetings of the Joint Rivers Commission but the gridlock persisted. (Eventually a joint approach was made but no one had an answer of what benefits would accrue to Nepal.)

By the end of 1979 I was displaced from my post as Foreign Secretary. In 1980 Mrs Gandhi was re-elected, and in May 1981 Zia-ur-Rehman, who had become President, was assassinated.

As far as my own personal involvement in Farakka is concerned, I felt satisfied at having negotiated the agreement in 1977. I must here acknowledge the disciplined cooperation of Muchkund Dubey who was then Joint Secretary dealing with Bangladesh and later became Foreign Secretary. Even though at that time he thought my thrust was a needless compromise of national interest, he brought his great ability to the finalization of the agreement. I was quite overwhelmed when years later, he voluntarily acknowledged to me that the compromise reached was consistent with our enlightened national interest. Subsequently I proposed his name for High Commissioner in Dhaka. Though a Bihari, he speaks Bengali fluently. It would be even more appropriate for me to acknowledge with gratitude the ability, expertise and eventually flexibility of B.M. Abbas, who most of the time was my opposite number. He very kindly records in his book as follows: 'Mr. Jagat S. Mehta, the Indian team leader and I could establish good rapport. He could take confrontation with good humour without embittering personal relations.'[6]

[6]Abbas, *The Ganga Water Dispute*, op. cit.

Years later, when I visited Dhaka, I went to call on Abbas, he was almost ninety then. He very kindly gave me a copy of his book—inscribing it 'Jagat S. Mehta for whom I have the greatest respect, admiration and friendship'. Leaving aside this mutual admiring duo, I want to underline that a personal rapport is always essential so that while remaining vigilant for respective national interests both could become the spokesmen for the rationality to their own colleagues and benefited by joint efforts at problem-solving.

POST-1980 DEVELOPMENTS

Let me try to summarize the subsequent Farakka story. (As I retired in 1980, this is not based on first-hand inside knowledge.) In 1982 when the agreement was due to expire, India removed the guarantee clause, which had provided that regardless of the quantum of flow reaching Farakka, we would not allow the flow for Bangladesh to be reduced below 80 per cent of the specified amount. Farakka was conceived disregarding the needs and claims of Bangladesh during the lean months. The Government of India, in the larger foreign-policy perspective, should not, in my opinion, have modified the guarantee clause. It would not have been done if Sheikh Mujib were in power; the penalty was to fall on the millions, mostly poor, who bank on these flows to contain saline intrusions. But myopia allowed anti-Indian sentiments to be aggravated. Relations naturally deteriorated: the removal of this clause was seen as confirming India's propensity to hegemony because of its size and specially where it was the upper riparian.

With the promise of improvement when a Memorandum of Understanding was concluded between Mrs Gandhi and General Ershad, when he became President, there was no serious follow up on either side. Another effort to give vitality to resolve India-Bangladesh cooperation occurred when Rajiv Gandhi and General Ershad met at Nassau in the Bahamas at a Commonwealth Heads of Government meeting. In November, a new MOU was concluded. It focused on alternatives and sought to bring within its scope joint efforts at flood control; but the long-term solution of Farakka diversion was deflected. There were other problems which were bedeviling the relationship, such as India reneging on giving leasehold to enable access for Teen Bigha, a Bangla Desh enclave surrounded by India. To give it the air of a new beginning, a joint office of experts was established, but after a year or so, the attempt made no progress.

The years 1985-96 were a sort of vacuum period with no substantial attempt at improvement of our relations. In 1996, however, there was a major breakthrough on the long-standing dispute. A new approach was evident in the treaty signed in December 1996 between Prime Minister Deve Gowda, helped by I.K. Gujral, the Foreign Minister, and Sheikh Hasina, focusing on the development of a barrage to divert waters within Bangladesh. Salman Haider deserves full credit for this breakthrough. A signal of stronger political commitment was transmitted when it was revealed that the agreement was valid for thirty years. The issue of augmentation of waters for Bangladesh was recognized in the preamble but the treaty did not make it central to the water-sharing arrangements. The share of the two countries was raised and reduced in alternative ten day periods. Farakka was a *fait accompli* but the major problem of optimizing growth and stability through available water utilization remains.

BILATERALISM VERSUS MULTILATERALISM

Before concluding it may be worth digressing to discuss the advantages and disadvantages of bilateralism versus multilateralism in negotiations on international waterways. Multilateralism is the running thread of the recommendations of the World Bank study by Salman and Upreti.[7] They hold up the Indus Treaty as an example of success in resolving deadlock and imply that in determining rights on international waterways, help by third party mediation should be followed. The Indus Treaty has, no doubt, worked; it should be looked upon as ending in the lesser evil; but it is not strictly consistent with Helsinki principles of optimum utilization and potential future developments. It is far removed from David Lilienthal's

[7] Salman and Upreti, *Conflict and Cooperation in South Asia's Internal Rivers: A Legal Perspective*, op. cit.

original proposal, made in 1951, to *supplement* (not substitute) the existing canal network of the Punjab rivers. In the Indus Treaty, it is true, the Bank mediated only when two contending parties were far apart in their own solutions. Bank urged, indeed more or less imposed, a simplified solution so that after transitional arrangements, three rivers each were assigned to India and Pakistan for permanent future utilization.

The solution, however, overlooked (or was obliged to do so) the long-term optimal potential of the Indus. Let me mention some of them. There is limitation on the hydro-electric and navigational potential on the Chenab and Jhelum, which could satisfy the needs of the inhabitants of Kashmir and other parts of India; under the treaty, this is made subject to Pakistan's veto even though no reduction of downstream flows is at risk. India did manage to get hydel power from the Chenab at Salal, but only after resolving an eight-year deadlock showing that the apprehended fears were unwarranted. The Chenab has sufficient water, which even if diverted through a link canal to the Ravi and the Sutlej could improve the potential of agricultural development in Haryana and Rajasthan. The Indus Treaty was facilitated because Pakistan had become an ally of the West, whereas India was non-aligned, but statesmanship and technological expertise lost heart prematurely. The world today is very different from the paranoia of the Cold War. The scope of constructive diplomacy sacrificed the vision, which in 2004 looked not so unrealistic to both sides. As stated earlier one billion dollars (at 1960 prices) mustered by the Bank and from some affluent countries would have yielded far greater benefits to *both* countries if the vision of supplementing had not been abandoned. Multilateralism was not an exemplary success. One might add that with the experience of the reference of intrusions into Kashmir to the UN in 1948, no government in Delhi could readily agree to the provision of arbitration or third party mediation for dispute settlement or conflict resolution. Sovereign powers are reluctant to consign access of a vital resource to a third party even if a genuinely neutral one could be found. Bilateralism may be difficult, but can be kept confidential. The irony is that following the political failure of US intervention in Iraq and the worldwide rise of suspicions and irrationality in the West, India and Pakistan are bilaterally exploring the potential of functional cooperation with generally supportive international encouragement.

HINDSIGHT REFLECTIONS

The world, and notably South Asia, faces the major problem of water conservation. The policy of mega projects of dams and diversion in river flows is not now looked upon with the old confidence. There will have to be greater decentralization of planning and decision-making; we will have to do better riparian management by re-bequeathing decisions to the local level and better rationalization of scarce availability. The story of Farakka illustrates the opportunity costs where short-term national perspectives overlooked and permanently damaged the long-term benefits which could flow from enlightened internationalism. As it happened, this did open up subsequently. Hypothetically speaking, as mentioned earlier, had the assertion of independence by Bangladesh from West Pakistan occurred in 1951; in other words, if East Bengal was not perceived as permanent part of an irrevocably hostile Pakistan, I cannot help wondering whether the Farakka diversion would have been taken in hand after the transfer of power in 1947. Going further into the past, if Partition had not occurred, the imperative of saving Calcutta by additional flow into Hooghly would have been set aside. Following the opening of Suez in the last quarter of the nineteenth century, the importance of Calcutta port had increased for the British empire. All post-Independence analysis was based on the unending hostility between the successor countries, spurred by populist sentiments to support a project serving only one side and with no hesitation about the harm done to the neighbour. The inherent economic flaw in the two-nation theory based on religion, where one half of the country with a population of 60-80 million (in 1947), different in language and culture was separated by a 1,000 miles, remained. Upstream diversion was predicated on the concept of absolute sovereignty over water flows; it ignored the consensus on international riparian experience. It overlooked that India was also a lower riparian to Nepal and a middle riparian on the Indus and the Brahmaputra. The engineers, discounted the adverse economic and human costs downstream. These entrenched attitudes were brutally exposed in 1971.

After Bangladesh became independent and during the ascendancy of President Mujib, the logic of many-sided economic (including riparian) cooperation based on geographical contiguity gleamed before the decision makers in both India and Bangladesh. It fructified in the constitution of a Joint River Commission, but a quarter century of hostile relations had left a difficult legacy, and statesmanship and constructive diplomacy could only make tentative beginning from the myopic narrow self-righteous view point. Anyway the honeymoon of friendship with India was too short, and came to an adrupt end with the assassination of Mujib even before the suspicion had been concretely unscrambled and the promise of common interests fully explored. Given a few more years and the uninterrupted pursuit of an enlightened vision, who knows but wide-ranging cooperation with beneficial results on many shared rivers might have led to several projects with potential advantages to both sides. Restored navigational transit through Bangladesh to Assam and the north-east by now might have become a reality, giving enormous benefit to Bangladesh and India. The ugly fact is that relations reverted to old anti-India suspicions. Instead of husbanding, or at least wanting and working for, the return to this possibility by assuaging unwarranted fears of hegemonism, we adopted revanchist attitudes that only reinforced the prejudice towards a small dependent neighbour and vice versa. Mujib himself was never fearful of subordination to India but he did not manage well the independence he gained to strengthen democracy. There was excessive centralization and the virulence of corresponding increase in militant extremism, including by his own old supporters, laid him open to the charge of tutelage to India. I have already referred to the encouragement given to the Mukti Bahini (and Shanti Bahini) being used to undermine the government of the successor in Dhaka, but this only strengthened anti-Indian nationalism. The virus of communalism, surfaced against the Hindus. The fault and damage was on both sides and harmed the potential of beneficial bilateralism.

In brief, India played into the inherent suspicions of being not only the bigger country but a callous, selfish upper riparian, and this permeated the talks on Farakka. The project, of course, could not be undone in 1974 or even in 1971-2, but we need not have been as insensitive to the needs of those traditionally dependent on the Ganga/Padma flows. It was a far cry from the claim of our engineers that 40,000 cusecs in a steady flow was necessary for effective flushing action, which on the basis of the area commanded by the Ganga flow in India was ours by right. Abbas told me in 1975 in Mujib's time, he had mentioned to our delegation that Calcutta was bound to be clogged up whatever may be the quantum of flow in the Hooghly. Our plan projected to bring in ships of deeper draught could only be viable for a few more years. Whether such a limited benefit was sufficient justification for jeopardizing a permanent neighbour with almost 80 million population (at the time) should have been examined objectively. In the long run the much greater economic and environmental interest was in the prosperity of Pakistanis/Bangladeshis in the Ganga delta. It was myopic to limit or neutralize the augmentation of the neighbour's economic capacity. The more optimal results were in enhancing the productive use of the water both within India and in Bangladesh whether the country was friendly or masochistically hostile.

I was involved in the Farakka negotiations only in 1976-7, by which time we did not have as clean a slate as may have existed in 1951 or even in 1971. However, while Indira Gandhi's attitude was not understanding towards the post-Mujib regimes, the approach of Jagjivan Ram, the chief negotiator, and Prime Minister Morarji Desai—even while accepting the inherited position and the prevailing deterioration of the political climate after it became a military dictatorship—showed more enlightened appreciation of the problem of Bangladesh or at least as it affected the ordinary people of the country. In general, the Janata government had openly placed more emphasis on improving relations with all of India's neighbours. At the stage when I was leading the delegation to the UN in November 1976, the UN conference in Mar-Del-Plata in March 1977 and in the three sessions between April and September 1977, I negotiated hard but in the spirit of government's policy, which was closer to my own approach. I tried to show patience and understanding for the Bangladesh viewpoint. To me, assuaging fears and reaching compromise promised better protection of India's interest than a self-righteous unthinking attitude. The diplomacy of rationality and sensitivity did moderate adversarial polemics in New York and Mar-Del-Plata. We were saved the embarrassment of a resolution in New York and pointed mention in Mar-Del-Plata. It was the cumulative effect of constructively motivated approach that enabled us to obtain a last-minute change, urged by a member of the Foreign Affairs Committee of the Indian Cabinet on the proposed duration as late as September 1977. (It was a short-sightedness on the part of India to remove the guarantee clause in 1982, in the event of an emergency low flow, to substitute it with time-specified governmental consultations.) The more positive and accommodating attitude was of course only possible because of the confidence of my negotiating adversary and his conviction that I was not trying to score points on his country, but it was also facilitated because diplomacy was kept bilateral and both sides kept the process confidential.

Our crystal balls should not have obscured that Bangladesh was inevitably in the womb of time after partition in 1947. When the political configuration changed dramatically, we found that we had ourselves constricted our options. The irony is that the rationale of bringing a guaranteed amount of water upstream of Farakka from the Brahmaputra (India's proposal) or storages in Nepal (Bangla Desh's proposal) to enable traditional flow was really unrealistic. Since I inherited it, I dutifully advanced the idea of the link canal, but I always knew it was a non-starter. So was bringing water from storage through the parched, highly populated provinces of India. It was also really too much to expect consent even in the Mujib period for such an inter-basin transfer, which would bifurcate a young over-populated country. Moreover, it was always unlikely that Nepal could agree to the Bangladesh proposal.

But the distant vision should not have been abandoned. It offered advantages—ethical and economic—of raising the living standards of the entire region. It would have given maximum benefit to all the peoples and would have been in the spirit of Helsinki principles and the UN Convention on Water (1977). Hydel projects in Nepal would remove the curse of poverty and, incidentally, moderate the prevailing insurgency, but whatever is surplus—and there could be tens of thousands of megawatts of power—could have helped the present demand for power in India, and also made Nepal rich. In my view also, India should overcome its hesitation over the navigational canal through the Siliguri gap in India so that some part of Nepal's seaborne trade could go through Chittagong or other Bangladesh ports. In other words, there must finally be an end to decades of politics based on self-destructive nationalism. The India-Pakistan Accord of January 2004 may justify our dreaming again after sixty years of suicidal myopia.

All this would be in the spirit of cooperation envisaged by the SAARC and SAPTA declarations, where all partners, directly or indirectly, depend on the Himalaya and the monsoon. Salman and Uprety urge conflict resolution and cooperation through treaties. They do not mention that SAARC was born at the initiative of Bangladesh because the latter suspected the propensity—justified or not—of hegemonism on the part of India. The crunch is not despair, but greater confidence in purposeful diplomacy. In the early years, India was looked upon as the spokesman for all nationalisms but in fact we alienated all our neighbours. India has failed in recognizing that it is central to the entire region; its very size is its diplomatic handicap.

South Asia as a whole has turned a blind eye on the opportunity costs of delay in optimizing the use of their separate and interlinked water resources. It seems to me that with the new century, we may be on the threshold of a new beginning. The twenty-first century will be the century of technologically determined processes. Increase in state power and organized militarism will confront (and be baffled by) the power of defiance of the people in the quest for greater social justice. Diplomacy is now throbbing with a sense of equality and wanting a fairer share of progress out of globalization and interdependence. As George Verghese concludes in his *Waters of Hope*, it is a time for statesmanship. Or, as Ramaswamy and Rangachari forthrightly put it, Bangladesh cannot be treated as a 'residuary' water taker; its right to a legitimate share of common rivers will have to be recognized. Bangladesh on the other hand cannot lay claim to the historic flows as a matter of unqualified right; it will have to accept the needs of the large upstream population of India.

Consistent with the spirit of the UN convention, the final message must be that even in the narrowest possible definition of national interest, there is no alternative but to equitably determine the sharing of international waterways through international cooperation. Power and coercion must be subordinated to the beneficial advantages of near and distant neighbour not only now but also in the future.

CHAPTER 7

Diplomacy between Landlocked and Unequal Countries

Separating Transit and Trade with Nepal – 1978

HISTORICAL AND POLITICAL BACKDROP

In September 2004, Nepal looks like another failed state; unlike Vietnam, Kampuchea, and Laos, it is cascading to instability with inevitable deterioration of its economy and the welfare of its hard working people. Without any exception, no two countries have such permanent common interests—strategic, economic and cultural—as have India and Nepal. This inter-dependence was evident through the millennia, but Nepal has never been formally a part of India. A standstill agreement was concluded prior to the transfer of power in India, but the Treaty of Friendship was only signed on 31 July 1950. It does not specify any limit of time that implicitly embodies confidence in the permanent identity of interests between the two countries. Although the leaders of the Nepalese Congress like B.P. Koirala had participated in India's own struggle for independence and were deeply hostile to the dominant feudal dispensation in Nepal and were also committed to democratization as in India, the treaty was signed with Mohan Shamsher Jung Bahadur, the Prime Minister of the non-representative Rana oligarchy and the Indian Ambassador, C.P.N. Singh. In effect, India disregarded the nature of the regime and pledged official dealings with the government in effective control of Nepal. Sardar Vallabhbhai Patel, the Deputy Prime Minister and the Minister of Home Affairs in charge of the 'States', had wanted Nepal, Bhutan, and Sikkim to also accede to the Indian Union, but Nehru firmly respected their distinct identity. The responsibility for these States was with the External Affairs Department and under Nehru's charge and not the old Political Department which became the Department/Ministry of States. (Considering how the USSR splintered and the Warsaw Pact disintegrated, I, for one, am glad that the distinct national identities were respected and the Nehru view prevailed.) None of these States were included in the Constitution of India, not even Sikkim which had been a member of the Chamber of Princes. For Nehru, to integrate these states was too much like imperialism continuing in the post-colonial age. It is a rare example of the fundamental principle of equality of nations and non-interference on which the Law of Nations is based.

Nehru was, however, fully conscious that geography ultimately mattered and that the high Himalayan range—the most imposing natural frontier in the world—ran to the north of Nepal, Bhutan, and Sikkim, so that they were indissolubly linked with India. The Himalaya, in fact, forms a barrier for the monsoon clouds and the waters of most rivers and rivulets flow southward; environmentally these are thus indissolubly linked to the India-Gangetic plains. No doubt there was an ethnic and cultural transition zone along the Himalayas. Tibetan theocracy, for example, had monasteries and pockets of influence south of the Himalayan watershed but Nepal belonged to the Indian civilization. For most Nepalese, Hindu shrines were pilgrimages for worship and the banks of the Ganga was the preferred place for the last rites. While culturally, economically and spiritually Nepal looked southward, there was an understated incipient sense of political separation from India. The oligarchy of Rana rule in Nepal was content to accept that independent Nepal would have no external connections except with British India. In effect, Nepal was under British paramountcy, as were the princely states of India. For a long time, the British representative in Kathmandu was called the British Resident as in the princely states of India. This was upgraded to Minister Plenipotentiary and finally to Ambassador with the transfer of power in India.

The fuller aspiration of exercising latitude and discretion as an independent country was bound to arise once British control over the subcontinent and Tibet put imperialism on the retreat.

The anomaly of the introverted and restricted 'independence' of Rana rule also got unexpectedly exposed after King Tribhuvan broke out of his royal impotence in decision-making and took refuge in the Indian Embassy, from where he was taken to Delhi. Gyanendra, an infant grandson of king Tribhuvan was put on the throne by the Rana oligarchy but this was not recognized by India or any country. In 1951, after India's mediation, the King was restored to his throne and effective power. While an Indian Embassy was established—indeed took over the British residence as it was paid from Indian revenues—the British policy of not allowing China or any third country to establish a diplomatic or consular mission in Kathmandu continued. India saw it as its duty and interest to help and guide Nepal to modernization and progressive democratization. It is not always remembered in Nepal that it was India who encouraged breaking the imposed (and seemingly cherished) isolation of Nepal and financed the construction of the Tribhuvan Rajpath and Gaucher Airfield.

NEAR BLIND TRUST IN INDIA, 1951-1959

The confidence that Nepal was safe in calibrated modernization under India's guidance was brutally shaken only a few months after the India-Nepal Treaty was concluded. In October 1950, the People's Liberation Army marched and occupied Tibet. The strategic anxiety in Nepal, though muted, of Communism just across the Himalaya was patent but it was universally felt by the cognoscenti in Kathmandu that India provided the assurance of contingent defence. At the back of every Nepalese mind it is ingrained that in the final crunch, it is in India's interest to help preserve the faith and traditional personality of Nepal.

Nehru in theory believed that all nations have the inherent right to their own destiny, but he took for granted that independent Nepal was so much a part of Indian civilization that it would see its own best long-term future in never offending or harming India. What was good for India, he assumed, must be perceived as in the best interest of Nepal.

When British imperialism held sway directly or indirectly over much of Asia, Tibet was almost detached from China. The fiction obtained in Simla in 1914 at the tripartite conference of India, China and Tibet as equal participants with the British Indian Foreign Secretary Sir Henry MacMahon presiding was of Chinese suzerainty subject to the autonomy of Tibet. But this was only to keep Czarist imperialism away. After the Manchu Empire collapsed in 1911 and the Chinese Amban was obliged to withdraw, the Dalai Lama's government was virtually independent of China. Indeed, it was so independent that the Regency Council even refused transit passage of military hardware through Tibet for the defence of China, then fighting the Japanese. Nepal was in fact a safe and effective sub-buffer for British policies.

The defanging of the internal Rana oligarchy in Nepal and the military re-conquest of Tibet by the People's Liberation Army of China occurred simultaneously and this laid the seeds of complications as well as opportunities for India-Nepal diplomacy. We were slow to recognize that though Nepal subconsciously believed that its destiny and defence were linked with India, we underestimated the rise of political consciousness within Nepal. We failed to note the offence given by attitudes of overlordship in Indian diplomatic and expert-level behaviour which provoked the suspicions that contrary to statements and concrete gestures, India perceived itself as the successor to British imperialism in the subcontinent and genuinely believed that they knew better what was best for Nepal. After the King's return to the capital, C.P.N. Singh behaved more like a Viceroy than an envoy. He arbitrarily chose M.P. Koirala (rather than the better respected brother B.P.) to head an interim government in Kathmandu. Singh was succeeded by a senior ICS officer, B.G. Gokhale, who was diplomatically more correct and worked only through an Advisory Council on political and developmental restructuring. Bhagwan Sahay who followed was sagaciously active but tactful, and was able to persuade King Mahendra (who succeeded Tribhuvan in 1955) to approve the devolution of power to a democracy with his own position modelled on the British constitutional monarchy.

India's focus on development was assumed to be primarily Indo-centric. The project for flood control measures located in the Nepal's tarai hills on the Kosi and the Gandak rivers (which annually wrought havoc in Bihar) were blue-printed in

India without sufficient deference to the extent of submergence and damage in Nepal. The Nepalese, with no engineering expertise of their own, presumed on the enlightened motivation of India. Our engineers and administrators however ignored that the irrigation benefits for Nepal were minimal compared to the substantial advantages in flood control and extension of irrigation acreage in India. In the Indian decision-making process, the political aspects were never fully studied in External Affairs and never at a higher, much less at the political, level. It was not anticipated that it would be interpreted as the insensitivity of 'Big Brother' and would cast dark shadow on future cooperation with Nepal for decades.

The elections held in 1959 under the new Constitution gave a two-thirds majority to the Nepali Congress. King Mahendra was taken aback by this result. He had expected a splintered political spectrum, leaving the Palace to continue to play an active arbitral role. Un-reconciled to the weakening of his monarchial authority by a democratically elected government, in December 1960 the King suspended the Constitution and put B.P. Koirala and others in prison. In a spontaneous, reaction, Prime Minister Nehru expressed regret in the Indian Parliament at the smothering of democracy in Nepal. He was in fact, going against his own normal inclination not to pass political judgement on the internal affairs of independent countries. Without full reflection, he was articulating the inbuilt conviction that orderly political evolution in Nepal was of special importance for India. (I have always felt that if the ministry had, as a matter of routine discipline, given the draft of statements—as we have done for all subsequent Prime Ministers—Nehru would not have let slip a sincere but nonetheless indiscreet judgement.) Anyway this open criticism gave a nasty jolt to King Mahendra which smouldered for years until the resentment was assuaged by the visit of Prime Minister Lal Bahadur Shastri in 1965.

NEPALI VARIANT OF NON-ALIGNMENT

Following the escape of the Dalai Lama from Lhasa in March 1959 and, in its wake, the unexpected crisis in India-China relations, Nepal faced a complex problem. There was an undercurrent of sympathy for the feelings of Tibetans. Many thousands arrived on the Nepalese frontier—some through Mustang and other difficult routes—and camped in Nepal. But it also provided an opportunity for the country to demonstrate its independence from India. Nepal continued to rely on India's economic support, but agreed to increase the involvement of China in its development. King Mahendra went on to enlarge the country's diplomatic contacts. While other countries including USSR, if only as a matter of courtesy, had kept India informed of developing relations with Nepal, China had kept secret its talks with Kathmandu representatives even in the period of friendship with India. A China-Nepal agreement was concluded in 1956, on the same lines as that of the Indian Agreement in 1954 pertaining to the relations with 'Tibet as a region of China'. The deliberate secrecy was an early indication that China did not accept the British-bequeathed *status quo*. After the India-China crisis in 1959, Nepal readily agreed to the Chinese offer to 'settle' the Tibet frontier. The Chinese wanted to show that they were reasonable and accommodating with all their other neighbours. India's problem was of course larger in area and, in any case, parliamentary opinion was shocked by the accusation that India was responsible for the widespread disaffection and revolt in Tibet. In fact, the Nepal-China agreement only confirmed that the Himalayas had been the traditional limit of Tibet and that the border based on geographic features evolved even without formal delimitation agreements having been concluded.

After the constitution was superseded, a Palace-dominated 'non-party' Panchayati Raj was established, which continued till 1990. As time went by, popular disaffection grew against this non-democratic dispensation. Finally in 1991 King Birendra restored multi-party democracy, himself withdrawing to the position of a constitutional monarch. Through the 1990s, different complexions of governments have been tried but until 2004 none established lasting credibility.

Since the 1950s, India and Nepal relations have gone through many phases. It was all but forgotten that it was India which spurred encouragement for the fuller exercise of Nepal's independence consciously repudiating the British imposed isolation. After helping King Tribhuvan's reassertion to power and the confirmation of shared military perspective and even in intelligence gathering, India sought to husband Nepal to modernization and democracy. India sponsored Nepal's membership of the UN and also its participation in the Afro-Asian conference in Bandung (1955). But even during the 1950s, there was muted protest at the appearance of limitations in the exercise of Nepal's own sovereignty. When Nepal's neutralist detachment in the deterioration of relations with China, caused surprise in India, particularly when some leaders almost rejoiced in embarrassing India.

Nepal has suffered a succession of setbacks; and some avoidable ones. Democracy was prematurely overthrown and the momentum of development became slow spasmodic, and selective. The 2002 regicide, when most of the Royal family was gunned down, resulted in the decline of traditional unity around the old notion of divinity associated with the monarchy. Diplomacy between Nepal and India while throughout aware that there were greater stakes of mutual benefit in their co-operation than between any other two countries, have oscillated between confidence and advertised show of differences. The failure of governance in Nepal must be traced largely to their own sovereign mistakes in decision-making but it was aggravated by India showing disrespect for Nepal. Nepal assumed reliance on military and economic strength but India overlooked the need for 'soft power', avoiding misperceptions and diplomacy of non-ulterior persuasion. We did not make allowances for the sense of humiliation or inferiority and dependence at being an India-locked small neighbour.

As at present, next door Nepal is seething with deep anti-Indianism in all its centres of political power. Even those who depend on remittances from India, or escape from the local economic disabilities by migrating southward, are not immune to the sense of grievance. Nearly two-thirds of the country is now under the Maoist shadow and seems beyond the pale of law and order. Recently the capital itself was blockaded, and trucks carrying essential supplies were not allowed to enter the Valley. In these decades there has been little development but on the other hand rampant deforestation to satisfy India's demand of timber. Nepal has become a mountain desert, Indian policy makers never fully realized that being upstream, Nepal held India's own progress in the Gangetic states to ransom by the simple device of non-development and deforestation.

Nepal's near chaos was also aggravated by a near half-a-century of imitative hypnosis from the international bipolarity of the Cold War. Non-aligned detachment from the ideological and military confrontation between great powers, as first urged by India, was prophetic but instead of exertions for national development by disciplined domestic effort—which was its ultimate rationale—non-alignment frequently degenerated into flabby governance at home and reliance on competitive aid expectations internationally. The Cold War, in my long held view, was a gigantic folly and, at best, a needlessly protracted mutually reinforced paranoia. The present sorry state in most of Africa and much of Asia is that for some time it gave the poor and the weak countries of the Third World the temptation to play international politics and resort to easy punching above their own weight. After India-China relations deteriorated, unlike almost any other country, Nepal thought it had two strings to its diplomatic bow; it could take advantage not only of the East-West competition of communism versus anti-communism, but follow its own variant of being 'non-aligned' between two estranged neighbours and, imitating India, to supplement aid claims and get support from these regional antagonisms.

THE RISE OF ANTI-INDIANISM

The very dependence on India had provoked the ingredient of Nepalese assertives in the nationalism in 1950s. The 1960s was a period of maturing to awareness of its full independence as a sovereign state and its rights under international law as a land-locked country. As a Member of the United Nations General Assembly with permanent representation in New York and Geneva, the Nepalese diplomats rubbed shoulders on terms of equality with all member nations and could learn from the experience of other similarly handicapped countries. Nepalese scholars within Nepal, and many who availed of opportunities to study abroad became experts on the privileges of other land-locked countries. India, which had crusaded for the right of self-determination and equality for all countries in decision-making, was seen as obstructive of the same principle. The right of landlocked countries had come up directly when international fora had protracted discussions on the Law of the Seas. By 1969-70, opinion was crystallizing on a sort of 'alliance' between landlocked, and island nations, and the archipelago countries. The poorer landlocked countries got the support of the developed countries. This added to the confidence of Nepal. In due course after Mujib was killed Nepal developed sneaking affinities with Bangladesh. It became alive to the accusation of India's propensity of hegemonism. It joined other non-aligned countries including Pakistan in condemning Soviet intervention in Afghanistan (1980) when India under the Cold War logic had indulgently abstained. In doing so the *droit de limitrophe* advanced as defence by the Czechoslovak Communist government in supporting the Soviet sponsored Asian Security System implied that a big country had justification in intervening in a small country if the major power apprehended a threat to itself. This had somewhat frightening implications for Nepal. Nepal, of course, overlooked the very special privileges, unknown in international relations, that it enjoyed in India. Historical anomalies like Monaco aside, the fact is that no other country had such a non-reciprocal open border for goods and services including the option of military service as India provided to Nepal.

From 1960 to 1980 Nepal seized every possible occasion to wriggle away from the perceived straightjacket of being in a permanent dependent embrace with India and made deliberate efforts at diversifying its international linkages. By 1970 the resident diplomatic missions of many countries were already established in Kathmandu. Apart from being an advantageous observational perch from which to watch Tibet and China, most countries were basically interested in strengthening Nepal's domestic development and not necessarily in weakening India's pre-eminence. However, the presence of many Western embassies augmented Nepal's self-confidence and diluted the disproportionate cultural and economic dependence on India.

The PRC after rationalizing Nepal's old connection with Tibet took initiatives to balance the India connection, especially by agreeing to build the Kathmandu-Kodari Road. (It caused alarm when it was suspected that the bridges had the strength to bear the weight of medium and heavy tanks.) Amongst other projects, on Nepalese consent China took on development projects in the tarai bordering India. It made assiduous efforts to assuage entrenched fears of communism as a threat to Nepal's monarchy. The irony was that the royal palace in the only avowed Hindu kingdom came to apprehend less mischief from communist China than from the south. (We do not know if the so-called present-day Maoist movement and the official Communist Party of Nepal received only inspiration and surreptitious moral encouragement, or actual financial and material assistance, in diluting India's standing in Nepal.)

Indian diplomacy, at times, behaved as if Nepal had ultimately nowhere to go except rely on India's benevolence and so must willy-nilly acquiesce to our protection. Yet nations can assert their will to the point of suppressing their self-interest in order to demonstrate their independence. Sometimes, India showed punitive attitudes but the false suspicion aroused—which should have been professionally anticipated—became an embedded memory. For example, the well-intentioned assertion of India's 'special' relationship with Nepal was interpreted in the over-sensitive minds of the Nepalese, as signifying less than full respect for the concept of political equality. The rituals of friendship by periodic official visits including exchanges by heads of state, ministers, senior officials were of course maintained; every Chief of the Army Staff visited the other capital and the Indian chiefs were always bestowed with honorary ranks in the Nepalese Army. These had become routine and at times led to hypocritical semantics. For years, officially and more so non-officially, there has been a simmering demand to replace or amend the Treaty of Friendship of 1950 with one that would better reflect Nepal's independence, but thoughtful Nepalese officials realized that once negotiations were started, it could open a pandora's box on the freedom of movement, employment, and army recruitment. As far as I can tell, no consensus has emerged on how possible gains could be balanced by the inherent risks in re-opening negotiations.

In stressful anxieties or a burst of Nepalese nationalism, the deeper resentment come to the surface. Following the integration of Sikkim in the Indian Union, apprehensions were understandably aroused in Kathmandu. The local newspapers, some with inspired prompting, expressed confirmation of the hegemonistic propensities of India towards her immediate small neighbours: 'It is Sikkim today, Bhutan tomorrow and next it will be the turn of Nepal itself!' The fears were unwarranted but according to the Kathmandu gossip circle, the Indian Ambassador bluntly read the riot act to King Birendra himself, a sacrilegious offence in the minds of many Hindus as the occupant of the throne in Nepal was the Vishnu Avtar! It was in this sour mood that at the Algeria Summit of the Non-Aligned in 1973 King Birendra put forward a seemingly innocuous proposal of Nepal being recognized as a Zone of Peace. This barely concealed an anxiety about India's heavy hand disciplining of Nepal. Since Nepal has only two neighbours and since it was overwhelmingly connected by geography, religion, culture, social ties, military training, and many regimental connections with the southern neighbour, the suggestion unmistakably reflected worry about India's intentions. Predictably the Indian government and public opinion were outraged. The result was that political relations plummeted even though aid and economic relations continued.

II

This paper concentrates primarily on the problem of de-linking transit and trade between Nepal and India. The inherited position originated in history and geography and the difficulties were traceable to unequal size; old politics got catalysed by the non-comprehension of the evolution of twentieth-century nationalism.

Up to the 1950s, Nepal had no international sea-borne trade; Nepal's demands were met by British India which had links with banks and suppliers in London. Whatever requests for foreign luxuries were there—they really emanated from the royal family and the extended rich Rana oligarchy only—were purchased or ordered through agents and shops in India, mostly in Calcutta. In 1960, five years after Nepal joined the UN, a separate foreign exchange account for Nepal had been opened with the Reserve Bank of India. The 1961 Trade Agreement itself had recognized that Nepal had the freedom of independent exports and imports and that necessary transit facilities would be provided at Calcutta port for bonded transport to a point of entry in Nepal, but Trade and Transit were still under the common umbrella agreement. However, by the mid-1960s, Nepal had become aware that transit is the right of all land-locked countries and that this right does not change with the complexion of trade or freedom of employment and services with the surrounding countries or even if the two neighbours are in adversarial relations.

The problem of Trade and Transit between India and Nepal has virtually unparalleled complexity. The nearest parallel may be England and Scotland before the kingdoms were united in 1601 when the Stuart James VI of Scotland became James I of England. Like Scotland, Nepal has got accustomed to take 'the high road to the South as its noblest prospect' but Scotland has always refused to accept the position of being a satellite appendage of England. As with Scotland and Ireland, the Nepalese nationals (Gurkhas) came voluntarily to enlist in the British Indian Army regiments and were never treated as a 'Foreign Legion' or as mercenaries. The fact that some Gurkhas continued in the British Army by the Tripartite Agreement at the time of transfer of power, did not detract from the unusual features of the relationship between India and Nepal. After Nepal matured to awareness of its membership of the UN, the legal disability of Transit being linked to Trade was deemed a slur on Nepal's independence and sovereignty. The right to commerce, it was argued, was part of the wider process of political emancipation following the withdrawal of European imperialism, regardless of the benefit, that came from belonging to a common employment or currency market. Unlike other landlocked countries and partially similar to the relationship between Canada and the USA, even under the India-Nepal treaties of 1950, India continued to allow not only full freedom of movement but eligibility to persons of Nepalese birth or origin to all but its highest senior civil services. As India sought to develop industrially, it imposed a strict import substitution regime; as a consequence the freedom of transit in the 1961 Agreement and the open frontier provided an easy temptation to import goods, ostensibly for Nepal but with the obvious intention to smuggle them into the larger lucrative Indian market specially as such foreign products carried higher prices in India. The benefits of the economic freedom uniting India and Nepal (and Bhutan) justified providing for controls against process, which then was to sabotage of India's industrialization committed to a socialist pattern of society. Transit control of the quantity and nature of foreign goods, which may not be for domestic Nepalese consumption, gave India an inbuilt contingent leverage against the large-scale abuse of the porous border. In other words, the right to control the transit of goods was theoretically a method of ensuring that our 'generosity' was not abused. Once direct air service to Kathmandu covered destinations such as Hong Kong, Bangkok, and beyond, a vast number of electronic goods, clearly not intended for the domestic market of Nepal, were brought in—often by Indian merchants themselves—and then smuggled into India. It was patent that the quantum of goods being brought to Nepal far exceeded the needs of the Nepalese people. The Nepalese government was fully aware of this illicit trade; in fact it connived at the diversion by introducing a system of export voucher credits by which Nepal-based traders were allowed foreign exchange for goods of high value which were in demand in India. On the other side, for Nepal this hypothetical control on its international commerce symbolized an onerous and humiliating limitation on Nepal's right to determine its own trade and so was perceived as repugnant to its independence.

In the face of evidence of substantial leakage of India's import control policy, it was understandable that the Indian Commerce and Finance Ministries, particularly the divisions dealing with customs and developmental policies, disapproved of conceding to Nepal the absolute freedom of transit brought in by 'Nepalese' importers. The demand for a separate Transit and Trade treaties had come up when eminent officers like K.B. Lall, H. Lal, and N.V. Alexander held the post of Commerce Secretaries in India. Though India had shown flexibility and generous accommodation in determining the schedule of primary products and even for Nepalese manufactured goods with substantial proportion of local value added, the Indian negotiators had remained firm in having an 'umbrella' agreement which covered trade, transit and commitment to control smuggling and unauthorized trade. The demand voiced in the 1960s turned into a deadlock in the 1970s; no new agreement could be negotiated in 1976 when the last composite treaty concluded in 1971 expired. The result was a sharpening in the undercurrent of hostility towards India.

The Ministry of External Affairs had taken a backseat in trade negotiations. If I remember correctly, even our Ambassadors in Kathmandu were not strident in support of the Nepalese political resentment. We possessed irrefutable evidence of high demand products being imported into Nepal and intelligence confirming that smuggling into India was being systematically planned. Stainless steel sheeting was imported in bulk in large quantities, and hammered into pots, pans and trunks in little factories just across India-Nepalese border, obviously for sale in the Indian market. I remember evidence (possibly exaggerated) was furnished that more zipper strips were imported than virtually the total population of Nepal.

Since I started reflecting on the broad foreign policy for India, it had long been my conviction that given our size, resources, and economic potential, the real challenge was to gain recognition that the exercise of power by India was principled; this *inter alia*, implied continuing to stand for the liberation and equality of all nations. The litmus test of respect was not just support for the liberation of Africa and colonized islands, but whether we enjoyed the trust of our immediate South Asian neighbours. However, in Indira Gandhi's mind was embedded the notion that Nepal was not being sensitive to Indian interests. She recalled being embarrassed in the international fora by the demand that India accept Nepal as a Zone of Peace. She felt that Nepal was making a mockery of the Treaty of 1950. The very fact that China endorsed the idea of Nepal being accepted as a 'Zone of Peace' lent credence to the suspicion that it was an anti-Indian conspiracy. The Indian Prime Minster was also irritated at the Palace-inspired criticism of the integration of Sikkim in the Indian Union. Anyway, she was not prepared to agree to the renewal of the Trade Agreement if Nepal insisted on de-linking the freedom/right of transit across India.

When I became Foreign Secretary, I could sense that India-Nepal relations were riddled with deep, expressed and unexpressed prejudice and resentment. (The shadow of Kosi and Gandak agreements and the harm they did in Nepal was not forgotten. Nepal had overlooked the fact that the India financed projects had also benefitted Nepal but the suspicion persisted that India's motivation was primarily selfish and exploitative.) Indian official attitude was not seen in Nepal as proof of well-intentioned commitment to ensure the economic development of the country. No real progress on Karnali Hydel Project had taken place since 1960s and, the Nepal's immense power potential would benefit to both countries in Pancheshwar had remained stalled even after feasibility studies had been completed.

Theoretically to effectively control smuggling into India, a customs cordon was needed all along Nepal's southern border but this would not only be vastly expensive but was likely to be ineffective and lead to the alienation of the two countries. It would require the deployment of atleast para-military forces over 700 miles of the common border. More than that, such an installation would summarily abdicate the notion of Himalaya being the strategic frontier of the subcontinent. In a worst case scenario, I was told it would mean that six additional military divisions would have to be notionally ear-marked, if not deployed, to defend India's north Gangetic plains, which could eventually amount to the severing of the civililzation unity of India.

India's resistance to a separate Trade and Transit was interpreted as a slur on Nepal's sovereignty. This played to the advantage of the anti-Indian political elements, possibly encouraged by the Royal Palace itself. Indirectly it gave a gratuitous advantage to China for its low-key but purposeful diplomatic inroads into what the world had generally recognized was India's natural sphere of influence. In brief, the Indian refusal to allow the freedom of Transit gave additional ammunition to Nepalese nationalism, which over the years had already developed a propensity to suspect India. Nepal saw itself as being nearer to the abode of Shiva in Kailash but oppressed by the proximity of an independent Hindu majority India!

The atmosphere of bilateral relations improved after the Janata government led by Morarji Desai came to power in March 1977. In his first press conference, he promised that his government would continue the policy of 'genuine' Non-

Alignment. His qualifying adjective raised some eyebrows but his approach made clear that he would stand by the inherited policies, which for him coincided with morality and Gandhian commitment to peace. Vajpayee, who took over as Foreign Minister, on his official visit to Kathmandu, moderated the prevailing prejudice against India. Speaking in chaste Hindi, instead of referring to 'special' relations with Nepal, he appealed to the Hindu sentiments of his Kathmandu audience: 'In a land where every pebble (*kankar*) carries the image of Shankar and all rivers flow into the Ganga, how can there be anything but close trust and friendship?'

Having myself been involved in the comprehensive normalization of relations with Pakistan in 1976 and been a witness to the crucial concession on the allocation of waters by Jagjivan Ram and having as a follow up hammered the agreement on Farakka in October 1977 and accompanied Foreign Minister A.B. Vajpayee to Pakistan in February 1978 and having been witness to the historic transformation of climate in that country, I strongly believed our policy goals would remain incomplete if Nepalese distrust of India continued.

As hinted earlier, the resistance to de-bracketing Trade and Transit had emanated from the Finance and Commerce Ministries. It was well-grounded in reason. However, considering our consistent sympathy for the least developed and landlocked countries and with the special political importance of Nepal for India this question had an over-riding importance. I decided to explain the pros and cons to Prime Minister Morarji Desai underlining that restoring mutual confidence in our relations with Nepal was absolutely vital; it was 'immoral' for us to appear to be placing limitations on Nepal's sovereign discretion in trade just because we did not, or perhaps could not, take effective measures to control smuggling into India. Foreign Minister Vajpayee and Prime Minister Desai saw the logic that conceding in principle to Nepal's demand of a separate right of Transit was expedient if for no other reason than to preserve the long-term strategic identity and civilizational personality of the Indian subcontinent.

Our Ambassador in Kathmandu in 1978 had established a reputation of friendliness and bon homie with the Nepalese hierarchy but he too had not recommended the liberalization of our leverage against smuggling. As it happened, Ambassador Kirti Nath Jha of Nepal on his farewell call on Prime Minister Desai politely mentioned that Nepalese public opinion wanted two treaties instead of one. This reinforced my plea. The Prime Minister responding positively said that the climate of relations should reflect India-Nepal interdependence and friendship.

We, in the Ministry of External Affairs, prepared a Cabinet paper and, if I remember correctly, marked it 'urgent'. It was duly circulated in accordance with the usual procedures. When it came up, it invoked heated discussions in the Cabinet Committee. The Finance Minister H.M. Patel (himself a retired distinguished civil servant), no doubt influenced by his departmental brief, felt that it would be naive to give discretion to Nepal to subvert India's economic policies. Surrendering the right of control of transit would mean abdicating the leverage which was built into the composite treaty that, in return for the open border, Nepal should respect India's policy goals. He pointed to evidence that these were being systematically flouted. Normally Civil servants, even when authorized to be present at Cabinet meetings, are expected to keep silent in the discussions unless some information was sought. When, however, the Finance Minister stated that according to his departmental estimates, the total value of smuggling from Nepal into India crossed Rs. 10 crore annually, I made bold to interject that, despite intervening Arabian Sea, the constant patrol by Naval Coast Guard, intercepting dhows and a whole string of customs posts along major and minor ports on our west coast, the rough estimates of smuggling of high value products from Dubai annually exceeded the figure of Rs. 10 crore. The composite Trade Agreement had not, in fact, inhibited the smuggling of scarcity goods into India. We had no comparable strategic or political stakes in the Gulf. Smuggling from Nepal must be seen as an unorthodox method for Nepal to earn rupees to pay at least partly for Rs. 300-500 crore worth of goods imported from India for Nepal's internal consumption. Indeed, to cover the rupee shortages, Nepal had even 'sold' convertible foreign exchange earned from tourism. Not by a composite treaty but by establishing customs posts every few miles and exercising vigilance along obscure pathways and hundreds of rivulets could we significantly reduce illicit trade across the

India-Nepal boundary. The dilution of our import regulations because of the diversion, with Nepal acting as an intermediary was really minimal when compared to the cost of the customs posts, and the contingent implications for the defence of India. Moreover, the electronic goods were frequently smuggled into India, were only meeting the unsuppressed demand beyond the allowance given to incoming travellers from foreign countries. The logic of economic damage was, in effect, very small compared to the political stakes, now bordering on barely suppressed hostility towards India. The latter was jeopardizing our ancient cultural, economic, and strategic interdependence. I submitted that India's recognition of Nepal's independence must not be seen as qualified as it was by British India. On the other hand, India must be seen to be unilaterally generous and full-throated as a friend of independent Nepal. I also mentioned that in 1955 when Pakistan obstructed the trade of Afghanistan through Karachi (because the latter had demanded Pakhtunistan) India had taken the position that transit rights of landlocked countries should not be politically interrupted. My intervention struck home and I am glad it carried the approval of the Prime Minister and the Cabinet Committee. It was agreed that we could negotiate separate Trade and Transit treaties with Nepal. I was authorised to lead the delegation. This gave us a chance to overcome a complaint that had simmered since the 1960s and turned into a deadlock in the 1970s.

The comprehensive treaty of Trade and Transit concluded in Kathmandu in 1971 was signed by L.N. Misra as Minister for Foreign Trade of India and by Navraj Sybedi as Minister of Industry and Commerce of Nepal but it was negotiated by the Commerce Secretary. In March 1978 however representatives of all the concerned ministries including commerce had accompanied me as leader of the delegation. Udayan Bhatt, the Foreign Secretary was my opposite number. We negotiated for three long days. There were some hurdles and problems to be overcome; some semantic and some substantive compromises were made by both sides. Apart from separate treaties, the Nepalese would have preferred that there should be no time limit prescribed for the Transit Treaty. Moreover the Nepalese wanted the *right* of Transit to be embodied but we had reservations that in possible security scenarios, India may be justified in exercising control on what went to Nepal. The important concession we made was to meet the basic Nepalese concern of cosmetically de-linking Trade from Transit; while the former was made valid for five years only—the usual limit—the duration of the latter was stipulated as seven years. This eventually satisfied the Nepalese negotiators. (They would have preferred that even if it was not permanent, the duration of the Transit agreement were for a longer period.) We agreed to the *freedom* instead of the *right* of transit. A third document (not called a Treaty but an Agreement) pledged that Nepal would take effective steps to control smuggling into India; in effect to restrict the illicit trade that violated our customs tariffs. We, of course, knew of their inability, if not reluctance, to do so effectively but, even so, the Agreement provided a commitment to exercise restraint.[1]

During the course of the discussions, I emphasized that India wanted Nepal to industrialize and develop independent economic viability. I had obtained the prior approval of George Fernandes, then Minister of Industry, to reduce the percentage of raw materials, labour and value-added contribution in Nepal from 90 per cent to 80 per cent in order to allow duty-free entry of Nepalese products into India. The number of agreed points to facilitate mutual trade was increased to fifteen and these were accepted as points of transhipment from one part of Nepal to another. These were all transparent improvements, which restored the damaged credibility of India.

In point of reality, as compared to the previous composite Treaty, the scope of the three documents put together—the separate Treaties of Transit and Trade and the Agreement to Control Illegal Trade—the difference was only cosmetic and

[1]Though the negotiations were conducted and the main treaty signed by me, in the published compilation brought out in 1997 by MEA (vol. 10) there is pointed omission of my name and that of Udayan Bhatt, Foreign Secretary of Nepal. I assume this was bureaucratic pettiness and jealousy but a needless distraction of the merited credit to the late Udayan Bhatt. The Protocol and the Trade Agreement and annexure are printed as concluded by Mohan Dharia, Minister of Commerce of India and Pitamber Dhoj Khati, Minister for Commerce and Industry of HMG of Nepal.

not much in substance. However, the psychological transformation in the political climate of relations was tangible. I was told that for the first time, India was treating Nepal as equal and sovereign as did Germany, Italy and France, which provided transit facilities for trade for neutral landlocked Switzerland even in wartime. I was received by HM King Birendra who thanked me profusely. The idea of Nepal being internationally recognized as a Zone of Peace was never again reiterated.

I was myself unhappy with some items on the list of goods permitted for import which included forest produce. Amongst the primary products eligible for preferential treatment included timber, which reflected the demands of the Indian Railways for sleepers and by the Indian furniture-makers. This amounted to Indian encouragement of deforestation in Nepal, which eventually would lead to erosion and downstream floods in the tributaries of the Ganga. The trade items were, however, all specified by the Commerce Ministry. The minister also unilaterally announced that the annual review would remain the responsibility of the respective Commerce and Trade Ministries (the implication was that the MEA would have no say).

As stated, notwithstanding the separate agreement, there was no significant increase or decrease in the 'illegal trade' until many years later when our own imports were liberalized and industrial capacity diversified. However, Nepalese public satisfaction with the freedom of transit was immense and palpable. I greatly cherish the photograph taken in 1992 in which I stand linking arms with Agha Shahi (Pakistan), Udayan Bhatt (Nepal) and Abbas (Bangladesh), all of whom had been my negotiating opposite numbers on separate issues. I was hoping that in the changed climate in Kathmandu, we may be able to make progress in obtaining the consent of Nepal for an agreement to go ahead on the hydel project on Karnali, which had been on the anvil for years. The delay was, at least in part, because of unwarranted prejudice and suspicions of India. Both President Carter and Prime Minister Callaghan, during their respective visits, had shown interest in financing Karnali as was done in the final settlement of the Indus waters dispute in 1960. The estimated potential of the Karnali Hydel Project was 4,500

MV at that time. Of course, it required further studies, specially against the danger of earthquakes in the fragile Himalayas, but the potential that one project could provide power equal to the then total electricity consumption of the state of UP with a population of 100 million was mind-boggling. (Since then with technological sophistication, the potential has, I am told, been increased to 12,500 MV.) The power and revenue forfeited must run into trillions of rupees. If the Karnali project had been completed by say 1990, if might have quadrupled the per capita income of the Nepalese and correspondingly reduced poverty in the adjoining impoverished states of UP and Bihar. (The sale of surplus power from Chuka has transformed the economy of Bhutan and its per capita income is at least triple that of Nepal, Bangladesh, and India). To this day India gets no surplus power from Nepal when the estimated proven potential may be between 85,000 and 1,50,000 MV of renewable energy.

The signing of the two separate treaties and an agreement against smuggling was not the end of the story on trade and transit with Nepal. Long after I had retired, by contrived manipulation, the Trade and Transit Treaties of 1978 were both made to expire simultaneously in 1989 and at least hypothetically we reverted to the pre-1961 position. The transit points mentioned in the Trade Agreement were closed and Nepal, was for a while, virtually blockaded. This enhanced the importance of the Kathmandu-Kodari Road and the appeal of China. (Later in contravention of the 1950 treaty, the road was used to bring an anti-aircraft battery from China through Tibet.) In 1989 India proposed that we revert to one composite treaty. There was diplomatic and public contention that landlocked countries are normally only entitled to one point of transit and so by conceding two points, India was being doubly generous! The government of Rajiv Gandhi was not re-elected in 1989 and the V.P. Singh government, which followed, with I.K. Gujral as Foreign Minister, restored the earlier number of transit points.

I do not have firsthand knowledge of the developments after I retired, but have maintained a distant interest in international politics from the Indian perspective. However, after the repudiation of what I thought was a successful effort at regaining mutual confidence in 1978, the developments in the late 1980s struck me as retrograde with serious adverse consequences. I wrote an anguished article in 1989 in the *Hindustan Times* that the two countries seemed to have a worm's eyeview of their national futures. Since 1989,[2] even after some improvements under Gujral's more enlightened approach, Nepal's internal political and economic situation has continued to deteriorate. The legacy of the 1960s and early 1970s has diluted Nepal's confidence in India. Multi-party democracy revived in 1991 but no government has stabilized. Even though, India is now diplomatically more suave and continues to be economically responsive, the anti-Indian suspicions have become so deeply ingraind that the positive gains (or rather the negative consequences of drift) have developed a strong constituency.

In 1996 there was a moment of hope when, after protracted and patient negotiations, the Mahakali Agreement was concluded. The credit must go to Salman Haider, the then Foreign Secretary and K.V. Rajan, the Indian Ambassador in Kathmandu. That agreement has, unfortunately, run into difficulties of implementation. Any progress on river related international projects now requires a two-thirds majority approval of the Nepalese Parliament. As mentioned earlier, in 2002, in a tragic episode King Birendra and many of his family were gunned down apparently in a burst of personal anger by the Crown Prince who later also shot himself. King Gyanendra has been crowned but he has yet to carve a policy to overcome the bleak situation overwhelming Nepal. With Maoists besieging Kathmandu the question being asked is whether monarchy has any future in Nepal anymore?

The focus of this paper was the 1978 negotiations where a gridlocked situation was overcome through diplomacy. Some lessons, however, can be distilled to rejuvenate India-Nepal relations to avoid the kind of mistakes which scarred our relations. In the twentieth and the present century military or coercive politics through sanctions or blockades—even when equations are unequal in size or strength—only end in

[2]See J.S. Mehta, *Rescuing the Future: Penalties of Misperceptions*, New Delhi: Manohar (forthcoming).

aggravated antagonism. Big countries like India can wield the big stick, but small countries like Nepal can frustrate punitive manoeuvres by adopting tactics that may become self-destructive but could also harm the big country. At the back of many Indian minds is the idea of a military attack by China on Nepal after which all hesitation and artificial hostility would be forgotten and Nepal would fall back into Indian embrace. In my own view, expressed in writing in 1965, soon after I received ultimata in Peking, the repetition of 1962 (or any variant like militarily overwhelming Nepal) is not likely. The more likely scenario is not military but political; there is no reason to force compliance or frustrate cooperation. Diplomatic experience shows that provocations are not forgotten; the sense of affront and bitterness remains to poison the future. Now suicidal terror has become the baffling weapon of the weak against organized societies and uniformed armies.

SAARC was born out of the sense of solidarity and an exaggerated fear of the hegemonistic propensities of India. There are six countries wholly or largely dependent on India. In the case of the Trade and Transit question of Nepal, for ten years both countries disregarded the benefits of mutual economic cooperation and its opportunity costs was, damage to the genuine self-interest of India. There was an unspoken competition in self-righteousness which was repugnant to efficacious diplomacy. The notion of punitive capability as a way of enforcing cooperation and docility is less rewarding today. These are all sediments of the history of the pre-communication revolution, when diplomacy was confined to the elite. In the episode of the hijacking of IC 814 in 1999, we showed our anger by shutting down the IAC services to Kathmandu for three months ignoring the economic fallout. This was a sort of repetition of the earlier episodes of insensitivity to the nationalism of our politically aroused neighbour. The cross-border raids in 1961 to pressurize for the restitution of the democratic government of B.P. Koirala failed but this is totally forgotten in India but it remains embedded in the recesses of the Nepalese memory. The ill-conceived near blockade of Nepal in 1989 lasted for a few months and its memory is still fresh in Kathmandu. Incidentally, because the frontier is so porous, the adverse effect of the blockade was diluted by Gurkhas on leave or on demobilization and ordinary Nepalese carrying kerosene and coal as head loads.) It is possible, indeed likely, that in the IC hijacking of 1999, there was planned mischief by the ISI of Pakistan but it would have been more sagacious to restrain our reaction so that we did not confirm Nepal's suspicion of India's inclination to penalize the Nepalese people.

In 2005, the ultimate paradox is that India and Pakistan are now rationally exploring avenues of cooperation that will be beneficial to both countries. It would be the height of irony if Pakistan agrees to a transit pipeline of gas from Iran through Pakistan but we still make no progress on the enormous potential of renewable hydel power from the rivers of Nepal or fail to reach agreement to import gas from Bangladesh. Would it not be far better to have a prosperous Nepal sending its surplus to the power-thirsty Indian market, than our quibbling as to whether there will be intelligence mischief by the outside powers? After all, the waters and the electricity generated will remain in the region even if the USA, Australia, Japan, or Russia made financial investments in the projects as part of the globalization process. Nepal-India relations, I repeat, are an unmitigated tragedy and the tragedy is that neither Nepal nor India has raised its head sufficiently above the worm's eye view.

As initially stated, no two countries by geography and in their national interests and personalities have been so enmeshed. Nepal and north India can prosper substantially by trusting each other. This realization has never been absent and that makes it the more poignant. Discussions and seminars are full of half-truths, explanations, cover-ups, scapegoats, and the shifting of blame. Elsewhere even in this dire situation, I have made bold to make some concrete suggestions for Indo-Nepal complementary development.[3] We have had peaks of statesmanship; mutual confidence alternating with callous indifference and down-right punitiveness. The entire period

[3]See 'Policy Guidelines' for Track II Diplomacy (p. 58) in the Appendix II of the proceedings of seminar organized by Press Institute of India and B.P. Koirala India-Nepal Foundation in the monograph on Nepal entitled *Maoist Insurgency*.

has been riddled with misperceptions, inconsistency, and lack of a long distance vision. Without exception India-Nepal relations can be encapsulated as the worst case of bilateral diplomacy showing total obliviousness of the opportunity costs involved. But the failures have been on both sides and were avoidable. Future generations will never believe that India could have made such a mess of the era of emancipation in a country which could not be closer or have greater economic potential by steady trust.

It bears repetition: we must recognize that in the twenty-first century, the exercise of military and economic power based on disproportionate size and coercive attitudes brings about unexpected political nemesis. We see it in the frustration of the US-hyper power in Iraq and of mighty Russia in Chechnya. Paradoxically, success in our century—in the era of terrible military capabilities, instant communications and both economic and political globalization—is greater reliance on diplomacy, sensitivity, and treating nations with deference to their sovereignty regardless of how feeble or fragile they are. The benefits of globalization must of course be calibrated to national interests. Success in diplomatic negotiations only comes with governmental authorization but, we as professional advisers have a duty, in good time to volunteer methodology in the long-term national interest. In the case described, old deadlock was resolved but also impetuously reversed, leaving lasting resentment. The simple lesson is obvious: until the Himalaya get flattened and the rivers reverse their flow, India and Nepal can only prosper together.

CHAPTER 8

Some Unforgettable Diplomatic Contemporaries

Enough of recalling my personal experience of difficult on deadlocked negotiations which, largely by happenstance came my way. Diplomacy involves not only dealing with other countries but also intense human contacts with 'others'; name-dropping becomes second nature but some encounters make a lasting imprint even during normal diplomatic tenures. Even at the risk of appearing to bask in reflected glory, some colleagues deserve credit for their personal qualities. They not only lubricated official dealings and negotiations, but also facilitated long-lasting and much cherished friendships.

Unlike when ambassadors were accredited to monarchs, envoys in our times have little more than ceremonial relations with heads of state. Even with Prime Ministers and Foreign Ministers, one cannot generally talk freely or speculate intellectually. Anyway there are now too many ambassadors around to meet such dignitaries. In my limited experience, there were two exceptions. The first was Julius Nyerere of Tanzania who was President throughout my posting. The second was Marti Ahtisaari of Finland whom I met initially as an ambassadorial colleague, but 20 years later, he was elected as an unusually respected President of Finland. Both deserve special homage.

Julius Nyerere for all the years when he was President, came to work to the State House (the former Governor's residence), but throughout lived modestly in a small cottage on the beach. His developmental strategy of socialism, especially the collectivization of lands around Ujamaa villages to accelerate social progress, proved a disaster for agricultural productivity, but his integrity made him stand tall as an intellectual and moral giant—a veritable Nehru of Africa and a predecessor of Nelson

Mandela. Because of his enlightened leadership, Tanzania received more per capita aid from diverse rival and neutral donor nations than any other country. When I was in Dar-es-Salaam, the Chinese aid for the Tanzam railway, as a single project, was second only to the Soviet aid for the Aswan dam. In the 1960s in China's policy thrust, Africa was deemed 'Ripe for Revolution', presumably the Maoist variant. China was determined to out-compete not only Western Europe but also USSR, India and others in the help for the liberation from the legacy of European colonialism. India had a unique problem with 3,00,000 Asian residents in East Africa alone (not including South Africa, Mauritius and other countries) but Asians were seen as the instruments of British imperialism. They were particularly adversely affected in Tanzania by the takeover of houses and property. Our standard diplomatic approach was to recall the Asian contribution to the opening up to the monetary economy in the interior Africa. Nyerere knew I had served in China; this also put me at some further handicap. I seemed to have made him sit up when I told him that India's greatest asset was transparency; our democracy being flawed, the incompetence at hiding our failures became an asset. Tanzania could learn from India what mistakes not to make in development. The implication of 'Potemkin villages' being shown in China was not lost on him. Anyway it eventually led to a secret delegation, including some military officers in mufti coming to India when the country was mentally mortgaged to China. (I won't digress further on Indo-Tanzania economic cooperation but when I left, we had the largest deployment of Indian experts, and they were cherished and commanded respect because they were not supported by loans or aid from India, but paid for by the host country itself.) President Giri on a state visit insisted on visiting Nyerere's beach home and was surprised to see Rama's Sociology books on his reading desk. (Before we left, Nyerere invited her to come back and do a study on women in his country.) I was envied by great power colleagues when I became the only diplomatic envoy to be asked to visit Nyerere in Butiyama, his upcountry tribal village. Some time after I had been transferred, when he was touring Guyana in the Caribbean, Nyerere paid publicly a tribute to me and my wife as the best envoys he had come across. This was undeserved, but gratifying to the ego; obviously, not boasting had paid off in contrast to covert superiority in a humiliated continent.

We met Marti Ahtisaari and his simple charming wife when he represented Finland in Dar-es-Salaam. Since then he has been called upon to hold high posts in the UN Secretariat, oversee and superintend the transfer of power in Namibia, and do Peace-keeping for the OECD in the former Yugoslavia and Indonesia. In 1994 he was elected President, which office he held until the year 2000 during which Finland joined the European Union. He now presides over a Crisis Management Institute with headquarters in Helsinki, and his reputation for objectivity, and political sagacity is still unmatched. We had frequent frank conversations in New York. I felt flattered on being summoned when he visited Delhi and repeatedly referred to our old friendship in his addresses.

I never had similar relations with any other holding political office abroad but some other diplomatic colleagues seemed to combine the virtues of professionalism with deep human and social sensitivity and transparent integrity. One such couple was Sir Paul (later Lord) Gore-Booth who was the UK High Commissioner in India for five years (1960-5). He and Lady Gore-Booth were life-long Christian Scientists and never took modern medicine for any ailment. He visited Peking in 1965 as part of the preparation for his future policy responsibilities as Permanent Under Secretary in the British Foreign Office. Terence Garvey, the British Charge d'Affaires (also later High Commissioner in Delhi), took him along to one of those special performances arranged occasionally for the Diplomatic Corps where we were provided with headphones with simultaneous translations in English, French and Russian. On this occasion, under the title 'Blood on the River Congo', the theme was the Lumumba killing. It was a tirade of hate against the European Imperialism. Paul Gore-Booth was utterly shocked and volunteered to me that even at the height of India-China or Indo-Pakistan wars, there was less blood thirsty hate in India. I said to myself that China had gratuitously confirmed a friend for India. While he was Ambassador in Rangoon, he and Lady Gore-Booth became the God parents of Aung San Sue Ky with whom their bond grew stronger when her mother got posted as the Ambassador of Burma in Delhi. The Gore-Booths helped Sue through an Oxford education and to this day Lady Gore-Booth continues her concern for her even after her own and Sue's husband, Michael Aris, an eminent Tibetologist, passed away. I was struck how a stiff front old style professional and an aristocratic lady really concealed a truly compassionate heart.

Sir John Thomson, also a High Commissioner in Delhi and later Permanent Representative to the UN was another impressive British envoy. His father and grandfather and one cousin were Nobel Laureates but instead of science, John chose the diplomatic service. What impressed me was that John readily agreed to be the President of Friends of Seva Mandir in UK (Seva Mandir is an NGO in Udaipur with which I am currently connected.) Martin Ewans (later knighted) and Mary, whom I first met in Dar-es-Salaam was brought along by John as his deputy, presumably because I had become Foreign Secretary. Mary as Secretary of Friends of Seva Mandir, raised Rs. 10 crore for rural development in 400 villages around Udaipur. After retirement, Mary paid annual visits to Seva Mandir for 10 years until she was forbidden by her doctors to fly long distances. This kind of voluntary support was proof of social concern going well beyond professional association with India.

Karl Karstens, in my time in Bonn, was State Secretary of the Auswartiges Amt (German Foreign Office). I was only a number two and normally could not hope to befriend a State Secretary. (Later Karstens became the President of Federal Germany). My wife as a Sociologist became a friend of Mrs Karstens who, before, during and after her husband's official responsibilities, continued her active medical-social service in a village on the east bank of the Rhine near Bonn. This gave me access to her husband and it developed into a life-long friendship and offered me unmerited insights into decision-making during the Konrad Adenauer period. I recall also Count Ostrorog who in the 1950s represented France in Delhi for almost seven years and became a votary of cultural India. We had many fascinating evenings with visiting French intellectuals. The Ambassador hosted a small dinner for Malraux at which Prime Minister Nehru and Secretary-General N.R. Pillai were chief guests. Most of the conversation was in French. Rama got most embarrassed when Panditji asked her to interpret for him (He himself felt shy with his rusty command of the language). Nirad Chaudhuri and I were asked to check Malaraux's written message for the All India Radio which had been suggested by Nehru. Ambassador Jorgensen, his successor when I was Foreign Secretary, was professionally shrewd and friendly but his wife—also a graduate of one of the famous Paris Ecoles—continued to write under the *nom de-plume* of Rose Vincent. She visited our house in Udaipur; wrote a book on Women in Rajasthan. She wanted to call it Rama but my wife refused and so the book was called *Mohini*. It is dedicated to Rama whose name is bracketed along side a host of other Indian women's names. Later she wrote other books including on Pondicherry and still remains an Indophile.

Ambassador Rob and Mrs Lot van Shaik—like us also a husband and wife diplomatic couple (the latter is now Ambassador to the UNESCO)—from the Netherlands were exceptional in their professionalism. We overlapped as Fellows at Harvard. Sitting in New York as a 'consort in residence' under suspended lien with the Dutch Foreign Service, Lot became fluent in Chinese, while her husband was discharging ambassadorial duties accredited to the UN. Lot as she had hoped got a posting as Cultural Counseller in Peking when Rob retired and she resumed her career. Rob introduced me to Prince Klaus, the husband of Queen Beatrice, as the Prince had deep empathy for the Third World development. Even after retiring, Rob continues as Honorary Consul for Bhutan in the Netherlands. The story of Ambassador Helb, also of Netherlands, is illustrative of the occasional intellectual agony in diplomacy. From India, on promotion he was sent to Moscow. He was mortified on being declared *persona non grata* as a reciprocal measure when some Russian engineers defected during a trip to Amsterdam. After a long wait and frustrated hopes to return to Moscow, Ambassador Helb was finally sent to South Africa in what in the sixties must have been considered as a very senior and exceptionally sensitive post in the Dutch diplomatic network. He was personally anguished at the then South African official policy of Apartheid. According to his wife Dees Helb, he died prematurely because of deliberate debilitation and she really suspected it to be suicide at having to show Dutch indulgence to the conservative persons of Dutch origin. After being prematurely widowed, Dees Helb came to China and stayed with us rather than at the Netherlands Embassy. In fact she was our only guest during the three years in Peking. Even the Indian audit party refused to come when requested to 'inspect' our accounts as, after the India-China War, rumours had spread that even visitors could suffer insults and worse from the Chinese officialdom. This, of course, was not true.

Way back in 1955, Tikhvinsky, a Counseller of the Soviet Embassy in London, was the first Russian, who came to lunch with me at Dorchester Hotel without an accompanying interpreter. I guessed then that he must be well above KGB suspicions. Before long he was the head of the Research Institute on China; Vorontsov, the Soviet Ambassador, when I was Foreign Secretary, was the first Ambassador who came regularly without an interpreter but that was 20 years later. He became a good friend and entertained me lavishly, even after I had retired, while he was the Ambassador to the UN. He was the only Soviet envoy in my experience with whom one could let one's hair down and speculate on mistaken professional judgements and their unforeseen consequences.

Many American ambassadors in Delhi were exceptionally distinguished. We got to know some contemporaries including Daniel Patrick Moynihan (who was in the US Senate for twenty-four years, and bequeathed his safe seat to Hillary Clinton) and his wife Elizabeth (Liz), Chester and Steb Bowles, Ellsworth Bunker, Robert and Margaret Goheen were envoys during my postings at headquarters. (I did not have a long overlap professionally with the Galbraiths.) Moynihan had a tough time after the American tilt at the time of Bangladesh operations. After he left Delhi, at times unthinkingly, he embarrassed India. He revealed that the only political party funded by CIA was the Congress and that Mrs Gandhi had approved cooperation with CIA in a mountaineering expedition to install a device in the UP Himalayas to monitor Chinese nuclear explosions. But basically 'Pat' remained a great admirer of India's democracy. After our general elections following the Emergency in 1977, he famously pronounced to the US Senate that 'Overnight the numbers in the world who are ruled by democracy had doubled.' Liz is an authority on Babur and the Mughal Gardens and unearthed the 'lost' garden near Dholpur in 1978. Robert Goheen before he came to India was the youngest President of Princeton and the least flamboyant of all American envoys but he came to command great respect for his modest style in the political and academic circles in Delhi and still remains an activist friend of India. Bob Goheen's parents were missionaries in Maharashtra and so he had a special attachment to India and chose the post in Delhi when tapped by his friend Secretary of State Cyrus Vance with the offer of a diplomatic assignment in 1977.

Ellsworth Bunker, every inch an US East Coast patrician was, perhaps the most effective American envoy in India. He was not a career officer, but had served as Ambassador for 30 years and conducted diverse negotiations for eight successive American presidents, both Republicans and Democrats and so he was sanctioned a pension from the State Department normally earned by career officers only. At the height of the Cold War in the second-half of the 1950s, he managed to smoothly husband relations with India. It was during his tenure that President Eisenhower visited Delhi and got a reception, which out-trumped the public welcome accorded to President Tito in 1954, Bulganin and Khrushev in 1955 and Chou-en-Lai in 1956-7.

Ellsworth Bunker's second wife Carol Laise for 35 years was one of our closest personal friends. In my experience, without exception, she was the most active First Secretary I have ever seen on the diplomatic stage in Delhi or anywhere else. My family and I were invited to the most unique marriage in history when two serving Ambassadors got married. Carol was then Ambassador in Kathmandu and Ellsworth in Vietnam. To persuade Ellsworth to go to Saigon—already a can of worms—soon after his second marriage, Lyndon Johnson gave him the use of a special jet which could land on the small airstrip in Kathmandu and carry him or Carol back and forth for weekends. In those days, unreasoned suspicion of USA was rampant in India. Carol with her extensive reach was frequently suspected as an Intelligence Agent and because of our friendship, I was supposed to be her mole in the ministry. But then she was also friendly and liked by Mrs Indira Gandhi,

B.K. Nehru, Khushwant Singh, General Thimayya, Inder Malhotra (then of the *Times of India*), the late G.K. Reddy (of *The Hindu*), Ms. Mukherjee (the Secretary of AICC) and many others of diverse political affiliations. Carol was deeply interested and became head of the India desk, later Director-General of the Foreign Service, and made tireless efforts to grasp and promote India.

It is worth digressing that through the Cold War, intelligence organizations of all countries got bloated and were responsible for a series of terrible misjudgements. They gave no warnings of the assassination of Indiraji, Rajiv, Mujib, Daud and the Saur Revolution in Afghanistan nor recently of Kargil. Amongst the many costly gaffs, the CIA nearly doomed the Kennedy Presidency in the Bay of Pigs fiasco. The KGB record could not be any better; they must have been taken aback at the persistence of nationalism in Eastern Europe and the Baltic, and the demolition of the Berlin Wall. In any of the negotiations here described, I do not recall any constructive help from these unorthodox sources. At least some American Ambassadors did not conceal their near contempt for the over-extended and over-funded and completely non-accountable CIA. Some non career persons could publicly denounce the CIA as not an asset but as a menace to reasoned diplomacy. Let me recall incidents of these two famous anti-Intelligence and anti-Cold War envoys.

Chester and Steb Bowles and Kenneth and Catherine Galbraith made no secret of their indifference to CIA analysis and activities. The couples were straightforward friends of India and had better access to higher decision makers than any confidential contacts. Ken had authored thirty odd books in his own inimitable style which will remain compulsory reading on contemporary economic, social and political problems. He summarily sent away Rositski the CIA chief in the New Delhi Embassy. All the Mehtas have enjoyed the Galbraith hospitality and affectionate friendship for decades. Our daughter Vijay is treated like a daughter in their household. Kitty visited us even in Dar-es-Salaam. Her elegant luggage including her passport, a 5-year diary and travellers cheques worth thousands of dollars were pilfered from my car while we had taken her down in a special four-wheel wagon into the Ngorongoro crater to see the wild life. For three days, Kitty wore my daughter's *salwar-*

kurta while we got her new travel papers and re-equipped her but her precious diary was not found. My wife co-authored a book with Kitty Galbraith entitled *India Now and Through Time*. Both Ken and Chet were distressed when the Emergency was proclaimed in India but showed their affection for the country by their studied silence.

Chet Bowles was, one gathers, the first choice for the post of Secretary of State in 1961, to which Dean Rusk was eventually appointed. When in declining health with Parkinson's disease, Chet completely surprised me when he said that his most cherished last hope was to see democratic India 'take off' and, secondly, that India and the USA find their natural complementarity. I interjected and said, 'Surely Chet you are reversing your priorities'. I will never forget with unmistakable emphasis with which he asserted that the triumph of democracy in India was for him the most cherished fulfilment in world politics. It is not uncommon for envoys to become overly-attached to the country of their accreditation—we refer to it as *localitis*. This was true of many we sent to the Soviet Union and to pre-1962 War with China. There were others who started with such deep aversion to Pakistan that they showed professional non-objectivity and forgot that diplomacy must always try to be engaged in problem amelioration and conflict resolution. Chet Bowles was an unashamed liberal with open lifelong partiality for India, but such blatant reverse loyalty has probably no parallel in diplomacy. Bowles was, of course, respected and popular in India but his identification with India got so well-known even in the Kennedy administration that he got sidelined and his own political future in the US was adversely affected.

When Morarji Desai was paying an official visit to USA in 1978, at my suggestion that he might telephone the ailing Chet, he instantly decided to cancel all the official engagements for the day and flew from Washington to Groton and drove to Essex to greet him in his home. At the time of Clinton's visit in 2000, I made bold to suggest that we name a road in Delhi after Chester Bowles, but even after Foreign Minister Jaswant Singh endorsed the idea, the Delhi Municipal Corporation could not clear the procedural hurdles.

Madelaine Albright and I overlapped as 'scholars' in the

Woodrow Wilson Centre in Washington in 1981-2. It is only after some months that I realized she was the daughter of Ambassador Korbel of Czechoslovakia, the nominee on behalf of India on the UN Commission for India and Pakistan and whom I had met in 1948. Twenty years later, Madeleine was to be Secretary of State but at the time in 1982, she had no insights to supplement her father's book *Danger in Kashmir*. I treasure a copy inscribed 'To Jagat, my good friend and colleague. The world is indeed small that you and I should be working together – Madeleine.'

The Indian Ambassador who impressed me most as sagacious and effective (and alas not from our service) was Bhagwan Sahay. He was a distinguished member of the ICS, who served as Ambassador in Kathmandu. I had to attend on him from headquarters as a Deputy Secretary. After making his calls 'on the first floor' to the 'Bengali Babus' (referring half-affectionately to Subimal Dutt, Foreign Secretary and Bejoy Acharya, the Joint Secretary), he habitually used to come and lie down on my office sofa. He would then 'consult',—really think aloud on his strategy of how to husband relations with Nepal. Panditji respected him greatly. Nepal may never have adopted the democratic constitution in King Mahendra's time if Bhagwan Sahay had not been our envoy. If only he could have stayed two more years, the B.P. Koirala government might not have been summarily dismissed in 1960—atleast so I believe. Anyway, in my view, his departure began the slide in India-Nepal relations.

Amongst those who were my negotiating opposite numbers, I must acknowledge with genuine deference, the negotiating skills of Agha Shahi of Pakistan, the expertise of B.M. Abbas on international riparian problems (the 'embodiment' of Farakka) of Bangladesh and the understanding support of Udayan Bhatt, Foreign Secretary of Nepal. One of my most treasured souvenir photographs is with all these three negotiating adversaries and myself standing in a row with hands interlinked when all four of us found ourselves in our respective retirements attending the same seminar in Kathmandu in 1992.

But without doubt, the most intelligent, the most suave and the most polished professional diplomat and negotiator in my experience was Zhang-wen-Chin who led the Chinese team. He was then the Director of the First Asian Division but continued simultaneously to guide the negotiations with both Burma (Myanmar) and Nepal, while he himself was my opposite number for the entire second-half of 1960.

Zhang-wen-Chin disclosed to me, as perhaps to few, if any, non-Chinese, his own aristocratic Manchu lineage and that his grandfather was a Minister in Yuan-shi-Kai's Cabinet in 1911 and that his father, a banker, who until he died, long after PRC was established, remained an anti-Communist. But Zhang's own Communist credentials went back to the Long March, where he met his wife, Hang-Ying, a niece of Chou En-lai. Later I found a book entitled *The Last Chance in China* and discovered that Zhang himself was Chou's interpreter in Chunking (1943). It was after many months of daily meetings that he confessed to my blunt question that he knew English!

During the Cultural Revolution, Zhang came under strong attack by the 'Gang of Four' and the Red Guards but he was saved from a humiliating denunciation, if not a worse fate, by Chou En-lai dispatching him post-haste as Ambassador to Canada. When the Cultural Revolution was over, he was recalled and appointed Vice-Minister. He was nominated by Chou to secretly escort Henry Kissinger from Islamabad in July 1971. Chang helped to draft the famous Shanghai communiqué at the time of the Nixon's visit in 1972 and later shaped USA-China relations. Kissinger agreed with me that Zhang-wen-Chin was in the same mould as Chou En-lai himself. In 1982 he was appointed Ambassador to the United States and, as mentioned in the chapter on India-China, I called on him in 1983.

The 3,000-page verbatim printed record, still confidential, of the official meetings covering six months will testify that he was a formidable adversary. He was tough as nails across the negotiating table but even in patriotic zest, he appeared rational and self-confident enough to agree to semantic compromises which enabled us to finalize the report on the India-China Boundary Question. (At one stage I was really afraid we might not even have a common forwarding submission to be addressed to the two Prime Ministers.)

As mentioned in the chapter on China, it astonished the Governor and the establishment in Texas when without an official state level invitation Zhang-wen-Chin came to visit the

University of Texas in Austin. The Texas State government hurriedly offered their plane to bring him from Houston to Austin. The University and the LBJ Public Affairs School were also taken aback when the Chinese Ambassador agreed to speak on China's Foreign Policy. Furthermore, it created quite a stir when the Ambassador was found sitting in the podium with no one else except an old Indian diplomatic adversary and that too when India's own relations with the US were at best lukewarm. I could not help feeling some little inner satisfaction when Zhang paid a public tribute, perhaps undeserved, both to my personal qualities and my competence as the negotiating representative of India. I cherish that as an epitaph to my entire diplomatic career.

Zhang-wen-Chin, passed away a few years ago.

This memorabilia is intended as a tribute to the personalities of professionals one met only because one had the privilege to serve India in the Foreign Service. It vividly illustrates what binds the non-existent international guild of Foreign Service professionals. Diplomacy has to combine the commitment to serve one's national interests to the best of one's ability but in doing so, one must observe civilized norms of intra-personal human relations. In principle, we must always seek to promote understanding and peace amongst countries belonging to the family of nations. Intellectually we are paid to duel all day (and often late into the night) but we continue to toast each other's country after sundown. This is our daily ritual but it makes diplomacy a unique calling.

Index

Abbas, B.M. 28, 121, 228, 230-1, 234, 236-40, 245, 268, 283
Afghanistan 30-1, 53, 186-8, 193, 215, 257, 266; and India 186; Mujahideens of 186, 215; Saur revolution in 30, 184-5, 281; Soviet intervention in 215; US intervention in 215
Africa 123-6, 144-5, 160, 230, 256, 274-5
Africa, East 124, 127, 130, 275; Asians in 275
Africa, South 123, 275, 278; and Apartheid 278
Afro-Asian nations 58; anti-imperialism of 116; solidarity of 124
Afro-Asian Conference *see* Bandung Conference
Ahtisaari, Marti 274, 276
Aiyer, Mani Shanker 183
Akbar the Great 150
Aksai Chin 59, 73-5, 79-81, 89
Albright, Madelaine 282-3
Alexander, N.V. 261
Algiers 129, 160
Ali, Iftikar 154
Ali Mazuri 126
Allahabad University 151, 164; Students' Union of 151
America Atomic Commission 200
Amin, Idi 23, 25, 28, 34, 125-34, 136-9, 141-6; and King's African Rifles 132
Arab armies 126
Arab countries 162, 178
Arabian Sea 217, 265
Arunachal 36, 86
ASEAN nations 185
Asia, East 21
Asia, South 30, 53, 197, 220-1, 229, 232, 262
Asia, South-East 57, 113
Asians 124-9, 133, 144
Assam 71, 154, 238
Aswan Dam 275
Athens 234-5
Australia 50, 142, 148, 202, 272
Awami League 225
Ayub Khan, M. 69, 104, 158, 191; proposes joint defence of the subcontinent, but rejected by India 69

Babur 150, 280
Baburi Masjid, demolition of 148
Baghdad 183
Baglihar 217
Bahadur, Mohan Shamsher Jung 249
Bahuguna, H.N. 151
Bajpai, G.S. 58
Bajpai, K. Shanker 171, 175
Bajrang Dal 190, 194
Bandung Conference 57, 160, 255
Banerjee, P.K. 105
Bangkok 261
Bangladesh 24, 26, 28, 30, 34, 119, 143, 162, 189, 220-1, 225, 227-41, 257, 269, 272, 279, 283; crisis of 173; proclamation of independence of 163; treaty of friendship with India 226
Barnala, Surjit Singh 237
Bay of Bengal 220-1
Beas River 202, 223

Beijing 51, 119, *see also* Peking
Bengal, East 243; West 85
Berubari, India-Pakistan Agreement on 85; Supreme Court judgement over 85
Bhagirathi River 224, 226
Bhakra Nangal Dam 199, 223
Bhandarkar, Ashok 111
Bharatiya Janata Party (BJP) 190
Bhasani, Abdul Hamid 227
Bhat, Maqbul 174
Bhatt, Udayan 266-8, 283
Bhutan 21, 26, 30, 34-6, 38-9, 41-53, 63, 70, 75, 83, 86, 88-9, 197, 216, 220, 249-50, 259, 269, 278; British policy towards 36; and China 51; and Colombo Plan 50; Communist Party of 55; development in 49-50; member of Universal Postal Union(UPU) 50; and SAARC 53
Bhutto, Benazir 167, 188
Bhutto, Shah Nawaz 167
Bhutto, Z.A. 22, 25, 158-9, 162-5, 167-8, 172-4, 177, 179, 184, 207-11, 233
Bihar 252, 269
Birendra, King 254, 259, 268, 270
Black, Eugene 201, 215
Bombay 126, 151-3, 165, 172, 183; state 141
Bowles, Chester 279, 281-2
Brahmaputra River 64, 219-20, 223, 226, 238, 243, 246
Brezhnev, Lionid 181
Britain, Asians in 143; Labour government of 127; Queen of 144
British colonies, problems of Asians in 124; Empire 123, 126, 243; government 126, 128, 131-2, 145, 250-1, 254; imperialism 251-2, 275
Buddha, Gautam 35, 37, 43-4, 62
Buddhism, Mahayana 63
Bumla 21-3; Pass 63-4
Burma (Myanmar) 57, 86, 93, 99, 132, 277, 284

Cabinet (India) 81, 110, 265-6; Foreign Affairs Committee of 81, 246; Political Affairs Committee of 163
Cairo 234
Calcutta 123, 221-2, 243, 245, 259
Cambodia 58
Cambridge 18, 153; Majlis (Tagore Society) of 153
Camp David Accord 182
Canada 32, 128, 142, 202, 216, 223, 260, 284
Carter, Jimmy 182, 185, 215, 239, 268; administration of 184
CENTO 203
Ceylon 153
Chamber of Princes 167, 250
Chamberlain, Neville 115
Chang-wen-Chin 88-9, 91, 96-8, 113-14
Chaudhuri General 108
Chavan, Y.B. 140-1, 175, 180
Chechanya 14, 273
Chen Yi 78-9, 88
Chiang Kai-shek 99
Chicago Convention 162
China 15, 19, 21-2, 25, 27, 29, 31, 33-4, 38-40, 46, 48-9, 53, 56-8, 60-2, 65-9, 73-7, 79, 83, 85-6, 89, 91, 93-6, 101-5, 107-20, 140, 147, 157-60, 201, 251-2, 254-5, 257-8, 262-3, 269, 271, 275-6, 279, 282, 284; accusations against India 106-8; agreement with India 57-8; attack on Vietnam 113; and Barahoti discussion 60; and Bhutan 51; blames India for expansionist designs 68-9; Communist Party of 55-6; Cultural Revolution in 109, 118, 157, 284; Foreign Office of 156; ideological differences with India 57; and

nuclear explosions 279; People's Republic of 56, 59, 68; reaction to Dalai Lema's escape to India 67-8; and Tibet 94-5
Chou En-lai 21, 26, 37, 54-5, 57-8, 60-2, 67-9, 73, 75-84, 88, 92, 96, 99, 103-4, 106, 158-9, 280; on boundary dispute with India 78; signs condolence book on Nehru's death 106; visits to India 40, 57, 78
Chuka (Bhutan) 269
Chuka Hydel Project 50
Chungking 19, 55, 99, 284
Churchill, Winston 58
CIA 49, 63, 101, 186, 279, 281
Clinton, Bill 188, 282
Cold War 15, 64, 101, 119, 149, 184, 195, 207, 242, 256-7, 280-1
Columbia 216, 223
Colombo 162; Plan 50
Commonwealth 55, 126, 240; Prime Ministers' Conference 125
Communist Party of India (CPI) 109-10, 173, 180
Congress, Indian National 67, 75, 77, 149, 151, 153, 183, 185, 220, 235; and Muslim League 153

Dalai Lama 21, 37, 39, 41, 61-70, 72, 74, 252-3; differences with Cabinet (Kashag) 61; differences with Chinese authorities 61; escapes to India 62-7, 70; reception in India 67-70; and reaction of China 67-8; and tension in Lhasa 62; visits India 37
Dange, C.P. 110
Dar-es-Salaam 126, 130, 147, 275-7, 281
Darjeeling 36, 71, 235
Das, Bipin Pal 141-3
Deng-Hsio-Ping 30, 112-13, 118
Desai, Morarji 23, 28, 79, 178, 180-1, 184-5, 210, 215, 233, 235, 237, 245, 263-6, 282; visits USA 282
Deshmukh, C.D. 153
Dhaka 162, 226-8, 231-2, 235-7, 239-40, 243; Bhutanese mission in 51
Dhar, P.N. 169, 172
Dharia, Mohan 267
Dhoj Khati, Pitamber 267
Dorji, Jigme 42, 45; 50; assassination of 50
Dorji, Wangchuk 43, 46
Dubai 265
Dubey, Muchkund 239
Dutt, Subimal 23, 38, 82, 88, 283

Egypt 230
Eire, Republic of 148
Eisenhower, D.D. 280
Eklingji, temple of 151
Emergency (proclaimed in India) 25, 161, 180, 210, 229, 233, 279
England 55, 260
Ethiopia 133
Euro-Asian continent 149
Europe 21, 56, 160, 278
European Union 120, 276
External Affairs, Ministry of (India) 20, 26, 62-5, 185, 205-6, 213, 228, 262, 265, 267-8; Africa division of 142; Pakistan division of, 142; Policy Planning Committee of 228; Policy Planning division of 109

Farakka Canal Project 26, 28, 221-6, 240, 283; agreement with India 238, 264; complaint to UNO by Bangladesh 229-32; issue of 177-8, 180, 193, 221-6, 228-30, 232-8, 240-1, 243-6; treaty with India 241
Fernandes, George 267
Ferozepur 200
Finland 148, 276

Foreign Secretary (India) 76, 81-2, 84, 87-8, 96, 99, 130-2, 139-40, 143
France 85, 125, 195, 268, 277

Gandhi, Indira 23, 25, 41-4, 47, 77, 112, 119, 129, 131-2, 136-7, 143-4, 163-5, 167-9, 172-4, 179-80, 182, 184-5, 206, 210-11, 213-15, 225-8, 231-3, 235-6, 240, 245, 262, 279-81
Gandhi, Mahatma 15, 32, 55, 123; and peace 264; started movement against racial discrimination in South Africa 123
Gandhi, Rajiv 61, 119, 183, 188, 269, 281
Ganga River 34, 220, 223, 225-7, 239, 245, 250, 264, 268, *see also* Padma River
Ganges *see* Ganga River
Gangtok 26, 39-40
Garo Hills 235
Gartok (Tibet) 40
Geneva 57, 86, 101, 179, 234, 256; Bhutanese mission in 51
Geneva Conference on Indo-China 57
German Republic, Democratic 156
Germany 28, 31, 103, 105, 115, 125, 195, 202, 268
Germany, East 156
Germany, Federal 277
Germany, West 156
Ghana 124
Ghana Embassy (Delhi) 158
Ghulam Mohammad 200
Gilgit 167
Giri, V.V. 126, 275; visits Tanzania 275
Goa 141, 194
Goalpara (Assam) 238
Godhra 194; railway station 190; torching of *karsevaks* at 148
Gokhale, B.P. 252
Gopal, S. 27, 74, 76, 78, 80, 87, 90, 92, 97, 100, 104
Gorbachev, M. 186
Gowda, Deve 241
Greece 234
Gujarat 141, 190, 193, 217; government of 194; Muslims in 149
Gujral, I.K. 241, 269-70
Gulf countries 174, 184, 186, 265
Gulf War 145
Gulmarg 61
Gurkhas 260, 272
Guyana 275
Gyanendra, King 251, 270

Hague, The 171
Haider, Salman 241, 270
Hang-Ying 284
Han-nien-Lung 112
Harman doctrine 216, 223
Haryana 212
Hasina, Sheikh 241
Hassan, Nurul 151
Heath, Edward 143
Helsinki 276; principles 203, 212, 223, 241, 246
Heng Samrin, government of 53, 113, *see also* Kampuchea
Hikmeteyar 187
Himalayas 35-6, 38, 45, 86, 89, 93, 197, 202, 220-1, 247, 263, 269, 273, 279
Hiroshima 14
Hitler, Adolf 115
Hoffman, Steven 103
Holland 148
Hong Kong 88, 110, 157, 261
Hooghly River 226-7, 233
House of Commons 144; of Lords 19
Hoyveda (Premier of Iran) 165
Human Rights, universal declaration on 120
Hungary 204
Hunza valley 104

Hussain, Saddam 145
Hydari, Akbar 154
Hyder, Sajjad 154, 156
Iyengar, H.V. 19
Illiff, W.A.B. 202
Imam, Akbar 153
India, and Bangladesh 240; and canal system 198-202; and communal riots 199; and riparian consequences 220-3; and China 37, 39, 42, 48-9, 54, 56, 58, 60, 62, 86, 94, 96, 103, 105, 113, 115-16, 119-20, 140, 253-4, 256; Chinese Embassy in 109-11, 116; and Commonwealth 55; Communist Party of 109-10; Constitution of 95, 97, 250; and Emergency 161, 233; and Kashmir 203; and Nepal 249, 251, 260, 262-7, 270-3, 283; and Partition 117, 149-50, 154-5, 191, 195, 243; Republic of 115; and Sikkim 262; and Soviet Union 112; and Tanzania 275; and two-nation theory 243
India-China War 54-7, 103
India-Pak War 106-7
India-Pakistan Accord 247
Indian Airlines 167; plane hijacked 22, 161, 206
Indian Army 158, 188-9, 191; Punjab Regiment of 152
Indian Council of World Affairs 70
Indian Navy 152
Indian Railways 268
Indo-China 119
Indonesia 276
Indus River 201, 203, 217, 220, 223-4; dispute over 214-15
Indus Waters Treaty 29, 189, 197, 201-5, 208, 212, 215-17, 224
International Civil Aviation Organization (ICAO) 22, 162, 167, 192, 206
Iran 166
Iraq 14, 32, 145, 273; US intervention in 242
Ireland 260
Irrawady River 98
Islamabad 163, 165-6, 170-3, 175-7, 181, 193, 206-7, 214-15, 227, 284
Israel 126, 182
Italy 132, 268

Jaipur 168, 174
Jammu & Kashmir 88, 104, 106, 109, 157-9, 180, 199, 204, 208; and Line of Control (LOC) 162, 180; problem of 170-1
Jan Sangh 77, 109; attack on Chinese Embassy by 110; and retaliatory measures by China and India 110-12
Janata government 113, 178, 180-2, 184-5, 210, 214-15, 235, 245
Janata Party 233
Jangpangi, Laxman Singh 59-60; awarded Padma Shri 60
Japan 21, 120, 272
Jha, L.K. 19
Jhelum River 202-3, 223
Jinnah, M.A. 153, 172, 199
Johnson, Lyndon B. 280
Junagarh 167

Kalimpong 68
Kampala 25, 28, 125-6, 128-31, 136, 141-3; Catholic Archbishop of 143; dissatisfaction in 124
Kampuchea 53, 113, 185, 249
Kandahar 176, 187
Karachi 104, 153, 165, 171, 183, 266
Karakoram 36; Pass 104
Kargil 188, 281; intrusion by Pakistan in 188
Karnali Hydel Project 263, 268-9
Karnataka 71
Kashmir 24, 107, 113, 147, 157,

177, 179, 181, 192, 214, 216-17, 229, 242; area (*see also*) Jammu & Kashmir controlled by Pakistan 188; Dogra rulers of 93
Kashmir issue 147, 200, 242; UN resolution on 188; White Paper on 177
Kathmandu 83, 112, 250-2, 254, 280, 283
Kathmandu-Kodari Road 257, 269
Kaul, M.G. 66
Kaul, T.N. 21, 62, 70
Kenya 123-4, 127, 132
Kashag (Tibetan Cabinet) 41, 61-2
KGB 111, 279, 281
Kham (Tibet) 23
Khampa revolt 45
Khampas 62
Khan, Rear-Admiral 228, 230, 233, 236-7
Khrushchev, N.F. 76, 280
Kissinger, Henry 31, 33, 113, 162, 173, 284
Koirala, B.P. 249, 252-3, 271, 283; imprisonment of 253
Koirala, M.P. 252
Kongka Pass 72, 74
Korea, North 21
Korea, South 21
Korea War 57, 119, 201
Kosi and Gandak Agreement 262
Kosi River 252
Kripalani, Sucheta 71
Kuen Luen (China) 89, 93, 257, 259, 261-2, 264, 266, 268, 270-2
Kuomintang (KMT) 27, 55-6, 58, 73
Kuwait, Bhutanese mission in 51

Ladakh 80
Laden, Osama bin 189
Lahore 161-2, 165, 167, 174-5, 188, 209; papers of 181
Lall, K.B. 261
Lamb, Alaistair 101
Laos 58, 249
Latin America 230
League of Nations 16
Lebanon, government of 155
Lhasa 21, 23, 36-9, 41, 48, 62-6, 94, 96, 253; Younghusband's expedition of 36
Li Zhisui 115
Libya 132, 174
Lilienthal, David 200-1, 203, 215, 217, 241
Line of Control (LOC) 25, 188
Lok Sabha 66, 72, 119
London 19, 113, 128, 132, 143, 171, 202, 221, 234, 259

Macnamara, Robert 239
Madhopur headworks 199
Maharashtra 280
Mahbub-ul-Haq 195
Mahendra, King 252-4, 283
Man Singh, Raja 150
Manchu Empire 94, 252
Mandela, Nelson 32, 274-5
Mangla Dam 202, 224
Mao Tse-tung 32, 55, 59, 67-8, 103, 108, 115, 117-18; and Long March 55
Maxwell, Neville 83-4, 101-2
McMahon Line 57, 74, 80, 89, 93-4; agreement on 95; McMahon map 94
Mehta, K.L. 21, 70
Mehta, Rama 155, 157, 159-60, 275, 277-8, 281-2
Menon, V.K. Krishna 79, 87, 96, 103
Men-Del-Plata 233, 245-6
Mewar, communal harmony in 150-1
Mexico 223
Migyitun 72
Misamari 70
Misra, L.N. 266
Mody, Narendra 190
Monaco 257
Mongolia 21, 58

Moscow 19, 20, 107, 181, 278
Mountbatten, Lord 149
Moynihan, D.P. 279
Mujib, Sheikh *see* Rehman, Sheikh Mujibur
Mukherjee, Nirmal 164-5, 172, 175, 237
Mukti Bahini 235, 244
Mumbai, riots in 148, *see also* Bombay
Musharraf, Pervez 33, 188-9, 191, 194; and modernization of Pakistan 194; takes over as President of Pakistan 191
Muslim League 149, 151, 153, 165, 220
Mussoorie 66, 71
Mysore 168

Nagaland 20-1
Nairobi 137
Najibullah 186-7
Namibia 276
Nanking 94
Narayan, Jayaprakash 70; and India's attitude to Tibet 70
Narayanan, K.R. 112
Nathula Pass 40-1
NDA 194; government 190
National People's Congress (Chinese) 59
Nehru, B.K. 187, 281
Nehru, Jawaharlal 19, 21-3, 26, 30, 32-5, 37-49, 51-2, 54-63, 65-84, 86-7, 92, 95-7, 99-104, 200-2, 277-8; visits Bhutan 35-44; visits Pakistan and signs Indus Waters Treaty 104
Nehru, R.K. 23, 38, 59
Nepal 23-4, 26, 29-30, 32, 34, 36, 48-9, 52, 70, 75, 86, 89, 93, 119, 189, 216, 220-1, 226, 238-9, 243, 246-7, 249-50, 253-63, 265-73, 283-4; and India 52, 249-53, 258-72; Maoist movement in 255, 258, 270
Nepali Congress 249, 253
Netherlands 278-9
New York 20, 51, 180, 231, 234, 238, 246, 276, 278
New Zealand 50, 202
Nigeria 124
Non-Aligned Foreign Ministers meeting 178-9
Non-Aligned Group 179, 230
Non-Aligned Summit Conference 129, 259
North Atlantic Treaty Organization (NATO) 14, 31
North-East Frontier Agency (NEFA) 20-1, 56, 63, 65, 70, 75, 81, 86, 95, 108, 159
North-West Frontier Province (NWFP) 20
Norway 148
Nu, U 75, 98
Nyerere, Julius 23, 130, 274-5

Obote, Milton 125, 130, 136
Oboth-Offembi 25, 131-2, 136-7, 143-4
Operation Gibraltar (started by Pakistan) 107, 159
Orissa 194
Oxford 167-8
Oxus 187

Padma River 221-2, 224, 227, 230, 232, 245
Padmasambhav, Guru 35, 43-4; and Mahayana Buddhism 34-6
Pakistan 15, 18, 22, 24, 26, 29-32, 34, 69, 102, 104, 107, 120, 142, 149-51, 153-6, 158-61, 163, 165-7, 170, 172, 174, 176-80, 182-3, 185-6, 188, 190-5, 197-217, 233, 242-3, 257, 264, 272, 282-3; and China 104; military camp in 190-1; relations with India 149-50, 161-205
Pakhtunistan, demand by Pakistan for 266

Pakistan, East 85, 107, 111, 147-8, 159, 162, 164, 207, 222, 224-5; migration of minorities from 199-200
Pakistan-occupied Kashmir (POK) 189
Pakistan, West 147, 199, 220, 224, 243
Palestine 193; partition of 148
Panchen Lama 37, 62
Panchsheel 85, 96
Pande, B.D. 174
Pandit, Vijayalakshmi 19, 160
Pant, Apa 26, 39, 45
Pant, G.B. 79, 81, 100
Pant, K.C. 100
Paranjpe, V.V. 78, 80, 87, 98, 115
Parliament (Indian) 29, 48, 66-7, 69, 72-3, 75, 79-82, 84, 89, 95, 97, 110, 123, 132, 140, 189, 215; attack by terrorists on 189
Paro 22, 43-4, 46-7, 50
Parthasarthy, G. 88, 105, 172
Partition (of India) 15, 18, 198, 200, 220
Patel, H.M. 19, 23, 265-6
Patel, Vallabhbhai 249
Pearl Harbor 115, 215
Peking 25, 27, 37, 49, 58, 62, 75, 87-9, 91, 97, 100, 103, 105-7, 110-13, 156-7, 159-60, 173-4, 271, 276, 278-9
People's Daily (Peking) 59, 67-8, 104, 114; accuses Nehru of hostility towards China 104-5
People's Liberation Army (PLA) 41-2, 62, 100, 251-2
Peshawar 187; Shura assembly in 186
Pokharan explosion 102
Poland 115; partition of 148
Pondicherry 278
Pon-zu-Li 67
Powell, Enoch 126
Prague 21
Prasad, Rajendra 58
Pratap, Maharana 150
Princeton 280
Punjab 141, 149, 157, 198-9, 212; rivers of 242
Punjab (Pakistan) 154
Punjab, East 199-200, 203, 214
Punjab, West 157, 198, 200; migration of minorities from 199; Upper Doab Canal in 199

Quit India Resolution 151

Radcliffe, Cyril 200
Radhakrishnan, S. 40, 58-9, 112, 115; addresses National People's Congress in China 59; visits China 40, 58-9
Raghunath, K. 29, 116; dubbed a spy by China 109
Rajasthan 151, 203, 212, 217, 242
Rajya Sabha 72, 100
Ram, Jagjivan 228, 232-3, 235-7, 245, 264
Ram Janmabhumi temple (Ayodhya), issue of 190
Ramchandra, Shri 130, 135-8
Rangachari, R. 208, 247
Ranganathan, C.V. 102
Rangoon 75, 91-2, 98-9, 276
Rao, B.N. 223
Rao, G.N. 87-90
Rao, Krishna 87
Ravi River 242
RAW 235
Rawalpindi 167-8
Reagan-Gorbachev formulation 16
Red Guards (Chinese) 29, 109-10, 284; militancy of 113, 118
Rehman, Sheikh Mujibur 162, 225-7, 235, 257; assassination of 226; and its effect on India 227
Rippentrop-Molotov talks 182
Rippon, Geoffery 128
Riyadh 178
Roosevelt, Theodore 32-3
Russia 55, 120, 272-3, *see also* Soviet Union/USSR

SAARC 271; declaration of 247
Sahay, Bhagwan 252, 283; and Nepal 283
Sahay, Vishnu 147
Salal 23-6
Salal Agreement 197, 210-11, 215-16
Salal Dam 176, 178
Salal Hydel Project 204-7, 209, 211-18
Saleem, Abdus 153
SAPTA declaration 247
Saudi Arabia, government of 179
Sayem, Abu Sadat Mohammad 226
SEATO 203
Shah Nawaz 175, 211
Shahi, Agha 151, 164-72, 175-6, 180, 206-7, 209-12, 268, 283; visits Delhi 211
Sharif, Nawaz 188
Sharma, S.D. 153
Shastri, L.B. 108, 159, 253; visits Nepal 253
Sherathang (Tibet) 40
Shillong 20-1
Sialkot 107, 205
Simla 25, 161, 179, 192, 200, 252
Simla Agreement 161-2, 165, 170-1, 173, 181, 206, 210-11, 215-16
Sind 223
Singh, Bahadur 115
Singh, Charan 28, 185, 237
Singh, C.P.N. 249, 252
Singh, Harmander 64
Singh, H.K. 131, 133, 136-7
Singh, I.P. 164, 169, 177
Singh, Jaswant 282
Singh, Karan 72, 109
Singh, Kewal 22, 161, 163, 166
Singh, Khushwant 281
Singh, L.P. 19
Singh, Manmohan 33; government of 183
Singh, Maharaja Ranjit 198
Singh, Natwar 115
Singh, Swaran 111
Singh, V.P. 269
Singhe, Shirley Amar 229
Sinha, Nirmal 40
Sinkiang 86, 91, 93-4, 120
Sobani, Lt. Ishaque 152-3; and naval mutiny 152
Soviet Union 31, 106, 112, 158-60, 184, 186, 219, 257, 275, 282; and Asia 257; foreign policy of 173; and Nazi Germany 182, *see also* Russia/USSR
Spain 85
Sri Lanka 30, 32, 230
Stalin, Joseph 32, 55
Sue Ky, Aung San 276
Sutlej River 199, 202
Swatantra Party 180
Sweden 148
Switzerland 42, 50, 143
Sybedi, Navraj 266

Taiwan 53, 95
Talibans 187, 189
Talwar, HMIS 152
Tanganyika 123-4
Tanzania 23, 125, 127-8, 130, 135, 274-5; Asian settlers in 127; and India 275
Tarbela Dam 202
Tashkent 160, 173
Taung Gye 98
Tawang 87, 96
Teen Bigha (Bangladesh enclave) 241
Tejpur 64-6, 70
Tennessee Valley Authority 200
Thailand, Bhutanese mission in 51
Thatcher, Margaret 102, 143
Thimayya, General 281
Thimphu 46, 49, 51
Third World 16, 32, 174, 256, 278
Thomson, John 277
Tibet 20, 21, 23, 35-8, 40-2, 45, 47-9, 51, 56-9, 62-3, 65-70, 86-7, 91, 93-5, 100-1, 107, 119, 202, 223, 250-2, 254, 257, 269;

Chinese occupation of 37; Khampa disaffection in 61-2; relations with China 62-3, 251-2; relations with India 37, 71; settlement in India of refugees from 71-2
Tista Barrage Project (East Pakistan) 225
Tista Multipurpose Project (India) 225
Tito, Marshal 280
Tiwari, N.D. 151
Tongsa Penlop (Druk Gyalpo) 36
Trevelyan, Humphrey 154
Truman, H.S. 201; Doctrine of 149
Tsering Shakya 62
Tsengpo *see* Brahmputra River

Udaipur 150-1, 278
Uganda 23, 123-6, 129-31, 134-8; Asians in 124-7, 129, 142; *coup d'état* staged by Idi Amin in 125; racist policy followed in 125-9; relations with India 144-6
United Kingdom (UK) 125-8, 142-3, 202, 227, *see also* England
United Nations Framework Convention 224
United Nations Organization (UNO) 17, 24, 88-90, 117, 178, 187, 193, 219, 227, 229, 231, 242, 245, 248, 259-60, 278-9; Charter of 14, 17; General Assembly of 74, 124, 128, 177, 180, 228-9, 232-3, 256
United States of America (USA) 13, 30-3, 69, 88, 112, 117, 119, 145, 149, 151, 158-9, 182, 184-6, 188-9, 200, 202-3, 215-17, 223, 227, 260, 272-3, 280, 282, 284-5; and China 284; involvement in Russo-Afghan War 186; and Pakistan 215; and Russia 101, 207
USSR 112-13, 160, 173, 184-5, 203-4, 250, 254, 275; intervention in Afghanistan by 184; relations with India 185; relations with Pakistan 173, *see also* Russia/Soviet Union
Uttar Pradesh (UP) 190, 269

Vajpayee, A.B. 30, 112-13, 150, 180, 182-3, 188, 193-4, 210-12, 215, 237-8, 264; on communal killings in Ahmedabad 194; visits Pakistan 181-5; visits Peking 112-13
Verghese, B.G. 153, 247
Versailles, Treaty of 16
Vienna Congress 13
Vietnam 14, 58, 77, 86, 101, 113, 145, 249, 280
Vishwa Hindu Parishad (VHP) 190, 194

Warsaw 86; Pact 13, 204, 250
Washington 19, 113-14, 202, 282
Watson, Francis 86
Wheeler, Raymond A. 202
Wilson, Woodrow 32-3, 74
World Bank 131, 201-2, 224, 231, 239, 242
World Trade Center (USA); attack on 188
World War I 55, 123
World War II 13, 16, 55, 71, 123, 130, 132, 182

Yang-Kung-Su 97, 115
Yatung 22, 40-2, 60
Yuan-shi-Kai 284
Yugoslavia 230, 276

Zaheer, Zafar 157
Zambia 128
Zanzibar 124
Zhang-wen-Chin 283-5
Zhongnanhai (China) 115
Zia-ul-Haq 181, 184-5, 191, 210
Zia-ur-Rahman 28, 226, 236, 238-9; assassination of 239